A HABSBURG TRAGEDY

Crown Prince Rudolf

BY THE SAME AUTHOR

This I Have Seen

Crusaders in the Secret War

The Making of Tanganyika

Dusk on the Danube

The Other Livingstone

A HABSBURG TRAGEDY

Crown Prince Rudolf

JUDITH LISTOWEL

ASCENT BOOKS

To Doreen
who inspired me to write
Rudolf's story

Printed in Great Britain by
Butler and Tanner Ltd
Frome and London
ISBN 0 9064 0701

Contents

Illustrations

Between pages 152/3

Prologue

I was fourteen years old when my maternal grandfather died. He had been a member of the Hungarian Upper House and also one of the DELEGATION, the group of politicians who four times a year met their Austrian opposite numbers to discuss joint Austro-Hungarian policy relating to foreign affairs, defence and finance. He had known the entourage of Crown Prince Rudolf of Habsburg both in Austria and in Hungary. I remember vaguely that once he spoke of Mayerling, and said something to the effect that Rudolf had not killed himself because of a chit of a girl. At that time this did not interest me. Years later I asked my mother about it. She was utterly unpolitical, yet her answer was that indeed Rudolf had not died because of a love affair, but because of some political plot. 'It was something to do with Hungarian independence,' my mother explained. 'Before World War I the Hungarians always wanted to break away from Austria.' I knew enough history to realise that this was not quite true—the Prime Minister at the time World War I broke out, Count Steven Tisza, surely wanted no such thing. He had visited my grandfather and I overheard something to the effect that Hungary needed Austria as much as Austria needed Hungary.

So much has been written about the death of Crown Prince Rudolf that the author who produces yet another book on the subject might be thought to have undertaken a profitless, indeed a foolhardy, task. But the tragedy of Mayerling has remained a mystery and for historians and journalists to attempt the solution of a mystery is irresistible—especially if there is a connection, however slight, between their families and the protagonists in the strange event.

The death of Crown Prince Rudolf in 1889, was high tragedy. When the heartbroken and humiliated Emperor Francis Joseph announced that his only son and heir had taken his own life the whole world was profoundly shocked. No one suspected a mystery—no one sought any secret explanation, but everyone in any way connected with Mayerling, the shooting lodge where Rudolf died, was sworn to secrecy. The coachman of the cab that was to have taken Baroness Mary Vecsera, the young girl who had died with Rudolf, back to Vienna, received a considerable sum of silence money. The woman whom Rudolf had really loved, and who had been his companion for many years, would not say one word; on her deathbed years later she destroyed Rudolf's farewell letter. The loyalty of all concerned, the Court, the aristocracy and humble folk alike, was astonishing. Even historians who discovered that all documents relating to the Mayerling tragedy were missing from the Vienna State Archives, kept their silence. Until World War I, which brought about the downfall of the Austrian Monarchy, almost the entire literature concerning Mayerling was based on guesswork and hearsay and gossip.

The years passed, World War II smashed the old order of East Europe; amidst the general destruction many old documents disappeared, but many others saw the light of day. The secret files of the German Foreign Ministry were brought to London and studied at the Public Record Office. Among these were the reports of the German Ambassador to Vienna in 1889, Prince Heinrich VII Reuss. They were of special interest to an Austrian historian, Albert E. J. Hollaender, working at the Record Office in London, who used them for an essay which threw new light on Mayerling. This essay was no longer hearsay or gossip, but a serious historical study based on the reports of a highly intelligent, well-informed ambassador, who was reporting to his chief, Chancellor Prince Otto von Bismarck. I read the Hollaender essay at the British Museum library in 1960, and for the first time began to wonder about the fate of Crown Prince Rudolf. Had he not committed suicide after all? And if someone had killed him, who was it and why? But I had no time to pursue this germ of an idea and was, anyhow, far from convinced that there was any mystery worth resolving.

In 1972, on my way to Budapest, I stopped in Vienna and remet an old friend, belonging to one of the great Austrian families. I mentioned to her that I thought of doing research into the Crown Prince Rudolf story: what did she know about it? She looked at me for a minute and then replied very earnestly: 'When I was eighteen years old, I asked my father what had happened at Mayerling. He answered that he had given his word of honour to the Emperor never to speak about it. He made me give my word of honour that I would never discuss, never even mention, this subject. Therefore I cannot tell you anything.'

After a silence—for I had been taken completely by surprise—she went on: 'And will you do me a great favour? Do not tell any of my friends that you are researching Crown Prince Rudolf's life. Promise. Please.'

This was a difficult one. I promised that I would not tell those with whom we were going to have lunch, or any of her friends, to whom she was going to introduce me. But when I reached Budapest I did ask questions among my Hungarian friends and men and women employed in the Hungarian Archives and in various libraries. The friends had been told nothing by their parents or grandparents because of the same pledge of secrecy extracted from them that I had run into in Vienna. Archivists and librarians were puzzled that they had found nothing relating to Mayerling, even the Károlyi papers (Count Pista Károlyi had been one of Rudolf's friends and allegedly fellow plotters) had been pruned of every Rudolf letter. Apparently on imperial orders, all documents remotely connected with Mayerling had vanished from Hungary no less than from Austria.

Yet here and there I picked up a few disconnected items. I found out that Count Samuel Teleki had been a close friend of Rudolf's. Samuel Teleki was the great-uncle and godfather of my sister-in-law. Alas, not only had he died years ago, but when I went to Transylvania to see what I could find at his country house, Sáromberke, I discovered that in 1944, when the Russians occupied Transylvania, the Soviet Army had carried out of the house its entire contents, including the three wooden chests in which Teleki kept his confidential papers, and burnt the lot. Then I heard that Rudolf had had many Jewish friends. The man closest to him throughout his adult life had been Maurice Szeps, a brilliant Jewish intellectual of Polish descent. Szeps had been editor of the best Viennese daily newspaper, for which—so my Hungarian friends asserted—Rudolf had written pungent articles anonymously. I heard that when quite young, Rudolf had been devoted to the Czechs and full of understanding for their grievances; later also to the Hungarians. Again and again there were references (though never anything tangible) to a meeting at Sáromberke, Count Teleki's country house, where Rudolf was supposed to have signed some document disloyal to his father. For the first time I sensed that there had been something more than just talk to be followed up. Perhaps my mother had been right after all.

Back in London I heard that a distinguished Austrian aristocrat, well in his eighties, was visiting relatives in England. I rang him up and asked whether I could see him and would he tell me something about the old days at the Hofburg. When he enquired why my sudden interest, and I told him, he politely but frigidly replied that he could not discuss the Crown Prince. He said he sincerely hoped I would give up the idea of writing about him.

By now I was convinced that there was a secret to be elucidated. What was it that had to be hushed up at all costs? It had to be something worse than suicide which the Emperor Francis Joseph had admitted. What sort of man had Rudolf been? The heir to the most romantic throne of Europe had Jews as his closest friends; he was anti-clerical to the point of going out of his way to annoy cardinals and bishops. Yet he loved the army and dreamt of expanding the Austrian Empire to the Aegean Sea. He loathed the Prussians who had defeated his father and undermined Austria's position. I found more and more contradictions. I decided I would have to make a start by reading the classic biography of Rudolf by Baron Oskar von Mitis, first published in 1928, and then work my way back through books and pamphlets to the secret file of Vienna's police chief in 1889, found among the effects of a little-known actor who died in Berlin in 1953. The most vital quest was to try and find the secret Mayerling dossier which the Emperor Francis Joseph had entrusted to his Prime Minister, Count Eduard Taaffe. He in his turn had left this dossier to his son Heinrich under the same seal of secrecy; Count Heinrich in 1929 on his deathbed had entrusted it to his son, Edward. In 1938 Count Edward Taaffe returned to Ireland, from where an ancestor of his had gone to Austria in the 18th century. Edward had died in 1967. But there were Taaffe relations still alive; I hoped that they would be able to tell me why Edward

Taaffe had left Czechoslovakia, and what he had done with the secret dossier.

I have found the answers to most of the questions that I asked myself when I was first confronted by the conspiracy of silence of those who knew something and by only empty spaces in the archives where the Mayerling documents should have been. During World War II an ace of the Polish Secret Service told me: 'If you want to solve a problem, you need two things: hard work and luck.' I have worked hard for three years on the problem of Rudolf's life and death, and I have had some luck.

I

The Birth of a Crown Prince

Rudolf had a difficult birth. His mother, the Empress Elizabeth, was desperately worried lest she should bear a third daughter instead of the much-wanted Habsburg heir. She enjoyed the advice showered on her from every part of the Empire as to what she should do to ensure that the child was a boy; it proved to her that she was popular. Everything worrying was kept from her; she was not told that on August 16, 1858, the great candelabrum in the throneroom of Schönbrunn crashed and broke into fragments. It was the second time within two years that this happened. Had Elizabeth heard of it, she would have interpreted it as an unlucky omen.

On August 20, 1858, Elizabeth's labour began. Her mother-in-law, the Archduchess Sophie, was informed by telegram and at once left Ischl for Schönbrunn. The first thing she did on arrival was to have the Blessed Sacrament exposed on the altar in the chapel.[1] As Elizabeth at her previous confinements had hardly uttered a murmur, Archduchess Sophie believed that all would again go smoothly. But this time it was different. At 10 o'clock in the evening Elizabeth gave such a heartrending cry that the Archduchess and her Mistress of the Household, Countess Sophie Esterházy-Lichtenstein, fell on their knees and began praying for her. In her delirium—according to one of the midwives—Elizabeth had prophetic visions in which she foresaw the fall of the House of Habsburg, and red flags waving in the streets of Vienna.[2] At last at 10.45 in the evening of August 21, 1858, she was delivered of a boy.

Francis Joseph was kneeling by her bedside when she asked anxiously whether she had a son. He replied, 'The midwife does not know yet,' for fear that the sudden joy might prove too much for her. Elizabeth wept: 'Of course—it will be another girl . . .'

'What if it were a boy, though?' he said. Elizabeth would not believe it until the midwife brought the baby to her and she had seen her son. He was baptised Rudolf Francis Charles Joseph, but he was to be called Rudolf, after the founder of the Habsburg dynasty, whose tomb, surmounted by his sad-faced effigy, was being restored that year in the imperial mausoleum of Speyer Cathedral.[3]

Archduchess Sophie took immediate control of the little boy, and chose as his nurse Baroness Karolina von Welden. She turned out an excellent choice, although the most important consideration in her appointment was that her late husband, General Baron Franz von Welden, had been Commander-in-Chief in the 1849 campaign against the Hungarian rebels, whom the Archduchess Sophie loathed. Rudolf became devoted to Wowo, as he called her, and in his farewell letter to his wife, written thirty years later, he asked her to give Wowo his fond greetings.

Elizabeth's recovery was slow, for she had such a flow of milk that she could not rest, yet she was not allowed to nurse the baby, for it was contrary to Spanish Etiquette for an empress to feed her own child. Indeed, she was hardly allowed to see him, for the Archduchess Sophie had moved Rudolf close to her own apartments. She rejoiced over the birth of the Habsburg heir as much as Francis Joseph. According to Spanish Etiquette, the day after Rudolf's birth the Emperor placed the chain of the Order of the Golden Fleece on his cradle; he also appointed him Colonel-in-Chief of the 19th Foot Regiment of Raab (Sopron by its proper Hungarian name), from then on known as the 19th Line Regiment of the Crown Prince. The Emperor invited the entire diplomatic corps to the baptism: tears of joy ran down his cheeks when he was congratulated, although he said that he did not think the baby good-looking, but 'magnificently built and very strong'.[4]

Francis Joseph's love for Elizabeth was, if possible, even greater than before. But he owed his mother so much and trusted her judgment so implicitly, that he would not stand up to her, even though Elizabeth was very unhappy that she had no say in the upbringing of her children. Yet Elizabeth's influence on Francis Joseph was growing; Sophie could see that clearly, but she had the poorest opinion of her daughter-in-law's ability to educate a future emperor. Her one object was to form the child in accordance with her own views as she had formed Francis Joseph. With Elizabeth's unbending character, conflicts between the Emperor's mother and wife were bound to continue, and to become more acrimonious.

In 1859, under the influence of his mother, Francis Joseph took a disastrous political decision. Piedmont (also known as the Kingdom of Piedmont and Sardinia), led by Count Cavour, intended to take advantage of Austria's isolation after the Crimean War. Francis Joseph, on Sophie's advice, had remained neutral when Czar Nicholas needed his support, and this although Nicholas had saved the Austrian throne in 1849 by sending 200,000 troops to put down the Hungarian uprising. For the Crimean betrayal Russia never forgave Austria. When Cavour pressed his nationalist claims, Francis Joseph issued a three-day ultimatum—drafted by his mother's favourite, Karl Ludwig Count Grünne—without informing his Foreign Minister, Karl Ferdinand Count Buol Schaunstein. When the ultimatum expired, on April 29, 1859, Austrian troops crossed into Piedmont.[5] It was all done with such haste that not even Prussia was notified, and Austria did not have a single ally. Piedmont for its part was backed by Napoleon III's France. Grünne[6] had appointed as Commander-in-Chief General Franz Count Gyulai, who missed his opportunity to engage the French and the Piedmontese separately before they could join forces. Then came the disaster of Magenta, a battle lost entirely owing to bad generalship. Alarming reports circulated and these came to Elizabeth's ears. She wrote endless letters to Francis Joseph, begging him to let her join him at Headquarters. Their correspondence has been preserved. In one letter Francis Joseph wrote: 'My dear, dear, only angel, I beg of you, in the name of your love for me, to collect yourself. Show yourself in the city often and visit institutions. You do not know what a help you could be to me if you could do this. It will raise the spirits of people in Vienna and maintain the good atmosphere which I so urgently need. Do take care of yourself for my sake, for I have so many worries . . .'

But Elizabeth was melancholic and shut herself up entirely, if only to see less of her mother-in-law, who prevented her from spending her time with her children. The unfortunate Wowo was in a most difficult position, for whatever Elizabeth suggested was promptly countermanded by Sophie. Elizabeth slept badly and ate scarcely anything; she was out riding all day, sometimes until late in the evening, accompanied only by her English groom, Harry Holmes.[7] The Archduchess Sophie did not consider this proper, and complained to the Emperor who in the midst of a calamitous war had to implore his 'dear, heavenly Sisi . . . my only beautiful angel . . . to be escorted by the Controller of the Imperial Hunts (*Oberstjägermeister*)'; but Elizabeth disliked him and disregarded Francis Joseph's instructions. She continued to scandalise Viennese society and the Archduchess by giving herself the small solace of the Englishman's companionship, sometimes covering as much as forty miles a day. This went on until the Emperor's return.[8]

Then came the defeat of Solferino, and trouble was brewing in Hungary. Elizabeth set up a hospital in the Laxenburg Palace, and spent most of her days there. She held her mother-in-law responsible for the Italian misfortunes and the last vestige of any respect she had for the Archduchess's political wisdom vanished. Anxious about the attitude of Hungary, she advised her husband to open negotiations with Napoleon III as soon as possible, in the hope of ending the war. Francis Joseph begged her not to grieve, and wrote, 'Your political plan contains some very good ideas, but for the present we must not give up hope that Prussia will, after all, come to our support, and till then there must be no thought of negotiating with the enemy . . .'

Poor Francis Joseph; none of his hopes were fulfilled, though negotiations with Napoleon were initiated through the intermediary of Prince Alexander of Hesse. Meanwhile he received long letters from Elizabeth in which she told him of her love for him and of her sufferings at the hands of her mother-in-law. Sophie also wrote, complaining about Elizabeth's senseless behaviour.

Anxious lest his own country might fall prey to the Prussian army while he lingered in Italy, Napoleon met Francis Joseph at Villa Franca and on July 11, 1859, they signed an armistice, according to which Austria had to cede Lombardy to Piedmont and pay an indemnity. At last the Emperor could go home to his beloved wife. He found her in an acutely nervous condition; the children were well, but Sophie would let her have no part in their upbringing. Elizabeth and Sophie clashed constantly, especially over what was to be done with Rudolf in preparation for his future duties. He was one year old.

As a result of the Italian defeats, Francis Joseph began to move away from the men and ideas with whom his mother sympathised and drew closer to Elizabeth's more liberal views. Buol had already gone, also Alexander Bach—particularly hated by the Hungarians because of his centralising system—and the Emperor was considering restoring constitutional government. Austria had lost prestige in the eyes of the world; her foreign policy was responsible for blunder upon blunder, she was threatened with bankruptcy[9] and possibly revolution; and now there was also grave discontent in the army because of Gyulai's devastating mistakes. The all-powerful, arrogant Grünne,[10] who had appointed him, was removed by Francis Joseph from the post of Adjutant General, which indicated to the Hungarians that their aspirations might be considered.

The Viennese blamed Francis Joseph quite openly. In the streets many no longer doffed their hats when they saw him; others when the police were not about shouted: 'Abdicate!' and 'Maximilian! Maximilian!' meaning the Emperor's younger brother.[11] There was a wave of suicides, some of which had serious repercussions. That of the Hungarian statesman, Count Stephen Széchényi, caused great bitterness because even in the mental institution to which he had voluntarily gone,[12] he had still been persecuted by the Habsburg police. Baron Karl Ludwig Bruck's suicide was even more resented. He had been an able and honest Minister of Finance, whom Francis Joseph had not supported wholeheartedly when he was accused, quite falsely, of being involved in the embezzling of funds by the Quartermaster. Grünne had insinuated that Bruck was capable of such a thing because, being the son of a humble bookbinder, he did not understand the lofty concepts of aristocratic honour.

Elizabeth observed with satisfaction that the structure built up by her mother-in-law was collapsing and her own hold over the Emperor was becoming stronger. She could see that even with the children she would eventally attain what she wanted. Yet it was at this moment that suddenly she left Austria and stayed away for two years.

Something happened between July 1859 and November 1860 which shook the foundations of Elizabeth's married life. After Francis Joseph came back from the Italian front, relations between them were excellent. Elizabeth was tender and compassionate; her husband, ashamed of failure and disappointed in the few men whom he had trusted, had become morose and suspicious. Most of that summer the Emperor and the Empress spent in Laxenburg.

After their return to the Hofburg, Elizabeth's wrists and knees were disfigured by curious swellings of the joints, which neither Dr Franz Seeburger, whom Elizabeth hated, nor Dr Joseph Skoda, could cure. They were not only painful and unsightly; clearly Elizabeth wanted to know what had caused them. In July 1860 she promised to visit her parents in Possenhofen. She travelled via Munich, where she took another medical opinion.[13] Joan Haslip, in her book *The Lonely Empress*, has written: 'Heavily veiled and under an assumed name, the doctor may not have guessed at her identity and therefore told her the truth—namely that she was suffering from an unpleasant and contagious disease. To learn that Francis Joseph had not only been unfaithful but had contaminated her as well, would have filled her with such horror and disgust as to explain not only her behaviour at the time, but her whole attitude in the future, for though later she might learn to pity, even to forgive, her lonely unhappy husband, she was never to admire or love him anymore. It would explain the unreasonable hysteria which drove her to flight, above all it would explain the Emperor's forebearance, his chivalry and generosity towards his wife, who in the eyes of the world disregarded her duties, but to whom he had a debt of conscience he knew he could never repay.'[14]

For Francis Joseph, who adored Elizabeth, to be told by her that her illness was gonorrhoea was an appalling revelation. In the 1860's there was no cure—those with good, strong health shook it off, the others gradually wasted away. In her state of nerves, Elizabeth was determined to flee to a southern climate and stay away till she was well again. Francis Joseph proposed Meran, Arco, or some sunny place on the Adriatic, but the Empress cried: 'No, no! I must go far, far away, right out of the country.'

She mentioned Madeira as being sufficiently remote. There, she thought, on an island, where spring was eternal, she had a chance to regain her physical health and mental equilibrium. There was no Austrian ship available at that moment, but Elizabeth refused to wait and said she must start at once. A request was sent to Queen Victoria, who placed her yacht, the *Osborne*, at the Empress's disposal for the voyage from Antwerp to Funchal and invited her to pay her a visit. Elizabeth, her face swollen, thanked the British Ambassador for the yacht, but declined the invitation on the grounds that she wished to preserve the strictest incognito. On November 17, 1860, Francis Joseph escorted her through Munich to Bamberg. And from there she went on alone to Antwerp where the *Osborne* was waiting for her.

It was a very stormy voyage but, ill though she was, the Empress bore the unusually rough passage better than the other travellers. Nobody appeared at meal times, but Elizabeth was not in the least upset by the heavy sea.[15]

The whole population of Madeira crowded into Funchal to watch the arrival of the beautiful young Empress, who had suddenly fallen ill. They expected a pale, wasted figure, or thought that she would be carried ashore. Instead Elizabeth disembarked with a grave face, but to all appearances fresh and well, and braced by the voyage. She was enchanted with her villa—Francis Joseph had given her an unlimited letter of credit—which stood on the top of a sheer cliff, in the midst of a luxuriant tropical garden with a fantastic view of the sea. For a while she forgot her worries and her health seemed restored—she hardly coughed at all. But having grown used to Funchal her melancholic moods returned, and she felt homesick for her children and her husband. Messengers came and went with letters. One of them, Count Louis Rechberg, wrote to his aunt, 'I am terribly sorry for the poor Empress, for quite between ourselves, I think she is very, very ill. Her cough seems in no way better than before her voyage here, though as a rule she does not cough much. . . . But mentally she is terribly depressed, almost to the point of melancholia, though in her condition this could hardly be otherwise—she often shuts herself up in her room all day crying. I can not imagine what the reason can be. . . . She eats alarmingly little. . . . She is so depressed that she never goes out, but simply sits at the open window, except for an hour's ride at a foot's pace.'

On April 28, 1861, Elizabeth started on her homeward

journey.[16] She sailed for Spain on the comfortable English royal yacht in glorious weather. She visited Seville unrecognised, but on her return to Madrid, the Duc de Montpensier, the Spanish queen's brother-in-law, came to meet her at the station in full uniform with decorations, afterwards conducting her to his state coach with its six horses, and offered her his palace at Sant' Elmo. Elizabeth who hated fuss, pomp and ceremony, declined the palace and confined relations with the duke to the minimum required by politeness. She also refused the King's and the Queen's invitation, and went alone to a bull-fight.

She passed by the Balearic Islands, paid a brief visit to Malta and landed in Corfu. She would have loved to stay there for some time, but the Emperor was on his way to meet her on board the yacht *Phantasie*. He welcomed her with tears in his eyes after their long separation, and after a visit to Miramar they returned to Vienna, where Elizabeth had a tumultuous reception. But her children had fallen entirely under the influence of the Archduchess Sophie, and when she ventured to raise objections, she was given to understand that she had been away so long that others had had to take charge of them, and that the system of education introduced in her absence must still be followed. Clashes with her mother-in-law occurred daily. Because of this, on May 23, 1861, Elizabeth and Francis Joseph moved to Laxenburg. Then there were rumours that Elizabeth's health was once more causing concern; on June 23 she left again, this time for Corfu. Once more her health improved, and when in October Francis Joseph visited her they at last reached a compromise. He promised to take her part in the matter of the children and, if need be, oppose his mother. Elizabeth agreed to return within the confines of the Monarchy, but not to Vienna. She arrived in Venice (then still part of Austria) on October 26, where she was met by Archduke Johann Salvator (later Johann Orth) and the young Ludwig Salvator. A week later Rudolf and Gisela joined their mother who was overjoyed to have them with her, especially Rudolf who, according to Princess Taxis, 'has become *ravissant*, jolly, natural, clever and very good looking'. Gisela was a dear little girl, plump, healthy and not very exciting. Elizabeth did her best to bestow affection on her, but not very successfully: throughout her life Gisela felt that her mother much preferred Rudolf to her.

Contemporaries believed that she married very young because she wanted to get away from a home in which she took second place to her brother and later to her young sister Valerie, Elizabeth's spoilt child.

In 1861 in Venice trouble arose again as Countess Sophie Esterházy-Lichtenstein[17] had received instructions from the Archduchess Sophie with which Elizabeth disagreed. This time she induced the Emperor to replace the Archduchess's confidant by Countess Paula Bellegarde, one of her former ladies-in-waiting. As Paula had meanwhile married Count Alfred Königsegg-Aulendorf, the Count became controller of the Empress's household.

In July 1862 Elizabeth finally returned to Vienna and was greeted with such enthusiasm by the population that the Archduchess Sophie's entourage regarded it as a demonstration for the liberal Empress and against the Emperor's reactionary mother. Elizabeth settled down in Schönbrunn and saw a lot of her children. Her feet were less swollen; she could again go for long walks, and restarted riding. Archduchess Sophie was away, so peace reigned in the Emperor's home.

Francis Joseph did everything possible to make life pleasant for his wife. He was most attentive; he sent her beautiful horses and anticipated her every whim. But she could not forget what had caused her illness. She was twenty-five years old, one of the most beautiful women in the world, yet her husband had been unfaithful to her and very nearly ruined her health. She could feel compassion, even gratitude for his generosity, but love him as she had before—no. Yet Francis Joseph adored her, and would go on adoring her to the end of his days.

2

Crises over Rudolf's Education

To plan the education of Crown Prince Rudolf presented a great problem. Much thought and heart-searching went into it, especially because the three people closest to Rudolf—his father, his mother and his grandmother—held such widely differing views.

The Emperor was anxious to maintain Habsburg family traditions, but in view of the mistakes made since he had come to the throne in 1848, Francis Joseph wanted his son to be better prepared than he had been. 'He must not become a free thinker, but he should be well acquainted with the conditions and requirements of modern times,' he wrote in his memorandum on Rudolf's education.[1]

Archduchess Sophie was an ardent reactionary, deeply religious, who would have allowed the Roman Catholic Church to run the Empire. She wanted to fashion Rudolf in accordance with her religious principles. Sophie was also a strong character, who had induced her feeble-minded brother-in-law, the Emperor Ferdinand V—maliciously nicknamed *Der Gütige*, the kindly man—to abdicate in favour of his nephew, Francis Joseph, passing over his brother, Sophie's husband. For her son's sake this ambitious woman had given up her chance of wearing the imperial crown.

Francis Joseph was deeply grateful to his mother—he understood the great sacrifice she had made for him. That is why he stood by her even against his wife whom he loved deeply. Elizabeth, with her views diametrically opposed to her mother-in-law, wanted Rudolf to have a liberal education, and become a man who could think things out for himself. And she was determined that he should not be hamstrung by the hated Spanish etiquette.

What Elizabeth was too indignant to admit—but what Francis

Joseph appreciated—was that Sophie tried to instil into Rudolf a sense of duty and of responsibility. It was not for lack of trying that she failed to transform her wilful, highly strung grandson into a paragon of all the virtues. And she was not altogether wrong when she said: 'How can Elizabeth, badly brought up as she is, and with no idea how to behave, bring up the heir to a great Empire?'[2]

Officially a strong child, in fact Rudolf's health needed careful watching. Wowo, completely devoted to him, knew how delicate his nervous system was. She also knew his wicked obstinacy; if any wish was not immediately granted, there would be outbursts of petulance, accompanied by screams and yells, and only Wowo could soothe him.

Naughty young Rudolf certainly was, but he was also a fascinating child, with his mother's soft voice and golden slanting eyes, a Wittelsbach much more than a Habsburg. And when he wanted, he was full of charm and affection. Aged three, Rudolf laid the foundation stone of the municipal building of Reichenau in the presence of the Emperor, to the delight of the onlookers.[3] Aged four he accompanied his father when he went to inspect the Military Academy of Wiener Neustadt. When the students shouted the customary three cheers for the Emperor, little Rudolf waved his hat and shouted 'hurrah!' with the best of them. Francis Joseph was so touched that he nearly cried with emotion —for several minutes he was unable to speak.[4]

As a highly intelligent child, Rudolf must have sensed the tension between his mother and his grandmother, between whom his father tried unsuccessfully to mediate. Nonetheless, when Elizabeth absented herself for two years from the Court, and Rudolf was entirely in the care of his grandmother, he had a happy time. The Archduchess Sophie had brought up four boys and she had a gift for dealing with children.

Elizabeth's restlessness had communicated itself to Gisela and Rudolf, especially Rudolf. This should have been a warning, but Elizabeth did not even notice. Partly to be away from her mother-in-law, partly to please the Emperor who liked Laxenburg, she spent the summer of 1863 there. This also suited Francis Joseph, because he was spared scenes between his wife and his mother. But the old symptoms of swollen ankles and wrists, of a puffed-up face with a rash, and of a constant sore throat reappeared. Deeply worried, the Empress's mother, aware that her daughter did not trust Dr Joseph Skoda who had replaced the hated Dr Franz Seeberger, sent the family doctor, Hofrat Dr Heinrich von Fischer to Vienna. He had known the Empress as a child, and had plenty of experience of the temperamental and unbalanced Wittelsbach nature.[5] Unfortunately his report, believed to have confirmed that the Empress had gonorrhoea, has disappeared, allegedly destroyed with many other documents of the Habsburg archives. Officially Dr von Fischer wrote that the Empress suffered from extreme anaemia, and prescribed a nourishing diet and an annual cure at Kissingen. That is where Elizabeth was when Rudolf tried to climb a tree from a ladder and fell down from a considerable height. He hit his head against a stone and was badly concussed, remaining unconscious for several hours. Francis Joseph, distraught with anxiety, hurried back from Bad Gastein where he was having important discussions with King William of Prussia and Prince Bismarck. Archduchess Sophie interrupted her holiday in Ischl to nurse her grandson. Elizabeth was not informed of the accident until her son was completely out of danger.

Rudolf was already convalescent when she returned and entranced him with her stories and indulged him in every possible way. She managed to laugh away his tantrums. But she was not capable of giving him the security and warmth he found in his grandmother's company. 'The Archduchess Sophie had only to come into the room for Rudolf's face to light up with pleasure and for Elizabeth to leave the story unfinished and the toys scattered on the floor. The mother, who was no more than a beautiful apparition, vanished and the Archduchess took control.'[6]

In December 1863 Rudolf had typhoid fever. Although this was hushed up, he was very ill indeed. He owed his recovery to his grandmother's and Wowo's excellent nursing. Elizabeth was again away from home, this time in Possenhofen, where Dr von Fischer was trying out new cures. She did not return for her birthday on December 18, nor for Christmas; only on December 30 did she reappear, accompanied by her mother. By then Rudolf was well on the mend, but after his concussion, he got out of unpleasant tasks by pretending to have a headache—and again there was no one to deal with him tactfully but firmly. When he showed intelligence, he wanted to be praised; if he did not get praised, he sulked. Again there was no one to pull him up and put him in his place with loving firmness. Spells of gaiety and high spirits were followed by melancholia and depression. Rudolf never told anyone, as far as is known, what made him unhappy—yet at times he was indeed unhappy. It may be that he missed the enchanting mother who passed in and out of his life like a beautiful fairy, yet never became the companion he yearned for. Here were the first indications that he could keep silent and hide his innermost thoughts from others.

In July 1864, when Rudolf was barely six years old, Francis Joseph, with his mother's approval, chose the man who was to supervise his son's education: Major-General Count Leopold Gondrecourt (1818–1888), a professional soldier, about whom Prince Anton Alexander Auersperg[7] had said in 1859: 'It is unbelievable what cruelty and foul language our colonel is capable of letting loose.'[8] Gondrecourt had privates flogged on the slightest pretext, such as careless saluting; he frequently used his horsewhip on his subordinates. During one campaign he personally thrashed an army chaplain. For this he should have been court-martialled but his influential Court connections (among them Archduchess Sophie herself) managed to have the case dropped.[9]

This man was to be Rudolf's tutor because he held the right conservative views, and was ostentatiously religious. Every morning Gondrecourt went, rosary and prayerbook in hand, to 6 a.m. mass. The prayerbook was in fact a cigar box. At his appearance the *Burgwache* (the castle guard) had to present arms to the rolling of drums, which Rudolf would hear. The general, however, did not go to church, but to his mistress, a blonde, buxom chorus girl from the *Theater an der Wien*.[10]

No one could have been less suited to supervise a little boy, described in official documents as 'physically and spiritually more developed than other children of his age, but very highly strung'. To toughen Rudolf, he not only forced him to wash in icy water, but had pistols fired off in the middle of the night in the boy's bedroom while he was sleeping. One morning at 6 a.m. the Emperor and Express woke up to hear drill orders being shouted in the courtyard. Looking out of their windows, they saw

Gondrecourt drilling the six-year-old Rudolf in deep snow by lantern light. Small wonder that in May, 1865, Rudolf became ill. Some doctors diagnosed diphtheria, others thought it was a different disease; all agreed that the Crown Prince was in a serious nervous condition.

Hardly had Rudolf recovered than Gondrecourt thought up an even more sadistic exercise to discipline him. He took him one afternoon to the zoo in Lainz. Approaching the exit, he quickly slipped out, locked the boy in an enclosure and shouted: 'Here comes a wild boar!' Rudolf naturally began to scream, but the more he cried for help, the more Gondrecourt and his attendant military escort tried to frighten him.[11]

This was more than Elizabeth could stand. This time she was determined to bring about a change—Gondrecourt must go, she must have the last word about the children's upbringing. Scenes with her mother-in-law, Gondrecourt's protector in spite of his incredible methods, yielded no results. The Emperor would still not countermand his mother's arrangements. Elizabeth sent her husband a written ultimatum.

On August 24, 1865, three days after Rudolf's seventh birthday, she wrote to Francis Joseph: 'I cannot stand by and see such things going on. It must be either Gondrecourt or myself. . . . It is my wish that full and unlimited power should be reserved to me in all things concerning the children, the choice of those by whom they are surrounded and of their place of residence, and the entire control of their bringing up. In short, I alone must decide everything concerning them up to their majority. I further desire that everything concerning my own personal affairs, such for instance as the choice of those about my person, my place of residence, all changes in domestic arrangements, etc., etc., should be left for me to decide. Elizabeth.'[12]

The Emperor, realising that Elizabeth was in bitter earnest, and that if she went this time she would not return, gave way. Gondrecourt was removed,[13] overall responsibility for the Crown Prince's physical well-being was transferred to a physician, Dr Hermann von Widerhofer; his education was entrusted to Colonel Josef Latour von Turmburg. Relations between the Empress and the Archduchess grew worse than ever; Sophie did everything in her power to estrange the Empress from Francis Joseph.

According to Elizabeth she was offered 'with devilish cunning, opportunities for wrongdoing.[14] By now Elizabeth was twenty-eight years old, aware of the power her beauty and her charm had over the Emperor, and men in general. Francis Joseph for his part knew that she had still not recovered from the after-effects of the gonorrhoea with which he had infected her, and was prepared to pay any price to make up for it. He let her have her way with the education of Rudolf. If hitherto it had been too conservative, now it became perhaps too liberal. The disastrous events of the year 1866, when Austria was ignominiously defeated by Prussia, were to play into Elizabeth's hand.

So Elizabeth had won, and the Archduchess lost, the battle for the education of the children, notably that of Rudolf. There can be no doubt that both women adored the little boy and would have made any sacrifice for his well-being. Yet neither of them (nor Francis Joseph, for that matter) asked herself how Gondrecourt's sadism had affected the sensitive, highly strung child. In Rudolf's mind, Gondrecourt's much-vaunted religion could not but be linked with his tutor's vicious qualities. Instead of instilling strong principles of religion into Rudolf, this is where his doubts on the subject must have begun.

Gondrecourt's so-called discipline also undermined Rudolf's will-power; lack of it was Rudolf's greatest weakness. Wowo could have borne witness to that: she was keenly aware that the little boy needed encouragement, gentle urging on, to help him to develop self-confidence and strength of character. Gondrecourt's violence achieved the opposite, and Rudolf's nervous breakdown in May, 1865, left lasting scars on his mind. For the rest of his life he would suffer from emotional instability; his tragic death may well have been in part a consequence of the Gondrecourt experience. It certainly strengthened his inclination to vacillate when it came to carrying out difficult decisions, to ignore what was unpleasant, and to dissimulate whenever it suited him.

3

The Right Man in Charge

Colonel Josef Latour von Turmburg was the man Elizabeth put in charge of Rudolf's education, probably on Francis Joseph's suggestion, whose A.D.C. he had been. Latour came from a very cultivated middle-class family; he was widely read, artistic and an exceptionally considerate character, devoid of any selfishness. Born in Vienna on February 3, 1820, he studied law; then he served in the administration of Steiermark, from where he was transferred to the Court Chancellery in Vienna. In 1848 he joined up and served in Italy, distinguishing himself in the battles of Vicenza, Custozza and Milan. In 1849 he lost the middle finger of his right hand at the assault on Gambolo. Several times decorated, when he recovered his health he was promoted to captain and seconded to the A.D.C. corps, where he again proved his ability, so that the Emperor entrusted him with several diplomatic missions. Since September 1865 he acted as *Ajo* (according to Spanish Etiquette *Governor*) of the Crown Prince's education, although his appointment became official only in 1870.

Latour had a remarkable understanding of young people, and became devoted to Rudolf. As Elizabeth was absent much of the time, and Francis Joseph was constitutionally incapable of communicating with his son, Rudolf was thrown back entirely on Latour, who fortunately gave him some of the affection he craved, and all his time and attention. Latour's only difficulty was that he did not belong to the high nobility and had no position at Court; at meals he was invariably placed below the salt, and had to put up with sarcastic remarks and ill-informed criticism from high-born courtiers. In spite of Francis-Joseph's backing, and his co-operation in Rudolf's school curriculum, the more reactionary members of the Court were hotly disapproving. For instance, the Emperor's first Adjutant, General Frederick Count Beck-

Rzikowsky, who later became Army Chief of Staff, noted in his diary: 'I could not approve of the whole tendency of these studies to introduce the Crown Prince to all branches of knowledge of public life, to give him professors and tutors of the most liberal conviction and to let him in accordance with the unfortunate Court regulations in existence, complete his studies in his 20th year.[1] The young over-excited mind of the Crown Prince, the immaturity of his conceptions, the extravagance of his undeniably high intelligence, cause me anxiety that he will assimilate ideas and tendencies which would not correspond to the conservative character of a future monarch.'[2]

Josef Latour was the best type of officer to be found in the Austrian Army; it was thanks to him that Rudolf's mental equilibrium was restored, and the damage done by Gondrecourt seemingly disappeared.[3]

Latour was put in charge of Rudolf's education soon after the boy's seventh birthday. He spent a considerable time working out a new plan for Rudolf's education, in which he had to incorporate Francis Joseph's memorandum. The Emperor was anxious that the traditions of the House of Habsburg should not be forgotten, and Archduchess Sophie also tried to have her say. But with great tact Latour disregarded anything—and anyone—of which he did not approve. In one of his reports to the Emperor he said: 'I am proceeding on my straight road without special consideration for any personalities, by which one does not gain popularity, but it is the only way to maintain an independent judgment at Court.'

Francis Joseph wrote on the margin: 'Quite right.'

Rudolf was eight years old when Austria suffered the defeat of Sadowa (Koeniggraetz). The boy took an astonishing interest in the war with 'upstart Prussia'. When his grandmother told him that things were going badly in the field, he wrote to his father to say how sorry he was 'that we had to retreat but I hope we will soon make up for this'. In June, 1866, Rudolf's nightly prayer was: 'Almighty, eternal God, highest Lord of Heaven and Earth, I beg you humbly in this time of danger, do not deprive our fatherland, Austria, of your help. Bless the weapons of our warriors so that in the fight for right and honour they should not be defeated, but with your grace attain victory. Especially now, oh Kindest Father in Heaven, let my Loved One be recommended to your almighty Power and Love. Protect him from all dangers, remove all suffering from him, and give his heart consolation and the joy of a favourable conclusion of the war. Holy Virgin, please pray for us. Lord Jesus Christ please hear us. Amen.'

Rudolf was completely shaken by news of the Sadowa disaster; young though he was, he seems to have understood what it meant, and it was a traumatic experience for him that the Emperor, his Fatherland, and all that Austria stood for, had been terribly humiliated. On July 4, 1866, he wrote to his father: 'I am upset beyond words by our defeat—I will pray very hard that with God's help we reconquer all that we have lost. I believe the Good God will help us because our case is just.'[4]

But the Good God did not help. After the Sadowa defeat, when the Empress suddenly rushed with her children to Buda, Rudolf realised that their trip was really a flight—Prussian troops were advancing on the Austrian capital. He also became aware of the economies introduced even into the imperial household when, an armistice at last signed, Austria had to pay a heavy indemnity to Prussia.

Latour's daily reports on Rudolf's educational progress were first handed to the Military Chancellery, then to the Adjutant-General, then filed and reference numbered; finally the Lord High Steward laid them before the Emperor, who read and initialled them, and made comments in the margin. One of the Habsburg traditions Latour had to accept was that of Rudolf's religious education. It had begun when the boy was not yet four years old. In March, 1863, however, the Chief Chaplain of the Hofburg, Auxiliary Bishop Dr Johann Kutschker, was entrusted with it; later he was succeeded by the Court Chaplain, Dr Laurenz Mayer. Neither of these well-meaning clerics, nor their assistants, was able to interest the little boy; the observant Latour soon realised that Rudolf deliberately resisted their teaching efforts. In his report of May, 1868, Latour wrote to the Emperor regarding Rudolf's mental apathy: 'he does not say his evening prayers as he should, he does not speak loudly enough, he, as it were, swallows his words; in short it seems he wants to get it over.' In another report he drew the Emperor's attention to the ease with which Rudolf passed over his religious tuition. He asked the Emperor to find an occasion to have a word with the boy. 'But please do not be severe with him, and on no account speak to him in the presence of his sister Gisela.' However much Francis Joseph may have loved his son, he had no understanding of the highly strung and sensitive child.

Rudolf was prepared for his first confession in April, 1870, when aged eleven and a half. It worried him a great deal and he asked Latour to help him examine his conscience so that he should not forget anything. Then Court Chaplain Laurenz Mayer brought Rudolf the Prayer of Repentance: 'My own God, I have provoked Thy vengeance. I am no more worthy to be called thy son. I have deserved to be for ever banished from thy presence.' After reading it, Rudolf burst into tears and sobbed. Latour told the Emperor: 'I was deeply touched, as the sins of His Imperial Highness are quite disproportionate to the content of the prayer, if taken literally. However, I did not venture any milder interpretation of the prayer, for despite his noble heart and gifted mind, it cannot be denied that his faith is rather fickle.[5] I was apprehensive that if I had done so, he might begin to take the whole matter too lightly.'

Francis Joseph ordered Court Chaplain Mayer to be consulted, and he agreed that as Rudolf took everything too literally, he would compose a more appropriate prayer.

Rudolf made his first communion in the Hofburg chapel on April 11, 1870, which happened to be Easter Monday. His parents, grandparents, Gisela, Wowo, and the entire staff filled the chapel which Antoine, the head gardener, had transformed into a floral bower. Rudolf knelt on a red velvet-covered *prie-dieu*, to his left stood the candle used at his baptism. He had to repeat the christening vow, and at the end of mass Canon Mayer preached a suitable sermon. Rudolf received many presents which pleased him greatly.

Latour was not blind to Rudolf's shortcomings. In 1867, when Rudolf was only nine years of age, he gave a disturbing example of self-assertion. Because he felt that Latour did not appreciate him enough, he sat down and made his first will. Latour took no notice of the moral blackmail in this gesture of morbid self-dramatisation. He just corrected Rudolf's spelling mistakes, and made him copy his will.

Latour knew that Rudolf used any and every means to wriggle out of a situation he disliked. Moreover, he often did not tell the truth, which Latour painstakingly pointed out to Francis Joseph. On December 15, 1868, for example, he wrote: 'I have already told Your Majesty that the Crown Prince does not tell direct untruths, but has repeatedly expressed opinions which I know he does not hold or which are even the reverse of his true opinion.'[6] Ten-year-old Rudolf had a readiness to forget unpleasant things quickly. To avoid difficulties, he tried to find the easiest way round and not infrequently lied in order to gain praise. For instance, one evening Latour took him to the ballet, and Rudolf was enraptured by the performance. Yet next day he told his grand-mother that he had been unable to look at the stage because the ladies had not been suitably dressed. Latour was shocked, as Rudolf clearly said this only to please his grandmother.

What is more, Rudolf knew exactly what would please Archduchess Sophie, because he had, like the Empress, an instinctive almost uncanny understanding of other people's feelings. For instance on November 6, 1870, aged twelve, he wrote to his mother: 'Now that the whole of the French Army is in captivity, what a dreadful experience this must be for the old French soldiers who had always reaped glory. This is terrifyingly sad.'[7]

The Archduchess Sophie died in May, 1872, Rudolf, fascinated by death from the age of twelve, wanted to know every detail. He had to be told again and again how his mother, forgetting old feuds and her mother-in-law's hostility, spent ten hours at the old lady's deathbed. When quite young, he had asked Archduchess Sophie all the circumstances of the death of her daughter, Archduchess Anna, who had died in infancy. And there was the occasion when Colonel Count Andor Pálffy took him for a walk in the public part of the Schönbrunn Park and suddenly they heard screams. A young man had tried to commit suicide by drinking caustic soda, and although help did come, it was too late to save him. For days Rudolf could speak of nothing else. The thought of death had an uncanny hold on him. He asked repeatedly what it would feel like, what it would be like 'on the other side'. It was a subject that constantly occupied him.

There was variety in Rudolf's life, and at this time he seemed to enjoy public functions. On August 11, 1871, the old Emperor William I of Germany visited Ischl. Rudolf received the victor of Sadowa at his father's side with accomplished grace. But he instinctively disliked young Willie (William I's grandson) only six months younger than himself and all he could think about was how to plan a bloody revenge for Sadowa. 'God's justice will overtake the Hohenzollern House,' he wrote in an astonishingly mature poem for a thirteen-year-old. When Tsar Alexander II visited Vienna, Rudolf—dressed in Russian uniform—again stood by his father's side and with equal courtesy received the Lord of all the Russians. In July 1873 Rudolf performed his first official engagement: in Carinthia he unveiled a memorial to Maria Theresa, and himself composed his speech. It was a good speech, genuinely and justly praised.

An intelligent and precocious child, Rudolf at the age of fourteen filled pages and pages of his diary with his ideas—ideas that would have profoundly shocked Francis Joseph and possibly even the much more liberal Elizabeth. For instance, in December, 1872, he allowed Latour to read what he had written in his diary: 'I am also convinced that mankind would have advanced much further without the terrible days of the Middle Ages. . . . The clergy, always hand in glove with the proud aristocracy, used their influence over the people and did not permit the development of any free ideas; the Church chose ways dangerous for itself, for eventually the people would realise how they were treated and recognise the sacrilege of those indulgences and other means which the clergy used to enrich themselves.[8]

In few European countries was the aristocracy further removed from learning and research than in Austria. The nobility and the Church—when Rudolf grew to manhood—defended themselves desperately against the forces of progress (which Rudolf backed throughout his life). He realised their hostility, and usually kept his thoughts to himself, but sometimes he wanted to show off by shocking people. '*Pour épater l'aristocrate . . .*'

Latour, who knew how the reactionary aristocrats criticised Rudolf's education, carefully kept his pupil's revolutionary ideas from Francis Joseph and even from Elizabeth.

During the Christmas holidays of 1873, when Rudolf was

fifteen, he dedicated to Latour a small notebook which he called *Various Thoughts*. 'Thoughts of all kind,' he wrote, 'roam through my head; all seem confused, all day long my brain boils and toils . . . all thoughts contradicting, sometimes serene and merry, sometimes raven black, crowded with frenzy, they struggle with one another and slowly truth develops from them. I always ponder: what will the end be?

'Are we spirits, are we beasts? Beasts, that is what we are. But do we descend from the apes as a special species of two-handed beings?

'Often I ask myself: are you already a madman or will you become one? I realise I shall know all I want to know, but one thing is certain: one must always strive, always endeavour to achieve more and always more, not titles and dignities nor riches. . . . No, I want knowledge.

'Love is certainly the most beautiful experience in the life of all organic beings; it is an emotion that man still possesses, pure as in an animal, when in love he is still at one with nature.

'Kings and noblemen made laws to suit themselves and among those many terrible devices of the Middle Ages was one according to which man could only marry within his own estate . . . so that man, the Lord of Creation, could not, as every animal does, follow his heart, he had to submit to laws—the beast of the forest is freer. . . . In our own time when after the long dark night the bright sun of freedom and knowledge has risen and an entirely new epoch lies before our eyes, how can we keep up such conditions? The scion of the highest house will be able to follow his heart as a commoner or an animal. . . .

'The priests did most harm because they understood well how to make the people base and submissive by supersitition and exaggerated piety, so that they as well as the nobility had an easy game, and could do with the poor people as they liked. . . .

'During the French Revolution the king, the nobility and the clergy were punished for their own iniquities, and for those of their forebears. The punishment was rough and bloody, but it was a necessary and salutary catastrophe.

'The Government has changed and is a step nearer to the Republic. Monarchy has lost its old power, and clings to the trust and love of the people. . . . Monarchy is now a mighty ruin which may remain from today till tomorrow, but which will ultimately tumble. It has stood for centuries and as long as the people could be led blindly it was good. Now its task is over, all people are free and the next storm will bring the ruin tumbling down. . . .'

These few examples of Rudolf's thoughts show not only that he differed profoundly from his conservative father, but also that he could not have absorbed them from his mother who never expressed any rebelliousness against the Austrian political system. It is fascinating to speculate what would have happened had the Crown Prince met Karl Marx and discussed with him Socialism and Communism . . .

Rudolf may have borrowed some ideas from earlier Habsburgs, like Don Carlos and Joseph II, but he thought matters out for himself. He had a social conscience—more aware of realities than most of the liberals who aired their views and influenced their contemporaries, yet ignored the sufferings of the artisans when—to take just one example—they were squeezed out of their small individual businesses, and forced to work for extremely low wages.

In spite of his intelligence and imaginative empathy, to which all Rudolf's teachers testified, he was rash and hasty in his judgements, as gifted boys frequently are. What was lacking in him was strength of character; as a result he did not live up to the high expectations of his tutor. The only point on which Latour failed him was that, having supervised his lessons—Rudolf had between 30 and 36 classes a week, plus riding, fencing and dancing lessons, home work and study of languages—he did not insist on time being set aside for the boy to assimilate what he was being taught.

Moreover—and this was truly astonishing—Rudolf was always alone with his teachers. He had practically no friends of his own age; apart from occasional cousins staying or the *thé dançants* to practice dancing, he hardly ever saw young people. The Crown Prince of Austria-Hungary was a lonely child.

On the technical level there were complications that caused Latour much concern regarding Rudolf's education. Should it centre around German traditions or should the Hungarian element be stressed? How far should the part played by the Slav nations, then awakening to national consciousness, be emphasised? Rudolf had to learn at least some of the dozen languages spoken in the Dual Monarchy.

Fortunately he had a marked gift for them. His command of Hungarian and its idioms was fair, although he never quite mastered Hungarian grammar. His Czech was fluent—he could address gatherings without difficulty and he had an excellent accent. He also spoke Polish and Croatian.

Yet the early 1870's were a propitious time for working out a curriculum for Rudolf—a liberal spirit pervaded Austria and in 1865 there had already been changes in the atmosphere. State–Church relations were to be newly defined; the Emperor—though a staunch Catholic—stood by the decisions of the new Austrian Parliament to reduce Church influence both over the schools and the universities, and over public life in general. Civil weddings had become possible in some cases; citizens could belong to no religious persuasion. But the vote for the new Parliament was based on income—only those who paid a certain amount in taxes were enfranchised. Still there was a general liberalisation of attitudes and institutions. Rudolf imbibed this spirit, and held to it during his brief life.

Latour, whom the Emperor loyally supported during the eleven years in which he had control of Rudolf's education, chose some fifty distinguished teachers, all eminent men in their respective spheres, to carry out his education plan. The world-famous Professor Alfred Eduard Brehm taught Rudolf zoology; Professor Karl Menger, founder of the Austrian School of Economics, his own subject; an eminent Czech historian, Dr Anton Gindely, the Czech language (he was succeeded by Hermingild Jireček); Dr Charles Rimely, Bishop of Besztercebánya (now Banska Bistrica), Hungarian.[9] Professor Alfred Ritter von Arneth, himself a distinguished historian, drew up the plan for 'the history department', and said in his *pro-memoria*: 'For a prince who through his birth is called upon to stand at the head of the greatest empire in Europe, and one of the most difficult to rule, the teaching of history is, without any doubt, the most difficult.' Arneth chose Heinrich von Zeissberg to teach Rudolf the history of the Austrian Empire. Zeissberg interpreted the subject with great tact, but the nearer he came to events through which he and the other teachers had lived, the harder it became to stick to facts and to abstain from judgments.

Political events made Latour's task more difficult and also had their bearing on Rudolf's mental development. Since 1859 the Hungarian question had been coming more and more to the fore. The Hungarians demanded the restoration of their constitution, an end to the centralising dreams of the Emperor and certain of his ministers, and full partnership with the Austrians. Elizabeth had an instinctive liking for the Magyars (already in 1859 she had suggested to the Emperor that he should come to terms with them), and she made great efforts to learn their language. With Rudolf she corresponded in Hungarian. Their letters are proofs of the charming relationship that existed between them at this time. Thanks to Latour, they are preserved in the Vienna State Archives.

The Hungarians were not slow to find out that they had, at last, a friend at Court. When the Empress occompanied her husband to Buda she was given a very warm reception. Her beauty enchanted men and women of all ranks, and when at her instigation (so it was believed) the Emperor pardoned the political exiles and allowed them to return, enthusiasm for her knew no bounds. Luckily the leader of the Hungarians, Francis Deák (1803–76), was one of the most remarkable men of the 19th century. He had begun his career as a Member of the Diet of Pozsony, but he had disapproved of Kossuth's revolutionary attitude in 1848–49 and realised that Hungary needed Austria as much as Austria needed Hungary. Deák wanted reconciliation, not revenge.

Besides the Hungarian problem Francis Joseph also had cause for anxiety in the aggressive rise of Prussia under the leadership of Otto von Bismarck, who was determined to bring Austria low—first by keeping her out of the *Zollverein*, the German Customs Union, on which Prussia began to work in 1818 in a small way, but which gradually embraced all the German States. In 1862 the ambitious, iron-fisted, rigidly conservative Bismarck was appointed Prime Minister of Prussia, and at last could begin to create the German Empire.

Francis Joseph knew that the Prussian army was better armed and better trained than his own:[10] how much better he found out in 1866, when on a flimsy excuse Prussia declared war and destroyed the Austrian forces at Sadowa (Koeniggraetz). The way to Vienna was open; Francis Joseph sent Elizabeth with the children to Hungary. 'Take them to Buda and be my advocate there. Hold in check [the situation] as far as you can, and we shall find a way,' he told her.[11]

It was then that Francis Deák, the Hungarian leader, showed his wisdom: in spite of Austria's humiliating defeat, he did not ask for more than he had asked before: restoration of Hungary's ancient constitution and what would nowadays be called civil rights, and partnership with Austria. The Habsburg dreams of an autocratic centralised regime, as well as Austria's leadership of the German nations, had died for ever at Sadowa. The Hungarian Count Julius Andrássy, who had by then already been pardoned, returned from Paris where he had been a glamorous exile nicknamed '*le beau pendu*'. He was attractive, brilliant, very handsome, very rich and had contacts with the high and mighty in all countries, especially in France and England. He backed Deák and fell completely under Elizabeth's spell. Between them the Empress, Deák and Andrássy worked out the *Ausgleich*—the Compromise—of 1867. On February 18 the restoration of the Hungarian Constitution was publicly announced in the Diet, and a responsible ministry formed under the premiership of Andrássy.

That same year Francis Joseph was crowned King of Hungary and took the oath on the Hungarian constitution. To express their appreciation of the role she had played, Elizabeth was crowned with her husband, although according to ancient Hungarian custom she should have been crowned separately a few days after.

And a year later Elizabeth made one of those wonderful gestures that endeared her for ever to Hungarians (even to some Communist Hungarians!): she chose the castle in Buda as the place where, on April 24, 1868, she gave birth to her third daughter, her eldest had died in infancy. The Hungarians reacted with typical emotion: their devotion to their Queen and to 'their Princess Mária Valéria' knew no bounds. As Elizabeth had expressed interest in a large country house eighteen miles from Buda, Gödöllö,[12] 'the grateful Hungarian nation' presented it to her on this happy occasion. Rudolf, Gisela and Valerie were to spend many happy days in Gödöllö.

With Andrássy Prime Minister of Hungary and Elizabeth in close touch with Hungarian affairs through her Reader,[13] Ida Ferenczy, the niece of Francis Deák, the Hungarian leaders placed among Rudolf's tutors a remarkable personality to teach him Hungarian history. His name was Father Hiacynth John Rónay.

4

Rudolf's Hungarian History Teacher

The man who was to teach Crown Prince Rudolf Hungarian history and much else besides, was born in Székesfehérvár on May 13, 1814. Jácint János Rónay,[1] the eldest child of well-to-do burghers, attended a Cistercian school from 1824 to 1829; his best friend was the son of the local librarian who lent him books he could never have obtained otherwise. Aged thirteen, J.J. decided to become a writer, but because of financial troubles his parents begged him to join the Benedictine Order. He agreed—reluctantly—yet it was partly due to his religious calling that the greatest opportunities of his life were offered to him.

He was ordained on July 20, 1836; taught for a few years at the Benedictine school in Györ,[2] then became liturgical supervisor to the Abbot of Pannonhalma (the leading Benedictine school in Hungary) and professor of philosophy. He also studied psychology.

During the national uprising of 1848, in Györ County J.J. united the clergy of all denominations to pray for the first Independent National Government. Then he was sent to Pest to report to Louis Kossuth that, owing to the extreme cold, Györ could not hold out.[3] When Government and Parliament fled from Pest to Debreczen, J.J. took refuge in a Benedictine monastery. Then came news of victories: Hungarian patriots liberated Györ; on his return J.J. had a rousing reception, which he used to save the life of an 'anti-Kossuth' Benedictine. The Government Commissioner, Sándor Lukács, took him to Pest, and he participated in the storming of Buda. Lukács appointed J.J. Commissioner for Religious Affairs in Györ County, but by the spring of 1849 Tsar Alexander had sent 200,000 Russian troops to attack the Hungarian insurgents in the rear. On June 28, 1849, the Austrians took Györ, and J.J. had a narrow escape. With his friend Lukács he was plodding towards Világos when a Jewish merchant[4] informed them that Kossuth had fled to Turkey in disguise, General Arthur Görgei had surrendered[5] and a death warrant had been issued against Father Rónay. J.J. went into hiding, thus not witnessing the execution of the thirteen Hungarian generals and of so many others that even the Tsar protested against Francis Joseph's cruelty.

After some months, however, J.J. managed with a forged passport to escape to Germany, and made his way to Hamburg, where he took a ship to England. He was allowed to land without a single document to prove his identity, without a penny in his pocket and without speaking one word of English. He and Lukács rented two rooms in Portland Street, London, W.1. Their landlady had a friend, a blind doctor called John Bird, who taught J.J. idiomatic English and proper pronunciation, and got him his first pupil whom he coached in Latin and Greek. He also earned ten florins a month by writing three articles a week for a Hungarian paper. Altogether 142 of his *London Letters* were published; they painted a truthful and dispassionate picture of mid-19th century English life and of Hungarian refugee activities.[6]

J.J. was fascinated by the English people and confided to his diary:[7] 'The English are industrious, they work with an iron discipline, together they form a great nation. Each person is only interested in one thing, but does that thing very well.' J.J. soon became popular with an increasing number of acquaintances. On September 30, 1850, Lady Mary Grey[8] told him that if he was willing to turn Anglican, she would assure him a living. Gratefully and in the most charming manner he declined. Lukács, who had become a freemason, implored J.J. also to join. But he refused to have anything to do with an organisation barred to Roman Catholics.

Meanwhile he had become a writer of note: he published in English *The History of Life* in five volumes; then he switched to geology—*The Wise Fireworshippers* was the title of his work dealing with *The Memories Of The Ancient World.* On December 9, 1850, Béla, the son of the great Count István Széchényi, unexpectedly called on him. He brought a manuscript of his father's, written in his voluntary retirement to the Döbling Lunatic Asylum; its title was *Blick—Rückblick* (A look forward—a look backwards) and was an analysis of Hungarian affairs since 1848, pouring scorn on the centralised system of Alexander Bach, Francis Joseph's austere Chancellor.[9] J.J. found a printer, George Barclay, who printed it for £250. In February, 1851, Béla Széchényi did the distribution with the help of the Marchioness of Stafford and Lord Loftus, both firm friends of the Hungarian liberals. Lady Stafford (later to become the Duchess of Sutherland) even learnt Hungarian from J.J. and visited Hungary.

J.J. was also in touch with Louis Kossuth and his two sons.[10] Kossuth asked Father Rónay to become his representative in Stockholm, but he refused, for he disagreed with Kossuth's radical ideas and believed that Hungary's future had to be evolved in Hungary, and not in foreign lands by emigrés and their backers. Nonetheless Kossuth asked him to teach his two sons Latin. He could only do this between 7 and 9 in the evening, and of course free of charge. When they left England, Ferenc and Louis Kossuth Jr. presented him with a golden pen, their names and the date—May 4, 1861—engraved on it. They remained J.J.'s friends all their lives.

Meanwhile Benjamin Smith, a Tory M.P. whose sons J.J. was teaching, came to like him so much that he took him on a trip to Jersey. There J.J. met Victor Hugo and made friends with him too. He now took up anthropology and travelled all over Britain. He had become sufficiently well-known to be asked by the Royal Geographical Society to review the book of László Magyar, the Hungarian Africa explorer, for their 1865 Yearbook.[11]

On March 27, 1862, the citizens of Györ petitioned the Hungarian Academy of Sciences to take steps to bring Father Rónay home. To show his appreciation, he sent six articles to the *Györ Közlöny* (Gazette of Györ); then he heard that the Hungarian Academy of Sciences wanted him to become its secretary. In 1865 the Hungarian Parliament was recalled, the first important move to bring about a reconciliation between the Crown and the Nation. On September 5 the Benedictines elected a new Abbot, whose duty it would be 'to move every stone to bring home J. J. Rónay'. The Abbot appealed for an amnesty for J.J., but he refused to beg for a pardon as, he said, he had not changed his views and never would. Eventually the Abbot induced him to apply simply for permission to return to Hungary, and on May

22, 1866, informed him with joy: 'His Majesty, having listened to your application, allows you absolutely to return to your Fatherland. May God bring you home soon.'

But J.J. could not leave London on the spur of the moment: he had obligations, pupils, the translation of Paul Hunfalvy's book —*Reguly*—commissioned by Prince Lucien Bonaparte; arrangements to be made with the Ethnographical Society which had elected him a member; and a lecture to deliver at the British Association for the Advancement of Science. And finally there was his love and admiration for the country where he had spent sixteen years and for his dear English friends who had taught him so much about liberty, constitutional government and what democracy meant. At last, on September 26, 1866, he reached Vienna and took a boat down the Danube—destination Pest.

The Minister of Education, Baron Joseph Eötvös, refused to let J.J. retire to Pannonhalma; he told him that in addition to becoming Secretary, the Academy would elect him a full member, and he was also invited to join the Committee that decided which plays should be performed at the National Theatre. Györ County elected him as one of its Members of Parliament.

In 1871 came one of the great moments of J.J.'s life: in a passage of the Parliament building, The Wise Man Of The Nation, Francis Deák, informed him that he would be appointed head of a section of the Ministry of Education. A few weeks later, an even more momentous encounter occurred: the Prime Minister, Andrássy, called him out of a session and informed him that His Majesty had entrusted him, Andrássy, to find a suitable person to teach the heir to the throne Hungarian history. 'I recommended you in the Ministerial Council, and it gave me great pleasure that all my colleagues agreed. Are you willing to undertake this illustrious task?'

Of course J.J. was willing. Everything fell into place: his past experience, his efforts to educate himself, his sixteen years in England. All these had prepared him for carrying out his daunting task. He resigned from his constituency, but not from the Ministry of Education.

Then he was summoned to Vienna.

5

Historic Truth instilled into Rudolf

On October 10, 1871, Father Rónay arrived in Vienna and put up at the former Hungarian–Transylvanian Chancellery, by then the Royal Hungarian Ministry.[1] He found a letter from Colonel Latour waiting for him. It told him that the lessons would be from 9 to 10 o'clock in the morning; a Court carriage would bring him to Schönbrunn and take him back to his lodgings. Latour invited J.J. to visit him the next day, when he showed him round and told him: 'It is the Emperor's wish that you keep to the truth and follow your convictions. His Majesty wants the Crown Prince to be well acquainted with all the conditions and requirements of modern times, but he does not want him to become a free thinker. There are no restrictions on your work.'[2]

Latour also asked Father Rónay for a plan of the lectures he proposed to give up till December 2, 1872. J.J. excused himself saying that he could not do this in so short a time; but he sent Latour an outline of the lessons to be given during the first three months. At the beginning of each lecture he proposed to sum up what he had said in the previous one and then to ask the Crown Prince to repeat it, thus both teaching him facts and practicing his Hungarian.

After the first lesson, on October 21, thirteen-year-old Rudolf invited J.J. to luncheon. 'The open, gentle, intelligent eyes, the friendly facial expression, the good humour and the childish ease and liveliness of Rudolf filled me with joy and high hopes,' J.J. wrote in his diary.[3] He was very pleased that Rudolf spoke Hungarian almost the whole time, and that he asked so many questions 'about our nation and its affairs. He is much more mature than his years; he also has humour and wit. Comparing the Austrians and the Hungarians, this is what Rudolf had written:

"The Germans are more reliable and more cultivated than the Hungarians, though the latter have hotter blood. The Germans are characterised by honesty and open-heartedness—except the Prussians, who are cunning. The hot-headedness of the Magyars is shown by their constant shouting—both young and old shout. Hungarians are good horsemen, but not much use as infantrymen. The Hungarians hang with body and soul on their fatherland, and are prepared to give the last drops of their blood for it. The Austrians are not prepared for this sacrifice." ' J.J. chuckled while writing what Rudolf said about Hungarian shouting in his diary. 'True, all too true . . .'

On another occasion Rudolf asked whether there were Hungarian families dating back to ancient times? 'I explained that he, himself, was descended through the female line from the Árpáds, the original Hungarian royal family. Rudolf replied he had heard that said, but he wanted to see proof of it. I hope I reassured him on this score—I drew a family tree to show him his Árpád blood.'

J.J. explained to Rudolf that there had been seven Hungarian tribes, each with an independent chief, and 108 clans. From the Etelköz—the present-day Bessarabia and Moldavia—they crossed the Carpathians and descended into the Hungarian plain by the pass of Vereczke.[4] The seven chiefs formed a blood alliance; each one cut his wrist and let fall a few drops of blood into a golden goblet, from which they all drank. This blood alliance was and is the foundation of the Hungarian Constitution. J.J. noted in his diary: 'Rudolf immediately understood the importance of the Hungarians' arrival: they divided the Svatopluk empire, and prevented the formation of a huge Slav dominion, reaching from the Arctic Ocean to the hot steppes of Asia. . . . I felt as though I were talking to a young man of eighteen or twenty, not to a boy of thirteen.'[5]

During the same luncheon, conversation turned to Transylvania, and J.J. explained how King Géza II (1131–61) had come to settle the Saxons in this principality 'to teach their crafts to the Hungarians'.

In 1147 the German Emperor, Conrad III, requested permission of King Géza II for his crusaders to pass through Hungary on their way to the Holy Land. He promised that his well-disciplined troops would keep to the main roads. Some 70,000 trained men did, but not the 100,000-odd 'followers'.[6] J.J. told Rudolf that the followers behaved not like Christ's pilgrims, but like tyrants and brigands, who robbed, looted and set houses on fire.' The genuine pilgrims were so shocked and disgusted that they refused to form part of this mob any longer. Géza II, who was only seventeen years old, felt sorry for them and allowed 'the refugees from the Netherlands and Saxony[7] to settle in Hungary,' on condition that they passed on their crafts to the locals—that is to say to the Transylvanians.

Rudolf, who had listened with wrapt attention, gave J.J. a long look and said, 'It would have been better if the Saxons had not settled in Transylvania, for there were already enough foreign elements in the country. Even if the Hungarians learnt crafts from the foreign wanderers, the endeavours of the outsiders had a harmful effect on political life, and this weakened the country.' To J.J.'s amazement the Crown Prince went on: 'Hungary's concessions to them are illustrated by the fact that after 800 years, they still speak their original language, and retain their original traditions. Yet they have not shown any gratitude for this generous treatment and have not become Hungarians.'[8] Father Rónay could hardly believe his ears when Rudolf concluded: 'We must keep together, because Austria without Hungary would melt into the German Empire, and without Austria, Hungary would be enjulfed by the Slav Empire.'[9]

J.J. looked in amazement at the boy who at the age of thirteen had such an understanding of the gravest problem facing the Habsburg Monarchy, and his own country, Hungary. Rudolf was completely different from what J.J. had imagined; no one had prepared him for his precocious wisdom.

J.J. was to make an even greater impact on Rudolf's imagination by explaining to him that the Emperor Ferdinand II, who ruled from 1619 to 1637, was largely responsible for the Thirty Years War. As for the elected Prince of Transylvania, Gábor Bethlen, a Protestant, he waged two successful campaigns against Ferdinand II and a third against Ferdinand III, in the name of religious freedom. Wherever Gábor Bethlen's flag flew, all religions—Catholic, Protestant and Moslem—could be freely practised. His negotiations with the Habsburg Emperor broke down because of Ferdinand's religious bigotry and his territorial ambitions. As they could not defeat him, Habsburg agents poisoned Bethlen when he was only forty-nine years old.[10]

J.J.'s analysis of Ferdinand's character and villainous intrigues incensed Rudolf so much that one day, walking through a passage in Schönbrunn with Latour, he caught sight of Ferdinand's picture and tried to shoot at it.[11] Latour could not understand why young Rudolf should have suddenly turned violent. Had he understood Hungarian, and thus what J.J. was telling the Crown Prince, he would have realised why.

Rudolf's maturity never ceased to surprise J.J., who came to realise that his own liberal, very English views had had a much greater effect on his pupil than he had thought. So he gave him a serious warning. 'When you will become Emperor and King, please bear in mind that you must not go too fast or attempt to do too much. Study the history of your remarkable ancestor, Joseph II. He was decades ahead of his time—and he genuinely wanted to improve the lot of the people, yet his excellent ideas proved a complete failure because he went too fast and too far.'[12] Rudolf studied Joseph II's life, but he did not tell J.J. what conclusions he reached for himself.

The most difficult task J.J. had to face was telling Rudolf the story of the 1848–49 national uprising. His description of conditions in Hungary before 1848 was absolutely fair: he was as critical of the Hungarian absentee landlords as of the Austrian refusal to live up to the Hungarian constitution. He castigated the devaluation of the currency carried out on Vienna's instructions—in the end a hundred crowns were worth only six. The inflation, the heavy taxes and the lack of comprehension for the Hungarian attitude ruined the country.

J.J. paid respectful tribute to Count István Széchényi, and to his three famous books—*Hitel* (Credit), *Világ* (The World) and *Stádium* (Stadium). Széchényi had gone to England and France to observe economic developments, new constitutional institutions and the lessons to be drawn from their respective revolutions. In *Hitel* (Credit), (1832), Széchényi analysed why the large landowners were not credit-worthy; the bankers of Austria (like the Rothschilds) refused them loans because of their antiquated agricultural methods. He spelt out the faults of the Hungarian landowners, big and small: conceit, maltreatment of the serfs, misuse of unpaid feudal labour, injustices to the peasants, etc. He described the necessary reforms—using as examples the methods by which English and French estates were run. He dwelt especially on England, where everyone with an income above a certain sum paid income tax and everyone was equal before the law. 'It was with an inner feeling of delight that I perceived in England every man's equality before the law,' was one of Széchényi's sayings which moved both J.J. and the Crown Prince. Another was the concluding sentence of Széchényi's speech, when in 1825 he offered his income for one year—125,000 florins[13]—for the foundation of the Hungarian Academy of Sciences: 'Hungary has not been—Hungary will be.'

In *Világ* (World) and *Stádium* (Stadium) Széchényi extended his analyses to economic conditions—to the need for the creation of industry and commerce; to the total overhaul and modernisation of the economic system, all on the basis of the English principle of *laisser faire*.[14] Under the impetus of his enthusiasm economic enterprises of immense importance were initiated; one in particular—the bridge between Buda and Pest, constructed by the English Tierney and Adam Clark—had direct political importance: nobles also had to pay toll for crossing it, the first breach in their cherished privilege of exemption from taxation. Széchényi wanted to achieve the regeneration of Hungary by evolution, as against revolution—here he clashed with Louis Kossuth, the other great Hungarian leader.

J.J. discussed with Rudolf the National Assemblies of 1832 and 1836, which debated religious freedom, the union of Hungary proper with Transylvania, the abolition of corporal punishment of the serfs, of feudal dues and Church tithes; the introduction of taxation of the nobles, and the adoption of Hungarian in place of Latin as the official language.

In 1835 Ferdinand V ascended the Austrian throne and was also crowned King of Hungary. In the spring of 1836 the National Assembly met in Pozsony; its young and determined members managed to get passed a number of liberalising laws. When it rose on May 2, without having toned down any of these laws, official circles in Austria were appalled and indignant, although ordinary Austrians warmly approved the courage of the Hungarians. To counter their influence, which conservative Austrian politicians called revolutionary, anarchistic, mad, dangerous, Vienna espoused Pan-Slavism in Slovakia—to turn the Slovaks against 'the Hungarian rebels'; 'Romanism' in Transylvania to alienate the Vlachs, who called themselves Rumanians and demanded autonomy, and 'Illyrism' between the Drava and the Sava rivers that the Serbs and Croats should 'break Magyarism'.[16] 'Never have politicians rendered a worse service to the throne than they did when they took up this dangerous double-edged weapon,' J.J. told Rudolf.

Father Rónay recorded in his diary that the boy listened with visible excitement. Then came the account of the reconvened National Assembly of 1839–40 and of 1843–44. Its members were exclusively nobles, yet these nobles voluntarily accepted general taxation, from which they had hitherto been exempt, and renounced their privileges of their own free will. J.J. rightly pointed out that this was largely the result of Széchényi's work; there were others—Baron Nicholas Wesselényi, Francis Deák, Ferenc Kölcsey, Louis Kossuth—who had also agitated for such reforms, but it was Széchényi's deeply religious attitude and the moral grounds on which he castigated and rejected privilege that had the greatest effect. Finally, in 1847 the National Assembly passed the laws imposing equal taxation and abolishing the entailed estate system. Then came news of the February Revolution in France; Kossuth came to the fore and forced the pace by introducing the parliamentary system and responsible government. On March 17, 1848, Ferdinand V gave in to the inevitable; on April 11 he signed the laws sanctioning the great reforms.

J.J. explained to Rudolf that there had been too much enthusiasm in Hungary, and too much fear among the imperial advisers in Vienna. In 1848 hundreds of thousands of Magyars took up the cause of their Fatherland with fervent patriotism, without anyone thinking of a final break with the Monarch, or an open fight against the dynasty. However, 'the irresistible force of circumstances, the fear and antagonism of advisers surrounding the throne (in Vienna) drove the nation to a point far beyond its original aim. That is how national self-confidence was transformed into open battle, and the fight for freedom into heart-rending bloodshed. The die was cast, and rolled irresistibly towards the bloody meadow where all understanding, all effort to save the constitution, proved vain.'[16]

Father Rónay has further described in his diary how, as he was talking and keeping a tight rein on himself in order not to say more than was necessary to inform the Crown Prince of the facts, he felt the atmosphere becoming tense, and watched the precocious boy sitting opposite him digging his hands into the arms of his chair. It was almost a relief when the lecture was over.

What J.J. did not confide to his diary is whether he ever told Rudolf about his father's extreme cruelty to the Hungarian insurgents. Between 1848 and 1853, Francis Joseph signed and confirmed more death warrants than any other European ruler during the whole of the 19th century. Did J.J. tell the young Crown Prince of the execution of the first responsible Prime Minister of Hungary, Count Lajos Batthyány? Batthyány did all he could to prevent the break between Hungary and the Imperial Government; he resigned from Kossuth's government and remained in Pest when the imperial troops entered. Prince Alfred Windischgraetz had Batthyány arrested in his palace, sent him to Olmütz to stand trial; Batthyány was duly condemned to death, but with a strong recommendation for mercy. After the tragic defeat of the Hungarian rebellion, he was sent back to Pest. Free for a few days, he was re-arrested by General Julius Haynau,[17] whose bloodthirsty cruelty shocked the whole of Europe. Haynau had Batthyány condemned not to shooting but to garroting. Petitions for clemency were sent from all sides to the Austrian Minister of State, Prince Felix Schwarzenberg, but he refused to relent; it was said that Archduchess Sophie had had several talks with Batthyány, and showed more than political interest in him. As Batthyány did not reciprocate her advances, she used her influence with Schwarzenberg that Batthyány should die by garroting.

Batthyány was very much in love with his beautiful sister-in-law, Countess Ede Károlyi, née Countess Carolina Zichy. She was in Pest, and one day, while sitting in the garden of the Károlyi town house, a gipsy woman managed to get in and foretold the death of Lajos Batthyány. In case this prophecy were to come true, she taught Carolina the words of a terrible curse, which called down the vengeance of heaven and hell for the innocent blood shed by the Habsburgs. Francis Joseph was to be struck through those dearest to him, in his children and his whole family.

Carolina visited Batthyány in prison and gave him a large loaf of bread, in which a sharp knife was hidden. Batthyány, who regarded garroting as a shameful death for a Hungarian nobleman, cut his throat with the knife, and therefore had to be shot. While he was being executed on October 8, 1849, in the *Neugebäude*, an enormous fortified barracks where Parliament now stands in Budapest, Carolina waited outside. The execution over, she managed to slip into the courtyard where it had taken place and threw herself on the body of the man she adored, and invoked the curse the gipsy woman had taught her: that all those Francis Joseph loved should perish by violent deaths. Batthyány's body was taken away by a donkey cart, driven by a gipsy.

At the spot where Lajos Batthyány is believed to have been shot, there is a commemorative plaque. It was put up in the 1930's, it was not destroyed during the siege of Budapest, and a red bulb is glowing over it to this day.[18]

Rudolf had to pass examinations in all the ten subjects he studied. On April 15, 1872, he had the first test in Hungarian history. Rudolf and J.J. sat opposite to each other at small tables, with a jug of water and a glass in front of each of them. To the right of Rudolf sat the Emperor and fourteen distinguished men, Austrians, Hungarians and Czechs, and of course Latour.

Father Rónay did not ask Rudolf to answer specific questions; in an easy conversational style he reviewed with him the whole of the Árpád period. Then J.J. told Rudolf to imagine himself in the place of St Stephen and to address the nation's leaders. Rudolf thought for about two minutes, and then began to speak. His argument was that if the Hungarians did not accept Christianity, and continued with their plundering expeditions, they would be chased back to Asia by indignant Europeans. Rudolf once more demonstrated his extraordinary maturity—also, he had a definite flair for acting. At this examination he spoke well and everyone in the room, most of all the Emperor, was impressed by his instinctive grasp of political implications. Concluding Rudolf raised his voice and addressed his audience as though he were truly St Stephen: 'If we do not accept the Christian religion, and the ways of peace, our best men will be killed in eternal wars; we will diminish in numbers and in strength, the whole of Europe will rise against us, and in the end we can return from whence we originated—Asia.'

On December 23, 1872, Rudolf passed his final examination in Hungarian history. Again it was a ceremonious event, which took place in Gödöllö, in the presence of Francis Joseph, many distinguished Hungarians such as the Secretary of the Hungarian Academy of Sciences, and two Austrian historians. Again J.J. did not ask specific questions, but in one hour and a half took Rudolf through Hungarian history to their own day. Rudolf told the story 'from King Venzel to Papa', and made two excellent extempore speeches. Francis Joseph's verdict was: 'Father Rónay, you have instilled the spirit of historic truth into Rudolf's heart, also love for your Hungarian fatherland and loyalty to the Monarchy. Thank you.'[19]

J.J. was pleased with the result of his tutoring. He believed that Rudolf would never deviate from his own statement: 'Austria without Hungary will melt into the German Empire; Hungary without Austria will be engulfed by the Slav Empire.' To this he added his own belief: 'We have gained our freedom, but that we should be, and remain, Hungarians—only the Hungarian nation can ensure for itself.' J.J. was aware of the disintegration that was going on in the Monarchy, and of the nationalities' problem in Hungary, he was afraid that if the Austrians continued with their undermining activities they would ease the road to Prussian hegemony.

Rudolf continued to pass exams, to learn facts and interpretations, to charm teachers and almost everyone who came in contact with him. J.J. was not the only teacher with whom Rudolf struck up a lasting friendship; he also got on very well with Dr Chlumecky, who taught him the Czech language and imparted so much affection for his people that for a number of years Rudolf was an ardent Slavophil. He became devoted to Professor Alfred Brehm, the famous zoologist, who aroused his interest in birds; and to Professor Karl Menger, the distinguished economist, who introduced Rudolf to his theories. Rudolf felt happy in the company of all these outstanding men. Had he been allowed to carry on with his studies, his life might have taken a very different course.

6

Rudolf comes of Age—his Foreign Travels

Crown Prince Rudolf came of age on July 24, 1877, one month before his nineteenth birthday.[1] In accordance with Spanish Etiquette, his father ordered him to stop his studies, so that Rudolf, whose mercurial temperament had always been an obstacle to methodical thinking and disciplined work, was denied the benefit of a university education. This was the greater pity as Rudolf had real talent for ornithology. Empress Elizabeth, whose modern thinking had so often shocked the Court, failed to understand how much her son cared about acquiring knowledge, and did not use her influence over Francis Joseph to let Rudolf continue his studies at least for another year. Nor did she put in their place the Camarilla—as Count Lónyay called the influential reactionary courtiers—who while pretending concern for Rudolf, poked fun at his enjoyment of nature, calling it 'provincial', and 'not befitting his high station'.

Young as he was, Rudolf judged the members of the Camarilla for what they were, and disliked most of them. With his highly developed social conscience, he took the measure of Austria's social ills practically on his own. To complete the training for his future position, he was sent on several journeys; in 1878 he spent two months in England, which made a tremendous impression on him. Three years later, on his voyage to the Middle East, he showed remarkable powers of observation and diplomatic insight, as illustrated by his official views published in his *A Trip To The Orient*,[2] and his personal views expressed in letters to friends.

Rudolf had charm and a great gift for sympathy. He was in Gratz on July 3, 1872, the anniversary of Sadowa, when the Emperor ordered him to visit General Lajos Benedek, the man who so magnanimously had taken upon himself full responsibility for the rout for which in fact he bore none.[3] But the general asked to be excused and the meeting never took place. In connection with this episode Benedek told his wife: 'It is too little and too late.'[4] To Latour he wrote a letter of thanks for Rudolf's visit. 'I know very well that only a very few people conceive correctly my fate as a soldier and my character as a soldier,' he began. 'This leaves me quite indifferent because I am at peace with myself. But you will surely understand me when I tell you that I nurse no grudge against anyone and that for my remaining days . . . I want nothing . . . only peace and quiet.'[5]

No doubt Latour, in his honesty and with the instructions of the Emperor to tell Rudolf the truth, explained to the prince the tremendous sacrifice the general had made, which was accepted by Francis Joseph, who never spoke up for him, or named those who were responsible for Sadowa. One can only surmise the reactions of a sensitive, generous young mind like Rudolf's to such injustice. He and his father could have little to say to each other. The Empress did not use her exceptional position to force father and son to talk to each other about problems like the treatment of General Benedek.

A year before the Emperor had sent Rudolf to Prague, where he had a full, ceremonial reception, which at first amused him. But he soon grew tired of formalities; also he found out that the purpose of the visit was to throw a sop to the Ultramontane Czech nationalists, and that his role was merely that of a pawn in a political game. He resented the part he had to play.

Very different was his visit to Buda in 1872, where the Vienna Diplomatic Corps had been invited to assist at the closing ceremony of the Hungarian Parliament. Then the Crown Prince was introduced to its members in Buda Castle. His youthful charm, his delightful manners, and his intelligent questions and answers made a most favourable impression. High praise about the future Habsburg ruler was reported by all the foreign representatives present.

Rudolf's next journey was to Berlin with his father, for a meeting with the Czar; from his letters it is clear that he liked the Emperor William's grandson no more than when he had first met him.

In July, 1874, Rudolf went to Bavaria, accompanied by the excellent art historian, Dr August Wilhelm Ambros. Rudolf had a warm feeling for his mother's native land, but little interest in the buildings and art treasures Dr Ambros showed him in Munich and Nüremberg. Rudolf was intrigued by his cousin, King Ludwig II of Bavaria, about whose eccentric way of life he had heard a good deal, and who referred to his mother as The Dove.

According to Latour's account, Rudolf's education from November 1, 1864, to June 30, 1878, had cost 388,564 *Gulden* and 55 *Pfennig*—the equivalent of £19,423 at that time. Of the fifty men Latour had selected to teach the prince, several were liberals who advocated economic reforms. But the ideals of progress and enlightenment which Rudolf described in his notebooks at the age of fifteen and sixteen, went far beyond anything his tutors could have told him. He realised that growing industrialisation uprooted and pauperised many small craftsmen; driven to seek employment, they earned pitifully low wages and their standards of living fell catastrophically. Unlike the leading liberals of the day, Rudolf was upset because nothing was done to ease the sufferings brought about by the transition from the old economy to the new; he knew that a large part of the profits had to be re-invested in modern machinery, yet so much was left over that the industrialists lived in great luxury, while the workers had to eke out their living on a pittance.

For the Crown Prince liberalism was wholly incompatible with the quick enrichment of the entrepreneurs. 'Uplifting the soul and progress will be difficult,' he wrote, 'when economic insecurity is so marked that the many poor see in the few rich their enemies and the wasters of public property; to the extent that hatred for them and the struggle for their own survival becomes demoralising. Therefore we should ideally consider more or less equal wealth and prosperity a source of moral development.... New ideas and principles emerged from the many corpses of the guillotine, and the nations of Europe arose from the period of revolutions and struggles for liberation rejuvenated, strengthened, ennobled and elevated.... Only during the upheavals of the last hundred years has man really become human.... There will always be wars until every race and nation has finished developing, until all unite and mankind becomes one great family in which each strives and fights for a higher spiritual life for all.'[6]

As for his political views: at sixteen Rudolf wrote an essay on

Vienna's Position and the Future.[7] It was based on two fundamental concepts. First, opposition to Germany. 'A cultured Danube State would form a fortunate counter-weight to the German Empire, whose dissolution it would expedite.' Secondly, sympathy for the Slav people. 'The future belongs to the Slavs, but Austria can preserve herself if she conceives her task correctly and puts herself at the helm of the Southern Slavs and thus becomes a mighty Danubian Empire.' To the first principle Rudolf remained faithful to the end of his life; it was both diametrically opposed to the views of his father, and—not surprisingly—anathema to Prince Bismarck, the creator of the new German Empire.

Francis Joseph promoted Latour to Field-Marshal-Lieutenant and created him a Count. In a warm letter of thanks he wrote: 'In the past, with my full confidence, I entrusted you with a difficult and anxious task. I here express my deeply felt recognition, for you have in every respect brilliantly justified the confidence I had placed in you and rendered great services to Me and My House. With rare understanding, with unlimited sacrifice and devotion, you watched over the physical and spiritual well-being of my son. From now on, you can look back with justified pride on the fruits of your activities, which assure you for ever my heartfelt gratitude and the unchangeable sympathy and affection of the Crown Prince.[8] This well-deserved praise was borne out by Rudolf's parting statement to Latour: 'What I want is to learn; I want to develop my mind and I want to know—I want to find all the answers.'

But underneath the surface the seeds of corruption had already been planted. According to the Hungarian psychographologist, Mrs Klára Ács,[9] who has recently examined many specimens of Rudolf's handwriting, he caught gonorrhea at the age of eighteen. One of his teachers, Captain Baron Max von Walterskirchen, who was uncannily perspicacious, noticed that changes had taken place in Rudolf in the months after his coming of age. He wrote to the Crown Prince:

'The portrait you sent me yesterday . . . shows that you have become strong and manly, none the less it does not quite satisfy me. I miss the trait of freshness of the spirit which always gave all of us so much pleasure.

'That horrible stubble on the chin, which during our time

together I hated so much, has—to judge by the portrait—thickened and given your face a mephistophelean expression which is entirely alien to your being.

'Also a sombre earnestness seems to have settled over your features which I had never noticed before. Surely in the short space of time since you came of age, life cannot have faced your inner eyes with something so cold?

'For goodness' sake, do not let the sweet illusions of your youth be wiped away; they will disappear fast enough. It is your duty to preserve your intellectual freshness for your very difficult future task.

'You have a beautiful, joyful youth behind you; you need not empty the cup of life greedily like one who had thursted for a long time. Enjoy life at a moderate pace. It is your right. Do not let your joy of life turn to gall by brooding speculation whose traces I believe can be seen in the eyes of your portrait. Your intelligence and your striving after higher things guarantee that you will not founder in the whirlpool of pleasure.' Signed Max Walterskirchen, dated Oktober 22, 1877.[10] Few courtiers would have dared to write such a letter. Unfortunately it had no discernible effect on Rudolf.

As soon as he was of age, the Crown Prince had to set up his own household. At the head of it, with the title of H.E. the Master of His Imperial Highness's Household, was placed Vice-Admiral Carl Count Bombelles. With a good record in the Austrian Navy, in 1856 Bombelles became A.D.C. to Archduke Maximilian and accompanied him to Mexico. The Empress Carlotta fumed that he had procured women for her husband, but Bombelles loyally and courageously supported Emperor Maximilian during the disastrous Mexican adventure.

It has always been a moot point as to how Bombelles came to his appointment. Oskar von Mitis, in his excellent biography of Crown Prince Rudolf,[11] says that Rudolf himself suggested it and that 'Bombelles was a real *bon vivant* and a typical Court official.' Bombelles certainly belonged politically to the Camarilla, whose members were afraid that when Rudolf came to power he would take drastic actions and that these would affect their own positions. They dreaded the intelligence and liberal thinking of the Crown Prince. Therefore, according to Lónyay, a malicious observer with an excellent memory, they entrusted Bombelles with the task of corrupting the Heir to the Throne.[12] Excessive indulgence would, they opined, make a young man, whose nerves were not of the strongest, in due course amenable to their will.

According to the Rev. Kántor, who wrote with hindsight, 'Bombelles did his job with masterly and devilish pleasure and vice. Now there was no more holding Rudolf. He rushed headlong into every possible and impossible escapade, with Bombelles at his side, his most ready and able mentor.'[13]

In fairness it must be added that Richard Barkeley, in his well-researched *The Road to Mayerling*, paints a much kinder picture of Bombelles as an easy-going man who enjoyed the good things of life, but who was devoted to Rudolf. This is also borne out by a letter Bombelles wrote to Latour on August 28, 1877, when he accompanied Rudolf on a trip down the Adriatic and then on to Corfu: 'The Crown Prince enjoys the beauties of the coast and the sea with enthusiasm. This is a new point of rapprochement between us, which again pleases me. The closer I can get to his tastes and likings, the more confidential will our relationship become, and the easier will it be, in a given situation, to provide support with my views or my advice. May God help me that my advice should always be right, or should I make a mistake, there should be no disastrous consequences.'[14]

The sad fact was that, whatever Bombelles' own politics may have been, he had no comprehension of Rudolf's philosophy of life, and to the end knew nothing of Rudolf's political activities. Hence, despite his excellent intentions, at the crucial period of Rudolf's existence, Carl Bombelles was unable to provide any advice at all.

In September Bombelles went to Switzerland with Rudolf, who wanted to have a look at the ruins of the Habsburg, the small castle from which his namesake, the first Rudolf, had started the family on its imperial career. And then he once more visited Munich.

Rudolf was not a success with his Wittelsbach cousins, who led simple, almost bourgeois lives, compared to the Habsburg Court. They thought him stuck up and conceited;[15] but Rudolf was greatly attracted by the strange, lonely king, Ludwig II, with whom he had been corresponding since the age of sixteen. Ludwig not only adored the Empress, he was also devoted to her son, who for his part was impressed, as is clear from the following letter he wrote the Bavarian king: 'You have so often in your great kindness expressed your friendship to me; and you ordered me to speak to you in honest speech of the heart instead of in the formal tones which your high position should impose on me. Therefore graciously forgive me when I assure you that you are my favourite and dearest friend, not because of the great office you hold, but because of your great intelligence, and your noble and truly lofty being. You can always count on me and on my loyalty. I do appreciate and am proud of it that a gentleman who locks himself earnestly into himself and into his knowledge, and so very seldom bestows his confidence and his friendship, has chosen just me as his friend.'[16]

But what really linked these two fundamentally different men was their antipathy to Prussia—their fear of Bismarck's plans and of Prince William's arrogance and ambition. On this subject they spoke the same language.

After a family Christmas at the Hofburg, Rudolf at last set out for England, with Bombelles, Professor Menger, and his A.D.C., Major Josef Ritter von Eschenbacher. The journey began none too happily. The Empress, one of the best horsewomen in Europe, demanded that Rudolf give her his word that he would not ride to hounds in England because his seat was not good enough. She told Rudolf of her misgivings in a wounding manner, which hurt him to the quick. He replied haughtily, 'In England I will indeed avoid riding to hounds. Our public does not regard it as heroic if one breaks one's neck while hunting. To me my popularity is worth far too much to risk losing it for such a thing.'[17]

And on the Empress's private train from Vienna to London, Elizabeth did not send once for her son to talk to him. As he wrote in January, 1878, to King Ludwig, who had asked him to transmit a message to Elizabeth, 'I could not possibly answer sooner as I could never speak to Mama alone. During our continued travel she did not feel quite well and withdrew entirely into her compartment and only emerged for meals which, however, we partook together with our respective suites. Here in

London I saw her even less alone; during the few hours she spent here, she was constantly in the company of Aunt Marie of Naples and Marie Larisch. Only now did I have time to go for one day to Cotebrook Park, where Mama is staying. I asked her at once whether she agreed to your plan to accompany her. She thanks you very much for your proofs of friendship, and it would give her pleasure if you, were you to be at Castle Berg next summer, would accompany her once on the train journey from München to Possenhof.'[18]

And worse was to come. Both Elizabeth and her suite, and Rudolf and his, stayed at a small hotel in Brook Street, called Claridges. The Empress had with her a niece, Countess Georg Larisch-Moennich (to whom Rudolf referred in his letter to King Ludwig), the morganatic daughter of her brother Ludwig, Duke of Bavaria. In 1859 he had renounced his right of primogeniture in order to marry the actress Henriette Mendl. King Ludwig I conferred the title of Baroness von Wallersee on her, and on her daughter Marie, born six months after the marriage. In 1876 the eighteen-year-old Marie went to live with her aunt, the Empress Elizabeth; eighteen months later Elizabeth gave her a royal trousseau and a grandiose wedding when she married Count Heinrich Georg Larisch-Moennich.

Marie Larisch was a great favourite of the Empress, yet her conduct during the events leading up to Mayerling made her the bearer of heavy responsibility. She may have done some intriguing already in London, but there it was the Empress's second confidante, her sister Marie, the ex-Queen of Naples, who was the main mischief-maker. She had received much attention until the Empress's arrival. From then on all eyes were focussed on the ravishingly beautiful Elizabeth, who rode so brilliantly. Her pilot during the previous hunting season had been Captain Bay Middleton, a famous rider to hounds and steeplechaser. There was—inevitably—speculation about a possible love affair between the dashing Captain and the beautiful Empress. Actually, under the circumstances the Empress lived, surrounded by ladies-in-waiting, detectives, servants, grooms, not to mention curious neighbours, it is unlikely that she was ever alone with Middleton for more than a few minutes.

The ex-Queen Marie, picqued by the popularity of her sister, which had put her into the shade, avenged herself by telling the Crown Prince about the Middleton gossip in an exaggerated form. The result was that at a party attended by the Prince of Wales, when Middleton was presented to him, Rudolf turned his back on him. This caused a first-class scandal. Middleton behaved impeccably, he never mentioned this studied insult from a prince aged nineteen either in public or in private; but unhappily Elizabeth shied off having the incident out with her son. She bottled up her feelings and avoided all contact with him.

As Rudolf was not on an official visit to England, he did not stay at the Austro-Hungarian Embassy in Belgrave Square.[19] But the Embassy's able commercial director, Karl Ritter von Scherzer, was seconded to the Crown Prince as a guide. Scherzer wrote about his plans for Rudolf: 'To see and learn how the gigantically growing urban population of London is ruled, fed and educated, how it nurses its sick, supplies its armed forces, punishes its criminals, handles trade and communications reaching far beyond the borders of the civilised world, disseminates useful knowledge, takes care of the arts and sciences, yes, even how it entertains and amuses itself, seemed to me no less interesting and educational than visits to those industrial establishments which as far as they aim at satisfying the needs of the masses, form the main sources of the national income.'

Rudolf was vastly impressed by all he saw. From Chester he wrote to Latour: 'England has far exceeded my expectations. Life here is magnificent and I strive to get to know as much as is possible.' This applied not only to the economic, commercial and social institutions he observed, but to meetings with important personalities like Lord Beaconsfield at a dinner party, and hearing the Prime Minister, Mr Gladstone, speak in the Commons about the Eastern Question. Unfortunately Rudolf's English was not quite good enough to understand every word the Prime Minister was saying, but the liveliness of the debate, the blunt yet civilised exchanges between Honourable Members, filled him with enthusiasm. Before his visit to England he had said that he was a firm believer in democracy, but did not like the parliamentary system. England changed his mind on that.

Another less beneficial influence of his English trip derived from the presence in Rudolf's suite of Professor Menger, with whom he had struck up a friendship in the course of his studies. A famous economist and a fascinating talker, Menger had founded the Austrian National Economic School. He had inspired Rudolf to insist on the trip to England, during which he had long talks with his imperial pupil, and their relations were cemented for ever. Menger, the son of a bourgeois Jewish family, had turned his back on his own Mosaic faith, did not only talk economics with Rudolf. To Latour's rage, it was Menger who acquainted him with the ideas of atheism. Menger's influence in this direction is clear from a letter Rudolf wrote that winter to King Ludwig of Bavaria: 'I respect religion where in a blessed manner it became the educator of the people and planted in the common man the first beginnings of a moral feeling. But I fear religion when it becomes the weapon and the means to achieve aims—as certain classes and parties do; when it sows blind faith and superstition instead of true education among the people. For the educated man who stands on a point of spiritual development so that he can raise himself from everyday life and begin to search and think systematically, for him—as I said—I consider the Christian faith in its narrow limits, as our Church demands it, totally unacceptable. He will have his religion, or better said: his moral laws, which he will set up for himself and according to which he will regulate his spiritual life; there can be no limits as our Church is trying to impose on us by exploiting our desire for heaven or our fear of hell, but only chains by which the spiritual life of a man controls the physical life of his body.'[20] In plain words Rudolf had rejected the Roman Catholic Church and for the time being become an agnostic. No wonder the good Latour was plagued by dark forebodings for his charge's future.

This change in the Crown Prince's attitude to fundamentals created an unbridgeable chasm between himself and the Emperor, and between him and the whole Austrian establishment, which suspected correctly that Rudolf had worked with Menger on a critical essay about the Austrian nobility, published anonymously in Munich in 1878 under the title: *The Austrian Nobility And Its Constitutional Profession: a Warning To Aristocratic Youth From An Austrian.*

The warning by no means contested the importance of the nobility as an element in preserving the stability of society. But its privileged position should be counterbalanced by special duties. Members of the nobility did not have the right to devote themselves solely to the enjoyment of life; they had the patriotic duty to prepare themselves for the posts they were to hold. As long as the nobility did not consider it an honour to do their duty, and not a disgrace to shirk it, so long would the position of the nobility remain seriously menaced.[21]

This—to a modern reader—eminently sensible analysis caused tremendous indignation in Viennese Court circles. Nor did they realise that if Rudolf leaned too much towards any extreme, 'that dreadful Jew, Menger' warned him not to stray too far off the golden mean.

The second area in which Menger's influence had far-reaching consequences was his attitude to the Press. He explained to Rudolf the potential power of the printed word, and the importance for him to get to know the leading figures of the Austrian Press—to whom no one in Court circles would speak.

Rudolf spent his days in England visiting institutions like the Bank of England, Billingsgate and Smithfield, the Corn Exchange, the Law Courts, factories and old peoples' homes; the ports of Liverpool, Glasgow and Belfast; Midland cities like Manchester, Bradford, Sheffield and Birmingham. His evenings, when in London, were spent at various men's clubs, those specially English institutions. He was naturally received by Queen Victoria, and made such a favourable impression that she invited him to Osborne, a rare sign of favour. Princess Margaret of Connaught[22] laughingly reassured the Austrian Ambassador, Count Frederick Ferdinand Beust,[23] 'The Queen has quite fallen in love with the Crown Prince, but do not worry, she does not intend to marry him!' Yet at that time Queen Victoria refused to confer on him the Garter. The Prince of Wales, who had become a friend of Rudolf, begged his mother to do so, but she remained adamant in her refusal for nine years.

Rudolf also went to Ireland, where at a ball at Dublin Castle the Viceroy, the Duke of Marlborough, representing the Queen, remained firmly seated when Rudolf came up to him. Next to Marlborough sat the Mayor of Dublin; neither of them offered a seat to the Austrian Crown Prince, who had to remain standing behind their gilt armchairs!

Relations between the Prince of Wales and Rudolf began as a social contact, which became closer every year. Gradually a real personal and political friendship developed between them. Although the Prince of Wales was seventeen years older than Rudolf, they had a warm liking for each other—both suffered from a parent unwilling to let them play any part in official life, or bear any responsible position—and both had profound misgivings about their mutual relation, Prince William. The Prince of Wales was his uncle, Rudolf his cousin. William disliked both; but found it more difficult to deal with his English uncle who, after all, was much older than himself. Rudolf he already regarded as irresponsible and ridiculously bookish. Not so Prince Bismarck.

On his way home from England, Rudolf stopped in Paris and then went on to Berlin, where he had talks with the German Chancellor. Bismarck was impressed by Rudolf's political acumen, his quick grasp of unexpected questions, his charm and lively interest. He knew that Rudolf and the Prince of Wales were discussing a possible alliance between Austria and France; another between Austria and England; and possibly a renewal of Austria's alliance with Russia. The purpose was all too clear: the encirclement of the German empire. Bismarck was deeply concerned about the future when this talented, determined young man, who held such views, would acquire full power in Austria.

One incident of the Berlin visit was, however, kept a secret until after Rudolf's death: on March 6, 1878, in the royal game reserve of Potsdam, the Crown Prince shot a white stag with a ten-point antler. The Green Guild of the Hunters firmly believed that a man who shot white game would meet with a violent death. Whether or not Rudolf and his entourage believed this, is not known; but neither they, nor their German hosts, mentioned the white stag killed by Rudolf.

In 1879 Rudolf went on a long trip to Spain, lasting from April 28 to June 25. He went to Madrid via Trieste, Venice, Milan and Genova; then to Andalusia, Tangier and Lisbon, and shot near Cadiz. There was gossip that he was looking for a bride—the Spanish royal family being Catholic there might have been some truth in this. In addition to Bombelles and his A.D.C., he was accompanied on this trip by his brother-in-law, Prince Leopold of Bavaria, his sister Gisela's husband; by Hans Count Wilczek, a most generous philanthropist, patron of the arts and sciences and Arctic explorer, and by Professor Alfred E. Brehm. Rudolf had got to know Brehm when they went shooting together along the Danube; he worked with him while stationed in Prague, and contributed to Brehm's great work, *Illustriertes Tierleben*. It was alleged that Brehm, an ardent freemason, had inspired Rudolf to join and that the Crown Prince was admitted to the Hungarian *Grossloge*, but there is no proof of this.

Of course the Camarilla was indignant over the Crown Prince's friendly relations with a mere commoner, so much so that Rudolf did not dare to become godfather to the new Brehm baby. He told Wilczek, who transmitted the request, that he was afraid he would be forbidden to see Brehm altogether if he accepted. When Brehm died, Rudolf sincerely mourned the loss of a man who had been a close and devoted friend.

The Spanish trip had few political undertones; Rudolf made an excellent impression on the Spanish Court by his manners and elegance; he was entertained and invited to shoot by several grandees. Professor Brehm showed him the animal life of Spain, and much of its botany; they went shooting together and Rudolf thoroughly enjoyed himself.

Rudolf's last great journey as a bachelor was to the Middle East two years after the Spanish trip.[24] This was usually regarded as a voyage of fun, but it was far more than that. According to the notes for his book, *A Trip To The Orient*, Rudolf had found out accurately the difficulties and tragedies of the nationalist movement in Egypt. Conscious as he was of the need to acknowledge the aspirations of national groups within the Monarchy, so, in Egypt, his sympathies were entirely with Colonel Ahmed Arabi, Minister of War in the Government headed by Mohammed Sami, a nationalist intellectual. France and England, intent on maintaining control of the Suez Canal, had provoked an intense nationalistic spirit among Egyptians of which Colonel Arabi became one of the leading spokesmen.

On February 16, 1881, Rudolf sailed into Alexandria harbour on board the imperial yacht, *Miramar*. On February 19 he took the train to Cairo, and met a charming Egyptian, Abd el Kader Hilmi Pasha, a highly educated nationalist and close friend of

Colonel Arabi. Rudolf was so impressed by him that he invited Abd el Kader to sail up the Nile with him. By the spring of 1882, European ineptitude and Egyptian indignation led to riots, in answer to which the English and the French sent warships to Alexandria and bombarded the town and the harbour. The Egyptians made a stand, but were ultimately overwhelmed by General Sir Garnet Wolseley at the battle of Tel el Kabir on September 13. Colonel Arabi surrendered as a prisoner of war to the English and in December was exiled to Ceylon. On July 26, 1882, Crown Prince Rudolf wrote with prescience about these events to the editor of the *Neues Wiener Tagblatt*, Maurice Szeps: 'I am extremely interested in this Egyptian entanglement as I know the country fairly well and expected the situation to develop in this way years ago. What these complications on the Nile will lead to in European politics is unforseeable. If Arabi were *the* Moslem since Soliman—which, in spite of his much talked-about energy he is not—the English and French could be disastrously defeated in a shameful campaign. For many long evenings last winter while we were on the Nile steamer I spoke to an intimate friend of mine, Abd el Kader Pasha, who is a mixture of the Ottoman and Arabic races and unites in himself the extreme fanaticism of both peoples, about the things that were really happening now, and what could be done about a European invasion. Arabi could have at his disposal an enormous fighting power, but apparently he does not know how to use it. Count K.[25] is a great diplomat! His remark that the bombardment of Alexandria was a real decision in the eyes of the English, but that the continuation of this action, which might have saved the unfortunate town from disaster, would not have been a fair undertaking, was immense. What a pity Europe wastes so much money on her diplomats. God knows the harm they do is greater than the good.'[26]

Of course *A Trip To The Orient* did not contain one word about Egyptian politics as the Emperor would not have allowed it to be printed. But Rudolf's social conscience none the less did manage to make itself felt. Not only did he express his shock at the terrible poverty of the *fellahin*, the dreadful housing conditions, the flies and the vermin and the maimed, but he drew a biting comparison between the pampered fat white donkeys of the rich Arabs, and the poor stunted grey animals of the *fellahin*. His remark that in spite of working half-naked at water-wheels, 'yet the *fellahin* kept their pride and dignity', showed which way his sympathy lay. When he wrote 'as though the ancient tombs had opened and the people of the Pharaohs have come forward to lean over the Holy River', and that the Alabaster Mosque, built by Mohammed Ali 'the heroic founder of the present dynasty' who without European interference 'would have conquered even Constantinople', it seems probable that Abd el Kader had put these ideas into his head. And Rudolf must have mentioned what the distinguished Egyptian had told him not only to Szeps, but to his cousin, Archduke Leopold Ferdinand, who later renounced his title and rank to roam the world as Leopold Wölfling. He wrote to Rudolf from Colombo, where he had landed on his naval training ship, that he had met the exiled Arabi Pasha,[27] and felt deeply for him. Rudolf differed from the overwhelming majority of his contemporaries by sensing that Arabi represented genuine Egyptian feelings, that he had so much backing among ordinary people that he could have got rid of the Europeans—primarily the English—had he been more resolute, better-informed and less credulous. Rudolf, unlike the English Liberals, realised that Egyptian nationalism would eventually win out.

From Egypt Rudolf went on to the Holy Land and to Beyrut, which was part of Syria inside the Ottoman Empire. This was a genuine shooting and sightseeing trip.

Rudolf's facility to express himself in speech as well as in writing, of which *A Trip To The Orient* is but one example, was a gift that his unimaginative father totally lacked. Francis Joseph had sent his son out to see the world; when he came back and proved how much he had seen and learnt, the Emperor resented it.

7

The Army and Marriage

After his return to Vienna Rudolf reported to the Emperor on his impressions, especially his meeting with Bismarck. Francis Joseph listened politely, but did not discuss the merits of his son's views. Rudolf chafed under this slight; Bismarck had not only talked, but discussed problems with him—why not his father? Was it jealousy, as some had suggested, or was it disapproval of his liberal views? He hoped to obtain a worthwhile sphere of activity, but the Emperor was not going to be hurried in coming to a decision. While his father was making up his mind, Rudolf went on a fifteen-day drip down the Danube to shoot birds as specimens for Professor Brehm. He was enthralled by his surroundings, by the immense arc of the sky, by the strange plants and fantastic light effects. The excellent essay he eventually wrote about this trip gained him not only popularity,[1] but an honorary doctor's degree from Vienna University. Typical of Rudolf, to Latour he wrote: 'The only thing that depresses me is the shaming feeling that my dilettante work and the smallness of my achievements hitherto in the service of science did not deserve the doctor's title as of right.'

Latour refrained from telling him that what had saddened him was that Rudolf had neither the inner peace, nor the imperial permission, to do serious scientific work.

At this time Rudolf suffered an accident which was hushed up: through careless handling of his rifle, he shot himself through his left hand in his own room. Elizabeth nursed him and this restored their friendly relations so badly upset by her son's rudeness to Bay Middleton. At last in July 1878 Rudolf heard from his father that he was to serve as a major in the K. und K.[2] 36th Jungbunzler Infantry Regiment stationed in Prague.

It was hardly the kind of appointment he had expected—at first he was bitterly disappointed. Yet it was not as unimportant as he thought: there was a serious purpose, if only the Emperor had explained it to his son. In 1874, in one of his reports, Rudolf's Czech history teacher, Anton Gindely, had said: 'It would make a wonderful impression on the Slav people of Austria if there were irrefutable, daily repeated proof to show that H.I.H. had full knowledge of one of the Slav idioms. Whether this would also be of great practical advantage to our State, can neither be affirmed or denied with certainty.' Francis Joseph took the suggestion to heart, and appointed his son to a regiment with headquarters in Prague to demonstrate his good will to the Czechs.

They had been distressed because the Hradžin, the Prague Castle, had been allowed to fall into disrepair. Now they heard that it would be put in order for Rudolf. Yet the Czech press was far from enthusiastic; Ladislas von Rieger's[3] *Politik* had the bad taste to remind the Crown Prince that the Hradžin had 'historic windows'—a reference to the 'Defenestration' of the imperial envoys in 1610. The Young Czech Party's *Narodny Listy* passed over Rudolf's arrival in silence.

The Crown Prince's appearance on July 28, 1878, at the recruiting centre may not have been sensational news; even less than that at the age of thirteen he had made a long trip through the Sudetenland, and at fifteen and sixteen had visited and re-visited Prague. But Rudolf was delighted with his reception. He soon adapted himself to military routine, as he told Latour in his letter of September, 1878: 'Work pleases me; I have always been used to it and it does not matter to me if I am occupied from 6.30 a.m. to 6 p.m., with only half an hour off for luncheon.' His Commanding Officer, Major Friedrich Hotze, had eliminated all the officers with liberal or freethinking leanings, so that Rudolf had as companions young men of conventional ideas, almost exclusively from modest middle-class backgrounds. He liked them and in his will of April 15, 1879, he referred to the 36th Infantry Regiment as 'my real home', where he spent the happiest days of his life. It is interesting that Rudolf, who detested the conservative point of view of his father's entourage, felt so contented in the company of officers who—had they had any politics—would probably have reacted in the same way. But it was characteristic of the K. und K. officers (generally of the K. und K. Armed

Forces) to have no politics. To quote General Folliot de Creneville et Poutet: 'Disinterested in domestic and foreign policy, an officer does not serve the State, his loyalty is only to his Emperor and War Lord.'[4] One of the reasons for trouble with the Hungarians was that many of them felt they could not give all their loyalty to the All-High, for they owed some of it to their own country.

Rudolf had accepted the principles on which the Austrian Army was based, and regarded the Army as the only institution that held the Empire together. In it there was no difference on the basis of nationality, wealth, family or position. Rudolf loved the Army and particularly the 36th Infantry Regiment.

The views of his colleagues were well summed up in a letter of Major Hotze, dated August 2, 1879: 'In a few days it will be a year since I have got to know H.I.H. It soon became evident that he was not an ordinary man—his is a rich mind, impetuous and impulsive, with a warm heart and a noble character, developed far beyond his years. For such a nature it is not sufficient to have an ordinary occupation or training, it must have an aim worthy of it.

'This aim was soon found. H.I.H. grasped the idea that he had to dedicate himself entirely to the Army; through practice, experience, observation and study to mature into an efficient instructor. . . . It is most fortunate when such a rich and vibrating mind sets serious aims before itself; it will lead to misfortune if these aims are thwarted, for as he cannot lie idle, he will land on an aimless zigzag course. As this is my conviction, I have supported H.I.H.'s aims to the best of my ability. . . .

'His lecture about the battle of Spichern (1870) would have done honour to an experienced officer; and it was H.I.H.'s work, expressing his convictions. . . . For months he has commanded the Regiment *ad interim*; what he does is well considered, his criticism is constructive, his calm and objectivity praiseworthy. . . . A factor almost equally valuable as the purely military for H.I.H. is the contact with men. . . . H.I.H. has on many occasions shown good judgment. His kind heart and his natural amiability will hardly ever permit an injustice. . . .

'And now let me draw my conclusions.

'I am convinced that H.I.H. will command a regiment so satisfactorily in every respect that there will be no need to make allowances. . . . H.I.H. will not be infallible just as I and others are not infallible, but he will play his part to the fullest satisfaction. I can vouch for that. He never will seriously fail, for that he is too well educated, too reasonable, too able, too deliberate, too kind-hearted. . . .'

On August 18, 1879, Rudolf wrote an enthusiastic letter to Count Bombelles: 'This morning Papa had the grace to nominate me as definitive Regimental Commander of the 36th, over which I am immensely happy, my most ardent wish has been fulfilled.'[5]

Rudolf was fiercely loyal to his comrades, and whenever he noticed a slight directed at them, he placed himself on their side. 'I belong to the Army with life and soul, every tactless remark against the officers' corps I consider my affair,' he wrote at this time. '. . . The Army needs real friends among members of the imperial family, men who feel, work and live with it.' And he acted upon his beliefs: when in Vienna the Court circles organised a carouselle at which the officers of the local garrison were passed over, he ostentatiously refused to attend. When he noticed that the high Czech aristocracy cut his comrades, he took up the cudgels on their behalf.

Rudolf also shared the Army views on other subjects: he approved of duelling; he castigated the parliamentary opposition for criticising the occupation of Bosnia and Herzegovina[6] and even considered the possibility of an unauthorised issue of bank notes to cover the cost of the occupation as Parliament would not vote the money. He hoped—as did his comrades—to fight in Italy to reconquer Austria's 'lost territories'; and he was indignant over the Austrian and Hungarian Parliaments which refused to vote funds for new weapons and new equipment. He also believed that, should there be domestic troubles, the Army would have to step in with the utmost firmness. 'In our present chaos,' he said in 1879, 'the Army is the only binding means that represents the imperial ideal; it is Great Austrian. One must protect it, nurse it, and win it over—in these dark times this should be the ambition of the Liberals. Our officers corps is almost exclusively of bourgeois background, imperial in its thinking and supporting the idea of a powerful state.' Rudolf was strongly in favour of a single service language—German—and at this time angrily anti-Hungarian, because the Hungarians wanted to use their own language in their own regiments.

Again Rudolf's social conscience came into play: he took an interest in the food provided for the other ranks; in the raising of the officers' pay; moreover he had the moral courage to protest against the long three years' compulsory military service. Appointed regimental commander, he suggested that the volunteers, who signed up for a limited period, received a State subsidy and served as n.c.o.'s, should mess with the officers. When it was pointed out to him that they could not afford fourteen *Gulden* a month for their meals, he set up a foundation of 18,000 *Gulden* so that each 'State volunteer' should be given enough money to pay his mess bill.

Rudolf's hostile feelings towards the Austrian and Czech aristocracy were closely linked with his sympathetic feelings for Jews—because of the anti-Semitic leanings of most noblemen. In 1879 an ugly incident took place in Prague. 'Unknown' individuals rushed through the streets of the Jewish quarter and smashed windows. Like the general public, Rudolf soon knew who these 'unknown' individuals were and in the *K.A. Verordnungsblatt* of August 19, 1879,[8] there appeared an anonymous article, naming them as Counts Silva Tarucca, Richard Coudenhove, and Heinrich Clamm. Rudolf had been heard expostulating in the mess: 'Why should middle-class or working-class people receive heavy fines for barbaric acts, while rich young aristocrats get off scott free?' No wonder that the belief got around that the Crown Prince was responsible for revealing the names although, in fact, for a long time the identity of the author of the article was not known for certain.

Rudolf was also fascinated by the Jewish ghetto, by the small houses of the alchemists (several of whom had been Jews) who tried to find the philosopher's stone and discover the secret of making gold. The famous Rabbi Loew, a great authority on the Cabbala,[9] guided Rudolf through the old Jewish graveyard, the Klaus cemetery, with its 13,000 broken and crooked tombstones. When Loew died, his seat in the Staronova Synagogue, the oldest in Europe, built in 1268, was left permanently unoccupied; the Jews considered no one worthy to fill his place. Today the Jewish graveyard in Prague is looking more dilapidated than ever.

Linked with his distaste for the aristocracy, Rudolf had an

almost fanatical dislike of clerical circles. His views were clearly expressed in a letter to Latour of February, 1881: 'I conceal neither the fact that I have no sympathy whatever for the influence of the Church on the State, nor that I detest all tendencies towards Church influence. I would much rather send my children to a school whose headmaster is a Jew than to one whose headmaster is a clergyman, a runaway protagonist to the "black" tendencies. The State has to treat all denominations equally; a strengthening of the Catholic hierarchy has, so far, brought evil consequences.'

With views such as these, no wonder Rudolf had a running battle with the Cardinal Archbishop of Prague, Friedrich Prince Schwarzenberg, who from the pulpit had forbidden shooting on Sundays. On January 16, 1881, Rudolf wrote to Szeps, 'In Germany and here reaction and clericalism are properly on the move; now we are to receive a rich measure of Sabbath observance. Here the high-born gentlemen, primarily the Cardinal, very pointedly favour legal prohibition of all work on Sundays and feast days. . . . The other day in the newspaper which is under the supervision of the Cardinal, they let loose an article attacking me because of my Sunday shooting. Of course this left me completely indifferent, but I am concerned by the direction of events such a manifestation betrays. What has been achieved in a long struggle—the concept of a modern civilised State (*Kulturstaat*)—is now endangered. Prussia sets that example, and we are apeing it.'[10]

And yet, during this summer of 1881, Francis Joseph did for once pay attention to Rudolf's views. It was on the occasion of ugly incidents between German and Czech nationalists, which were linked with Kuchelbad, the place to which the Austrian Student Association *Austria* made an excursion on June 30, 1881. It not merely came to blows but to bloodshed between the members of *Austria* and the Czechs. Already on June 29, when the *Austria* marched into Prague ceremonially, accompanied by a band, there were anti-German demonstrations. Next day occurred the fight in Kuchelbad, and then even more serious excesses in Prague. In Vienna and in Budapest there were strong press attacks against the policy of the Prime Minister, Count Taaffe, whose pro-Czech policy had provided the occasion for these lamentable events. As Rudolf hated Taaffe's reactionary ideas, he was bitterly opposed to the alliance of German and Czech ultra-conservative politicians. But his own sympathies for the Czechs were still strong, as he expressed them towards the end of 1881 to Latour: 'I have much sympathy for the great Slav race and just for this reason I am enraged with those feudal gentlemen who owe allegiance to no nation and who drag the Czech people down with them into the mud, to exploit them for the achievement of their reactionary and obscurantist aims. The Slavs are liberal and the day will come when they will thoroughly disown those gentlemen . . .'

Rudolf wrote his father an outspoken report about the Czech–German fights in Prague and Kuchelbad. Unfortunately this report seems to have disappeared; but on July 3, 1881, the Emperor wrote in Ischl in his own hand to Count Taaffe, 'Enclosed I send you a part of a letter from Rudolf I have just received. It deals with the occurrences in Prague. Even if he has painted a few things in too bright colours, yet the rest is very disturbing and shows the urgent need to act quickly and energetically.' The Emperor told Taaffe that having read his report to the Council of Ministers, he agreed with his interpretation of the cause of the excesses (that they had been organised as a provocation and had been carefully prepared by the Great Germans) yet the Emperor regarded it as the duty of the authorities to maintain order regardless of political parties and various nationalities, to protect personal security and to restore respect for the law. In Prague the disorders had lasted far too long, the Deputy Governor had vacillated instead of holding the reins firmly in his hands. Everyone gave advice—deputies, students, German and Czech professors, town councillors—yet no one acted decisively. Soon an Austrian general was sent from Vienna to command the troops and a new Governor was appointed, who took energetic measures and handed out punishments to troublemakers regardless of nationality or party. Even Prince Carlos Auersperg—who as Chief Land Marshal had, as ordered, closed the Land Council, but with surprising haste and with accompanying words which deeply hurt the Emperor—was reprimanded and the Crown Prince was forbidden to speak to any member of the Auersperg family. The showing up of Auersperg pleased Rudolf, whose conclusion was that the sooner the entailed estates were dissolved, the better it would be.

It was in 1880 that Crown Prince Rudolf met the two people who were to play such very important roles in his life.

In March of that year he paid a visit to Brussels as the guest of King Leopold II of Belgium. His daughter Stephanie was one of the few Catholic princesses of a suitable age for Rudolf to marry. He had visited Saxony—but found Princess Mathilde too fat; the Infanta Eulalia of Spain was too plain. It is inexplicable that the overgrown schoolgirl that Stephanie was—heavy-handed, gauche, poorly turned out, ignorant both of the ways of the world and of politics—should have won Rudolf's heart. Yet so it was. On March 7, 1880, Rudolf wrote to Latour, 'I have found what I sought; Stephanie is pretty, good, clever, very well bred, and will become a faithful daughter and subject of her Emperor and a good Austrian. I am very happy and satisfied.' On March 11, 1880, he wrote again to Latour an even more excited letter: 'I am intoxicated with happiness and contentment. The days pass all too quickly and I think anxiously of the moment when I shall have to leave. I have learned to love my future parents-in-law very much. I am on a very good footing with the King, we talk a great deal together. He is one of the most intelligent, the cleverest and wisest of men and one of the best orators I have ever heard. One can learn a great deal from him.'

Only the Empress judged Stephanie correctly and she was desperately unhappy about the match. When she received news of the engagement in London, she turned so white that the lady-in-waiting dared to ask what the contents of the telegram were. Elizabeth told her; the lady-in-waiting replied with relief: 'Thank God it isn't a calamity.'

'May it please the Lord that it should not lead to a catastrophe,' Elizabeth said miserably. She immediately left for Brussels and arrived looking ravishing in an elegant navy blue outfit—an utter contrast to Stephanie. The comparison between the princess and the Empress could only harm the bride. Elizabeth's entourage wondered whether Rudolf would not draw that conclusion for himself.

The Empress expressed her misgivings to her husband, who

told her not to worry unnecessarily. But Elizabeth never gave any warning to Rudolf. Not once during the intervening months—and the wedding had to be twice postponed because the bride had not yet reached full womanhood—did she talk to her son. She did not advise him that he was dealing with a very poorly informed young person; she did not tell him to introduce her gradually and slowly to his world, imparting to her his ideas little by little—in some ways training her like a loving brother or mentor. She did not tell Rudolf that it would take time to transform her to become the partner he longed for. Instead, Elizabeth went once more to England, to hunt with the Combermere hounds in Cheshire, with Bay Middleton as her pilot.

Elizabeth had failed her son many times, but this was her most fatal failure. Rudolf was in desperate need of real friends, of companions who understood him and were prepared to help him with his enlightened plans, and to keep up his spirits when enforced political inactivity seemed unendurable. An odd scene took place in Gödöllö on the occasion of the Empress's name's day—November 18; Countess Marie Festetics described it in her diary. Rudolf had come from Transylvania and could talk of nothing except what he had shot, how large his bag had been. Then a cart arrived with a cage on it, and a wild cat staring from it. As the animal was let out in the courtyard and jumped to the ground, Rudolf killed it with a well-aimed shot. 'The Emperor is horrified, as for Her Majesty, she is terribly upset. . . . The Crown Prince is engaged to be married, but he does not seem happy—the wedding has just been postponed for a second time,' wrote Marie Festetics. Again Elizabeth did not say anything to Rudolf—no one said anything, but gossip and critical remarks were seething behind his back.

On October 28, 1880, Rudolf also met the man who was to have the greatest influence on him and who became his true and devoted friend. This was Maurice Szeps, the celebrated publisher and editor of the *Neues Wiener Tagblatt*. This is how his daughter and secretary, Bertha Szeps, has described what happened: '(Vienna) October 28, 1880. . . . today we were sitting in Father's library after lunch, the butler announced Professor Carl Menger. He has often been to the house before, and has spoken to my father about Crown Prince Rudolf, whose tutor and friend he is. (He is also a famous economist, my father says.) He said the Crown Prince had sent him to arrange an interview between him (the Crown Prince) and my father. Today Menger said that Rudolf wanted to have direct contact with the leading men of the country, and he said that not only was my father one of these leading men, "but through his editorials in the *Neues Wiener Tagblatt*, the leader of many of the other 'leading men' in Austria." I was proud to hear Professor Menger say this to my father.

'They arranged for my father to meet Crown Prince Rudolf tonight. Rudolf usually lives in Prague, and though he quite often comes to Vienna he only stays here for a short time.'

Bertha Szeps added the following: 'For the next eight years, until the tragedy of the Crown Prince's end, Maurice Szeps and Rudolf used either to write to or see each other at least once a week. My father, who was much older—the Crown Prince died at the age of thirty-two [actually thirty and a half], exercised a profound influence on his intellectual and political development. Rudolf, who, like his idealistic mother the Empress Elizabeth, had from his childhood revolted against the narrow-minded clerical and reactionary atmosphere of the imperial Court, found at last a congenial friend and instructor in my father. Through him he was able to understand the real spirit of democracy; proof of this was demonstrated by his growing interest in the Western democracies, especially in the young French Republic.'[11]

Here was one more development to cause concern to the Camarilla and also to Bismarck.

Rudolf's sumptuous wedding to Princess Stephanie of the Belgians has often been described, so it needs no repetition here. But the prelude to the actual wedding is so eerie that it must be reported. In the days preceding the event, Rudolf was noticeably out of sorts, even at the big Habsburg family luncheon, which was also attended by the Prince and Princess of Wales, the Prussian Crown Princess whom Rudolf liked very much, and her son Prince William, whom he could not stand. Rudolf's depression grew worse after the arrival of Stephanie in Austria on May 8, 1881, with her family and innumerable Coburg relations.

This is what Countess Marie Festetics recorded in her diary on the morning of May 10: 'As I stepped out of my room in full dress, I saw a footman run past, carrying the fabulous bridal bouquet of the Crown Prince. I suddenly felt ice cold and as I took my train over my arm, I heard the dear, sympathetic voice of the Crown Prince: "Countess Marie, don't run away, wait a little!" I did, and I felt apprehensive for he looked so serious, no, so nervous and so despondent. "I am so glad that we meet once more as of old," he said and stopped and could not make up his mind to walk through the door. "The bouquet is waiting," I said. "Yes," he answered, "it was too heavy for me and this way it is also all right." He made a movement with the hand to which I said nothing. I felt so awkward, and he noticed it and asked, "Are you in a hurry?" "Yes, Imperial Highness, I am fairly," I replied. "I am not," he said earnestly, "I have time for it." "Oh Highness," it slipped out, whereupon he stretched his hand to me and said, "for God's sake, say something cheerful to me." Tears ran down my face and I said, "God bless you and may you be very happy, dear, good Imperial Highness!" "Thank you," and with a strong handshake he disappeared behind the door of the apartment. This was the prelude to the wedding.'

Rudolf and Stephanie were married in the church of St Augustin with the rings of Maria Theresa and Francis of Lorraine by Cardinal Archbishop Prince Schwarzenberg.[12] In full canonicals, surrounded by archbishops and bishops, and many other ecclesiastics, the Cardinal received the imperial wedding party on the threshold of the church. Francis Joseph and Elizabeth, with their son Rudolf between them, led the way to the altar; Stephanie followed with her parents on either side of her. Behind them walked an endless train of princes and princesses. In his address the Cardinal said: 'Marriage is not, as those whose thoughts are only concerned with this world often maintain, a contract which gives the marriage partners respective rights. It is a mystery which ties the souls of two beings for ever together.'

To quote Marie Festetics once more: 'In the church it was blindingly beautiful—and solemn—oh so terrifyingly solemn . . . His "yes" sounded serious and sad, and was spoken in a very low voice. Hers was nearly screamed.'[13]

Luncheon was a stand-up buffet, which was over in twenty

minutes. Then Stephanie held her circle, and according to Marie Festetics did it nicely. At last the young couple could be alone, and drove to Laxenburg, where, according to tradition—meaning Spanish Etiquette—all Habsburgs spent their honeymoons.

It will never be known whose oversight it was that Laxenburg was chilly, comfortless, without a single flower in the bridal apartment. It was exceptionally cold for the time of year, May 10; snowflakes were in the air, yet not a single fire had been lit; there were no carpets, no bathroom, and no water closet. In Stephanie's room there was no dressing table, only a washbasin on a three-legged iron framework. Stephanie was all the more upset for, as she has written in her memoirs: 'In the newspapers I had read that there were 14 rooms which during recent weeks had been done up and refurnished. But when we entered the rooms, a breath of air as cold as ice in a cellar met us, and the prevailing smell was that of mould.'[14] As for what followed: 'What a night! What torments, what horror! I had not had the ghost of a notion what lay before me but had been led to the altar as an ignorant child. My illusions, my youthful dreams were shattered. I thought I would die of my dissillusion.'[15]

After the tremendous celebrations and fairy-like wedding ceremonies, here was reality which she found desperately humiliating, while Rudolf shrugged his shoulders. The situation symbolised that these two very young people—Stephanie was just seventeen, Rudolf twenty-two—were strangers to each other, and strangers between whom no understanding was likely to develop.

8

Strain between Emperor and Crown Prince

Unlike Elizabeth and Francis Joseph, who were madly in love, and probably did not even notice their surroundings, Stephanie was full of complaints about the primitive conditions of the castle. She did not feel in the least grateful to Elizabeth, thanks to whose influence she did not have to appear after her wedding night at a Court breakfast to be stared at by everyone.[1] Rudolf experienced for the first time Stephanie's nagging and he did not like it.

Yet the local gamekeeper, to whom Rudolf and Stephanie went to arrange a shooting excursion for the following day, has described how eager the Crown Princess had been for her first shoot, and how happy they both appeared.[2] Coachmen and grooms thought that Crown Prince Rudolf and his young wife were a gay, contented couple. These eyewitness accounts by simple people are very different from Stephanie's sour descriptions written forty-five years later. For a time the couple got on well enough with each other, especially when Stephanie was not irritating Rudolf.

They next paid a week's visit to Hungary, where they were received among scenes of great enthusiasm. Stephanie's speech to the two Houses of Parliament in Hungarian (which she had memorised with the help of her mother, daughter of the very popular Palatine Archduke Joseph) met with wild cheers. Receptions and entertainments were so strenuous that she was ordered to rest for a fortnight. This was regarded as a slight by the Czechs, who wanted the Crown Prince and his wife to visit them immediately after Hungary.

When at last they got to Bohemia, all went well. 'Our reception in Prague was both ceremonious and also sincere in feeling,' Stephanie has written in her memoirs.[3] Through crowded streets they drove to the Hradžin, the great palace of the former kings of Bohemia, where Rudolf's aunt, the Empress Anna, widow of Emperor Ferdinand V, greeted them warmly in French. The daughter of King Victor Emmanuel of Sardinia, she had lived for fifty years in Austria without learning one word of German.

Stephanie was pleased with their quarters; the glorious view over the Moldau and the lovely antique furniture. It was a strenuous period for both her and Rudolf. There were deputations, dinners, audiences, visits to the theatre, the inspection of schools, of charitable institutions and museums. Stephanie's health broke down once more and she was ordered to rest. In September Rudolf was due at the imperial manœuvres in Germany; he was anything but pleased about this, but having refused to attend his cousin's wedding on a poor excuse, this time he had to go, and Stephanie went with him.

At the end of the month was the 500th anniversary of Trieste's annexation by Austria. Rudolf and Stephanie accompanied the Emperor to the celebrations. Of course the Italians took offence; fanatical irredentists organised counter-demonstrations against the imperial family. At Nebresina, near Trieste, a man called Wilhelm Oberdank was arrested. Oddly enough, he was not an Italian, but a German Austrian, who had deserted to Italy, and joined the irredentists. He re-crossed the frontier as one of a band of twelve who had sworn to assassinate the Emperor. He was carrying bombs, but was denounced by an Austrian agent who had infiltrated the Italian conspirators. Oberdank was executed; as the place of his burial was not revealed, irredentists made his mother's grave a place of pilgrimage. Rudolf reported the consequences of this incident to Latour as follows:

December 21, 1882, Budapest.
Dear Latour,

The execution of Oberdank has aroused a veritable storm in Italy, and the Italian papers say the most horrible things about the Emperor and Austria, and openly advocate revenge. The official committees in Rome and other Italian towns also manifest great activity, and here already a few days afterwards there are piles of threatening letters and announcements and such like from Italy. That would not be so serious, but from our best and most reliable sources of information in Italy, from spies who associate with these circles, came the definite statement that three people have left Rome with the intention of accomplishing the assassination of the Emperor and of myself; their track was followed across the frontier, and then they were completely lost sight of, which is not surprising considering the Hungarian police.

In Milan also there was a meeting of a hundred young people who were to decide by ballot which of them should avenge Oberdank. According to what I hear, on this occasion a very serious matter is involved as proved by the agitation among generally pacific people—even the Emperor can ill-conceal his anxiety. The Italians calmly let everything take its course, although important newspapers use horrible and unjustifiable language. In one paper there was a supplement containing a picture of our Emperor beside the body of Oberdank, and beneath was the inscription: 'You, who have grown up in blood and grown old in blood, shall now drown in your own blood.'

It is remarkable that this time the whole matter is not exclusively directed against the Emperor's life; here anyhow much apprehension is felt for the Empress and myself, for according to the reports of our spies, the people in question propose to inflict pain and grief on the Emperor in the most diabolical way. It is certain that during the last few days at the meetings of the Irredentists the suggestion was discussed that, as Oberdank's poor mother suffered such sorrow on account of the death of her son, the Emperor should be made to feel the same pain by the murder of his nearest relatives, in which connection my name was chiefly mentioned. As you see, a delightful New Year atmosphere.

I beg you to make no mention of all this to anyone, as too much fuss would ensue. I think anyhow that the whole thing will soon be public property. Unfortunately there is not even a semi-competent police force here, and one has to grope in the dark.

Rudolf understood the strength of nationalism, but no one in the Government, least of all his father, paid any attention to his views.

Back in Prague, Rudolf was glad to be again with his regiment and fellow officers. In the evenings he either worked on his manuscript of *Journey To The Orient*, or learnt Hungarian and Croatian with Stephanie. In her memoirs,[4] Stephanie complained of being neglected, and wrote: 'The Crown Prince was much occupied with his military duties. He spent most of his days with the officers in the barracks, as a rule not returning . . . until 3 o'clock. After that he would go out shooting, take a ride or work with his officers. I scarcely saw him unless I accompanied him on an occasional shooting expedition.'

She does not admit that she could have gone out with him every time, nor that she had no interest in his work—it was the impression of people who knew her or had dealings with her at the time that she was busy and excited about her establishment which she wanted to run perfectly. She did not seem aware of Rudolf's interests: neither of his writings, nor of his political thoughts.

On July 9, 1881, Rudolf wrote to Latour: 'As you know Stephanie is pregnant. She is very young, has been used to the moderate humid sea climate of Belgium and has now been transferred to a continental dry summer just when exposed to other changes as well. In Prague the heat is so great that staff officers send their families into the country. For Stephanie good air is now absolutely necessary. She looks already a bit poorly. I have repeatedly written to the Emperor; his reply is always the same "send her to the country". After two months of married life this is a hard sentence, I would have swallowed it, though with bad grace. But for her the separation would be terrible and might damage her health, and probably even more that of the child. If one wants healthy progeny, which reasons of State demand, everything must be done to achieve a favourable development of her condition, particularly the first time, without regard to personal considerations. But that may not be. She may not become a nuisance (meaning to his parents). So this young woman must remain in the hot unhealthy air of Prague.' The Empress had forbidden Stephanie to go to Schönbrunn, Rudolf wrote to Latour with some bitterness. This is one of the rare occasions when he was critical of his mother. He added that he could not go with Stephanie to the country as he would be considered 'lazy' by his father. But eventually he did rent a villa for Stephanie in Salzburg.

In her memoirs Stephanie said, 'The Crown Prince cared for little outside his own pleasure and sport.' Yet on September 2 Rudolf wrote to Latour, 'Life here is so pleasant and quiet, and I have become so used to married life that I am really afraid of eight days' separation.' When he went to the German manœuvres, he wrote to Szeps in identical terms, adding that he had been much looking forward to the manœuvres in Hungary, but now he preferred his home.

In October, 1881, when the King and Queen of Italy came on a second State visit to Vienna, for Francis Joseph and King Humbert to discuss the possibilities of a Triple Alliance,[5] Rudolf and Stephanie were much in evidence; Stephanie assisted the Empress, and was delighted to deputise for her. Elizabeth however had no high opinion of her abilities, she referred to her as '*Das Trampeltier*'.[6] Rudolf must have got to hear about it, and felt hurt because the slight to his wife came from his mother.

In November, 1881, Rudolf took Stephanie to Transylvania, where Árpád Kendeffy[7] lent him his countryhouse, Boldogfalva, as a base for his bear and boar-hunting in the Carpathians. Peasants, men and women, with their children, knelt by the road side wherever the Heir to the Throne drove, and kissed the hem of Stephanie's dress. The Hungarian magnates vied with each other in the splendour of their entertainment. Indeed many of them came to meet the couple at the station, driving their four-in-hands in Hungarian fashion. The warmth of this reception induced Rudolf to rent a large Baroque country house in Görgényszentimre which Stephanie decorated and furnished extremely well. In later years she told her intimates that this was the place where Rudolf plotted with his Hungarian friends against his father, but she omitted the passage, with the names of the persons concerned, from her memoirs.[8]

Whilst stationed in Prague, Rudolf corresponded with Szeps, who provided him with political information. But his own acute observations told him much about the difficulties of the Monarchy. Now that he had a happy home, he watched with more concern the Empire that he, and after him his son (he was convinced that the baby would be a boy), would have to rule. He felt that the cohesion, the very existence of it, was threatened by Count

Taaffe's[9] growing influence. Taaffe's reactionary ideas were anathema to him; one of Rudolf's sayings was: 'Reaction is perdition.' Because he felt so deeply perturbed, he decided to write a memorandum for his father, outlining not only how he saw the situation, but what should be done to improve it. It ran to some twenty pages; he wrote and rewrote every paragraph several times so as to make its phraseology acceptable to the Emperor, and he completed it by the end of November, 1881. He sent the first copy to Latour with the request to read and criticise it. The memorandum consisted of four parts.

1. In the first Rudolf indicted the Constitutional Party—the former Liberal Party—for bad organisation, lack of leadership, inability either to form a government, or even to support the governing party. Unaware that penetration into the Balkans was 'a vital need for Austria', the Constitutional Party had tried to prevent the occupation of Bosnia and Herzegovina by voting against the military grants required for this operation.

2. Taaffe tried to rule without the Constitutional Party, thus excluding from his government the most important German elements. Taaffe had obtained his majority by making concessions, or by outright corruption.

3. There had to be no more concessions to the Slav nations.[10] Yet it was impossible to form a viable government either with the Constitutional Party, or with a coalition of German parties. The only solution was to dissolve Parliament, and appoint a Ministry of progressive and understanding Civil Servants. These Ministers would be above party and would end the disgraceful quarrels in Parliament. The Budget should be balanced, and if necessary taxes on bankers and stock exchange jobbers increased.

4. The main task of the new Ministry should be improvement of education and re-conciliation of parties—so that ideological differences should become more important than national diversity. It should be organised on the British model, based on a Liberal Party and a Conservative Party—the two-party system promised the most healthy development.

Finally, the last word on foreign policy should be reserved for the Monarch.

Read nearly a century later, Rudolf's analysis and his suggested solution do not bear the touch of great statesmanship. Any trained journalist would have been able to turn out a similar study; some would have done a better one. It was a superficial diagnosis of Austria's ills, yet it deserved serious consideration from the Emperor. Rudolf was his son and twenty-three years of age; Francis Joseph, never very talented at expressing his own views in writing, should not have allowed himself to be put off by infelicities in Rudolf's wording.

Rudolf had toned down his views, and his biting remarks were all edited out: he wanted to convince his father of his earnest attitude. As far as is known, however, the Emperor did not even reply. He may have spoken to Rudolf about his memorandum, but there is no indication of it in the Vienna Archives. Francis Joseph certainly did not act upon his son's suggestions.

If Rudolf's memorandum is of no great political importance, his letter to Latour, in which he laid bare his own feelings, is an extremely human document, revealing not only of Rudolf's own attitude, but of that of his parents.

On December 9, 1881, Rudolf wrote: 'Dear Latour, I was very pleased with the praise which you gave my humble work, and the manner in which you grasped the whole thing. It is not written to play the *frondeur*, or to earn praise, or to make an impression, but solely out of conviction. I see the slippery slope down which we are sliding. I am very close to affairs but I cannot do anything. I am not even allowed to speak up, and say aloud what I feel and believe. Our Emperor has no friend, his whole character and disposition do not permit it. He stands lonely in his eminence; to his servants he talks about their duties, but a real conversation he studiously avoids, that is why he knows so little about the thoughts and feelings of the people, about the views and opinions of his subjects. At present those in power are the only people who have access to him and they naturally interpret matters in a way which is most convenient to them. He believes that we are living in one of the happiest periods of Austrian history, he is officially told so. In the newspapers he only reads passages marked in red and so he is divorced from every human intercourse, from all impartial and really loyal advice.

'There was a time when the Empress frequently concerned herself with politics, whether with luck or not I will not now discuss. She also talked with the Emperor about serious things, motivated by views diametrically opposed to his. These times are past. The great lady no longer cares for anything but sport; and so this access to outside opinions which were on the whole tinged with liberalism is now also closed. . . . Three or four years ago the Emperor was already liberal to a certain degree and reconciled to the 19th century. Now he is again as he was at the time of poor Grandmama, bigoted, harsh, distrustful. . . . I am distrusted—I have noticed it for several months and latterly increasingly. . . . I have the reputation of a Liberal, I have the closest association with people who are not popular, even have a bad name. . . . If I wanted to play an evil, harmful part, if I wanted to become a rebel, I could do it in the most far-reaching manner. I am offered this from all sides. From this essay speaks no voice of revolt, no tendency to play a part, only the voice of distress, the voice of the adviser, who in deepest incognito wants to bring about changes, and have their fruits enjoyed, with no one knowing where the salutary improvements have come from.'

And then a significant passage: 'I have never been as happy as last summer, when, surrounded by blissful domesticity, I could devote myself quietly to preliminary studies and to work on my *Journey To The Orient*. Now if I am left in peace I want to work on Spain.' Compare this with Stephanie's remarks forty-five years later.

But to continue with the letter to Latour: 'Now to the reason why I am writing today. Do you believe—you know our master very well—that my essay will be taken amiss and interpreted as a presumption that will be repulsed? That, moreover, I could from this moment onwards be treated coldly and sternly and that this treatment could be extended to my wife? She is clever, very attentive and sensitive, full of ambition, a grand-daughter of Louis Philippe and a Coburg! More I need not tell you! I am very much in love with her, and she is the only one who could lead me in many ways! This is also to be considered!

'Will the Emperor take this little work seriously, or will he just glance through it in the evening before retiring and lay it in the file, take the whole for the eccentricity of a dreamer whose attitudes follow no consistent pattern: I often notice he has become used to taking my whole way of living, thinking and writing in this way. Will he show it to some of his favourites—Taaffe,[11]

Braun,[12] Archduke Albert,[13] or Beck,[14] who will oppose it with the sacred fire of baseness? Shall I let the Empress read it first? She is an inactive but thoroughly wise woman. Please be good enough to answer these questions. I will wait for your opinion, and act accordingly, or before that discuss it with you in Vienna. Yours gratefully, Rudolf.'

It is not known whether Rudolf showed his memorandum to his mother; she was at home at the time, so he could have done it. He and Stephanie spent Christmas with the Emperor and Elizabeth in Gödöllö. When they arrived, the sharp-eyed Marie Festetics wrote in her diary: 'The dear Crown Prince who used to bring a kind of sunshine with him, has become quite different . . .'

9

Rudolf misses his Greatest Opportunity

During these months, when Rudolf was being rebuffed by his father, a plan was being cautiously worked out that could have changed his entire future, and that of the Austro-Hungarian Monarchy. The Hungarian Prime Minister, Kálmán Tisza, made serious overtures towards conferring on Rudolf the position of Junior King of Hungary.

Kálmán Tisza[1] was a forceful personality. A Hungarian country squire, he had built up the Hungarian Liberal Party, which he led with undisputed mastery. He was impetuous and stubborn, yet his judgment and his policy were moderate, and avoided extremes. He despised doctrinaire slogans; his practical thinking and his adherence to national aims were combined with a capacity for compromise. A brilliant debater, a first-class tactician, he had immense will-power and tough tenacity; and a brain like a corkscrew. He was shrewd and hard, arrogant and very courageous.

Kálmán Tisza wanted to revive the Junior Kingship, an ancient Hungarian institution, with roots in pagan days, when the Hungarians had two leaders: Kende and Gyula. Kende was the priest-witchdoctor-rainmaker, Gyula the administrator and military leader. From this division developed the institution of King and Junior King, especially important when the King went abroad, or was for some other reason unable to exercise his powers. It went into oblivion after the Árpád dynasty died out in 1302, except for one occasion in 1490, when King Mátyás Hunyady wanted to crown his illegitimate son, János Corvinus, Junior King. After 1526, when the Turkish occupation began, and the Hungarian Crown fell into Habsburg hands through the female line. this position was never revived, in fact it was forgotten.[2]

I have found no written evidence as to why Tisza offered the

Junior Kingship to Rudolf, although from the time at which he did this—mid-summer 1881—the main reasons which prompted his thinking can be deduced. At that time Hungary's most serious problem was the new, rebellious attitude of the nationalities—as the national minorities were then called. Rumania had come into being in 1878, by the Congress of Berlin linking Moldavia and Wallacia into a country, of which in May, 1881, Prince Charles of Hohenzollern became king. The Rumanians of Transylvania thereupon demanded complete autonomy, naturally encouraged from across the border. Equally in 1881 —as described in Chapter 7—there were open fights between Czechs and Germans in Bohemia and Moravia, with the Czechs for the first time demanding that the Germans should remove themselves from their country Also in 1880 and 1881 there were nationalist agitations in Slovakia.[3] Finally there was trouble in Croatia, as described later in this chapter.

Kálmán Tisza was casting around for some imaginative, unifying link that would draw together Hungarians, Slovaks, Rumanians, Germans and Croats. It is probable that he wanted Rudolf as Junior King because he was devoted to the Slavs yet also very fond of the Hungarians. The popular Crown Prince would have been the ideal person to smooth over steadily growing frictions and enmities.

Both the grand-daughter of Kálmán Tisza, Mrs Joseph Patay (née Countess Jolán Tisza) and his great-niece, Countess Michael Teleki (née Countess Aimée Tisza), have told me that Tisza was an exceedingly cautious politician, who would not have put in writing a proposal of such weighty character as the offer of Junior Kingship to Rudolf. But had Rudolf accepted, Tisza would have known how to present the situation to the Hungarian Parliament, to Francis Joseph and to the world.

What actually happened, is known from the account Maurice Szeps dictated to his daughter after his interview with the Crown Prince, lasting from midnight January 30, until 2 a.m. January 31, 1882. 'I thought I would terminate our long conversation by saying how late it was, and that I understood that he had to leave in the morning for Prague. The Crown Prince said, "I am never tired. I never sleep well, especially in Vienna. I always feel better and more at home in Prague than here." And then he began a strange story, sometimes hesitatingly and sometimes hurriedly. . . .

'The Crown Prince said. "For many months the Hungarians have been very worried about the turn things are taking. It is the Hungarians who are the only support nowadays for Liberal and constitutional ideas. But they are unable to move. Here in Vienna, they are afraid of Tisza. But his power and influence are limited too. Last summer Tisza, with two of his ministerial colleagues and a third important political personage, who at the time held no official appointment, met and discussed the idea of having me crowned Junior King of Hungary.[4] They took a formal resolution to that effect. Now although there were only five people present at that meeting, Archduke Albert must have known about it a few weeks later, when he came to me and said, 'Rudolf, I understand they want to crown you Junior King of Hungary. I must warn you against it, Rudolf, because the title of Majesty which you would acquire would only flatter your vanity, but *au fond*, it would mean nothing. Moreover, if you were crowned, you would have to take a solemn oath to conform with the Hungarian constitution, and then your hands would be tied for ever. Think about your own future and that of your family, and don't take any oath. Don't let yourself be crowned. Don't make any promises. One never knows what might happen, and in certain circumstances such an oath would be an unsurmountable obstacle."

'The Crown Prince added bitterly: "Since then Tisza is no longer free to make a move. He lives under incessant threat of blackmail. And naturally, Szeps, you can imagine that there has been no more mention of the possibility of my being crowned Junior King of Hungary." '

Tisza was not a man to be easily frightened, let alone blackmailed. And blackmailed for what? The institution of Junior Kingship, though obsolete, was perfectly legal, and the idea of Rudolf being crowned Junior King would have been immensely popular in Hungary. Of course his appointment would also have strengthened the hands of Tisza and like-minded Hungarian patriots, which was the last thing anti-Hungarian Austrians, like Archduke Albert, desired. Albert had not forgotten 1848–49 (nor had Francis Joseph for that matter) and detested the

'Hungarian rebels', as he called them among his intimates. Hence his advice to Rudolf to refuse the offer, on the grounds that he would have to take an oath on the Hungarian Constitution. Considering that the oath to observe the Hungarian Constitution was the essence of the Hungarian coronation, every Habsburg ruler of Hungary had to take it, including Francis Joseph! And had Rudolf lived and been crowned, he would have had to take it too.

Alas, the twenty-three-year-old Crown Prince had neither the will-power nor the strength of character to stand up for his beliefs, and perhaps he did not fully understand what was at stake—the chance of transforming the Austro-Hungarian Monarchy into a federation or confederation, the only grouping of countries that could have protected itself against its two neighbours, the Germans and the Russians.

What Rudolf should have done was to have accepted the offer on two conditions: (1) that the Hungarian Government would put a stop to the agitation for Hungarian as the command language in Hungarian regiments, as only a unified army, commanded in one language, could provide the defence needed by the Monarchy; (2) that the Hungarian Government made the necessary concessions to the nationalities. Tisza would have argued indignantly that whatever he offered would be insufficient as the nationalities did not want concessions but independence. To this Rudolf should have pointed out that, for instance, in Transylvania a lot could be achieved by restoring the privileges of the Saxons who had lost their semi-autonomy (their schools, university, books, newspapers, justice under their own magistrates, etc.) when the Principality became an integral part of Hungary in 1867. Hungarians and Saxons together would have outnumbered the Rumanians, and the Saxons, apart from a short period in 1848–49, when they dreamt of a special role in a Greater Austria, were loyal to the Hungarians, and their deputies in the Budapest Parliament were solid supporters of Tisza's Liberal Party. Tisza would have had the wisdom to accept this cogent argument, and in view of the advantages of having Rudolf as the political link he so badly needed, made other consessions as well.[5]

The Crown Prince could also have pointed out that Francis Deák, backed by Baron Josef Eötvös had, in 1868, forced through

Parliament a nationalities law, which stated in so many words that every citizen of the fatherland, to whatever nationality he might belong, had equal rights, and that this law was being less and less scrupulously implemented. Tisza would have found it difficult to answer this challenge—but as Rudolf never made it, this is speculation.

For Kálmán Tisza, Rudolf's refusal of the Junior Kingship—for it must have been that—was first a personal affront, secondly proof that the Crown Prince did not have the moral stamina to visualise the change his coronation as Junior King would have meant in his position and in that of the Monarchy, and to fight for it. With Rudolf crowned, and his two conditions carried out, the Hungarian half of the Monarchy would have been strengthened; and Kálmán Tisza—and later his son Stephen Tisza,[6] also Prime Minister—would at least have put into effect Hungarian policy consistently and strongly. Stephen Tisza was the only member of the Austro-Hungarian Crown Council who voted against the unacceptable terms in the ultimatum presented to Serbia in 1914, because he was opposed to a war from which he could see no advantages accruing to Hungary (or to Austria either). Had Rudolf been alive and Junior King, by 1914 his position would have been extremely powerful, and he would have been sixty-five years old. Together with Steven Tisza, they could have decisively influenced the eighty-four year-old Emperor, thwarting the arguments of Counts Antal Forgách and Leopold Berchtold, the *Kriegsgrafen* (the 'war counts'), who insisted on the ultimatum being sent to Serbia after the Serbs had complied with practically all Austrian demands. With Rudolf and Tisza standing together on that historic occasion, there is reason to believe that World War I would not have broken out in 1914.

His refusal of the Junior Kingship had a traumatic effect on Rudolf. He thought about it a great deal and eventually came to realise that this had been his only chance of obtaining a great and responsible position legitimately. In spite of his immense power, Francis Joseph (who was extremely legalistic) could not have prevented it, for the Junior Kingship was part of the Hungarian Constitution—though in abeyance, it had never been abolished. Later on it added greatly to Rudolf's despair that he had thrown away his only opportunity lawfully to obtain the power for which he yearned, and which would have enabled him to influence events in the Monarchy. And he had committed this folly on the advice of his reactionary uncle Albert, who detested him for his liberal ideas . . .

Rudolf's relations with Hungary were, until the last years of his life, always ambivalent. He liked the Hungarian temperament and vitality; he knew the Hungarians liked him and he responded to them with all the warmth of his generous nature. He approved of Hungarian liberalism—it was the Hungarians' stand that brought Austria's absolutism to an end; on their own, the many quarrelling nationalities of Austria could not have achieved it. The Hungarians had many well-wishers because of what they had done for liberalisation. Finally, Kálmán Tisza was not only a strong Prime Minister, but he put into effect his centralisation policy, which in Austria could not be done.

But there were points on which Rudolf violently disagreed. First, the Hungarians wanted to have their own army with Hungarian as the official language. This was counter to Rudolf's ideas, for he believed that the Army—a united Army— was the only guarantee that the Monarchy could be held together. When the Hungarians obstructed by insisting on their own methods and language in their regiments, he was extremely angry, and would even have liked to carry out 'a coup' to force the Hungarians to conform.

No less did he disapprove of the Hungarian attitude to Austria's civilising mission in the Balkans. After his death, among his papers was found one, written about this time, in which he stated: 'The Danubian Empire must be extended to the Aegean Sea, to Salonika. That is only possible with Slav help. . . . Only by cultivating the Slavs can Russian influence be paralysed.'[7]

The Hungarians had little interest in Austria's 'civilising mission'; Tisza was far from enthusiastic about the occupation of Bosnia and Herzegovina; and the Hungarian Parliament refused to vote funds for it. Rudolf was indignant. He said—and in this he was a true Habsburg—that under such circumstances 'it is over with dualism'.[8] He stood by his old belief, expressed to Father Rónay at the age of thirteen, that Austria could not exist without Hungary, and Hungary could not exist without

Austria. (Originally, this had been Metternich's thesis.) In Prague on one occasion Rudolf said, 'What do the four million Hungarians think they can do in the midst of many more million Germans and Slavs? They seem to have forgotten that their Serbs and Rumanians have neighbouring countries of their own people to look to.' And in a letter of August 29, 1883, to Szeps he wrote, 'Hungary is badly administered; it is a country like Russia or Turkey; it has no well-educated bourgoisie, but instead many rotten civil servants, Israelites, impoverished peasants, and a disgruntled rabble. The middle class, which constitutes the true basis of a modern state, is lacking. Hungary will drift towards complete disintegration, and a time will come when they will find it necessary to interfere from Vienna. But here, where there is a sound basis for the establishment of a modern state, political power is being systematically destroyed by all this "Slavonifying", so that very soon Austria will be in the same case as Hungary.

'Here, however, in addition, there is a reactionary tendency, and personally I prefer the crumbling Hungarian liberalism to Taaffe's Austria.'[9]

At that time, under Tisza's strong leadership, Hungarian liberalism did not seem to be crumbling—but this was only on the surface. In 1883 occurred an incident in Croatia and, to quote C. A. Macartney, it was one of those incidents which 'absurd and trivial in itself, raises fundamental principles which end by rocking empires'.[10]

This is what happened. In 1880 a new Director of Finance, the Hungarian Antal Dávid, was appointed to the Croat Administration. The Croats had a Government and a Parliament of their own, as well as being represented in the Budapest Parliament. Dávid introduced courses in Hungarian for his staff, and made promotion dependent on proficiency in Hungarian. Over this there were murmurs of dissatisfaction. Then Dávid added the Hungarian coat of arms to the Croatian one on public buildings, such as schools and post offices, in villages and small towns. This was hardly noticed. But when on the night of August 15, 1883, he ordered the same thing to be done in Zagreb, Croat nationalists regarded this as an effort at magyarisation, and took to the streets. They tore down the Hungarian coats of arms, and the demonstrators degenerated into riotous mobs, so that troops had to be called out. Many people were injured. The *Banus* (Governor), Baron László Pejačević, himself a Croat, refused to bear responsibility for force being used to disperse civilian demonstrators, and resigned.[11]

The Hungarian Government under pressure from Francis Joseph, made amends of a sort, and feeling ran high on both sides. Eventually Tisza suspended the Croat constitution; Croatia was administered by a Royal Commissioner until order was restored; then he appointed a cousin, thirty-three-year-old Count Károly Khuen-Hédervády, a man of his own ilk. A good politician, a superb tactician, Khuen-Hédervády ran Croatia for twenty years. He kept law and order, and created prosperity and later on made concessions about schools and newspapers. But the feeling which had burst forth over the escutcheons was only driven underground and came to the surface towards the end of World War I, when as a result of it Croatia was made a part of Yugoslavia.

In 1883, the Crown Prince was extremely well-informed about Croatia because his friend, Szeps, had sent his best reporter, Dr Berthold Frischauer, to Croatia to find out what had happened. Having interviewed a number of politicians and other important personalities, Frischauer submitted to Rudolf a detailed report about the situation. Rudolf's views were expressed in an anonymous article published by Szeps in the *Neues Wiener Tagblatt* of August 28, 1883[12]: 'The Hungarian nation is too small alone to play a dominating part, it must lean on a powerful Austria. Therefore it was a shortsighted policy on the part of the Hungarian Government hitherto to have faced Taaffe's policy with arms crossed, as it was pleased in its struggle for Hungarian independence to deal with a weak Vienna Government. But now the fire has spread, and for the first time the Hungarians feel the need to pay close attention to their own Slavs. The Croat incident will force Tisza to stand up openly to Taaffe.'

But the Hungarians did not take to heart the demands of their own Slavs, nor did they stand up to Taaffe's reactionary policy. It is significant that no history book published in Hungary before 1945, not even the five volume Hóman-Szekfü *Hungarian History*, as much as mentioned the Croat escutcheon affair.

Perhaps Tisza himself misjudged it. Rudolf understood it very well indeed. He saw that Hungary's weakness lay in the Government's attitude to the nationalities, and that Hungarian blindness in this respect would lead to catastrophe.[13]

But Rudolf also had his blind spot: his hatred of Taaffe. As time went on, getting better and better informed, and more and more involved in political affairs, Rudolf was by no means the impartial observer the Crown Prince of Austria-Hungary should have been. In his struggle against Taaffe he leaned increasingly on the Hungarians, and perhaps backed some of their more extreme plans. But this belongs to a later period of his life.

1883 provided one more great event in Rudolf's life: at last Stephanie was really pregnant. He was delighted and wrote her affectionate letters whenever he had to leave her and begged her to take good care of herself and Vaclav—again he was convinced that the baby would be a boy, and he wanted him to be called Wenzel (which is the Austrian version of Vaclav). On May 11, 1883, he wrote to Szeps; 'Tomorrow afternoon we are coming to Laxenburg to remain until the happy event.' At the Hofburg the first decision was 'Stay in Bohemia'. Rudolf pointed out that it would be more suitable for the event to take place in Vienna. Only then did the Emperor decide that Stephanie should bear her child in Laxenburg. The Czech nobility was very upset that Stephanie did not have it in Prague.

Stephanie's mother came from Belgium to be with her daughter, who had a very difficult time. After forty-eight hours of pain on September 2, 1883, a baby girl was born and baptised Elizabeth in honour of both her famous ancestress, Saint Elizabeth of Hungary, and her beautiful grandmother. Stephanie sobbed desperately when she heard that she had not produced the much-wanted son and heir; Rudolf in his most charming manner said: 'Little girls are nice and affectionate', and on September 4 he wrote to Latour, 'Stephanie looks as blooming as ever, as though nothing had happened, and the little one is a strapping girl weighing seven pounds, completely healthy and strongly developed, with lots of hair on her head. She is very lively, screams madly and drinks a lot without any fuss.'

Of course he hoped that there would be a second and a third child and he would thus assure the succession. Although, strange as it may sound, it was soon after Erzsi's[14] birth that, at a shoot in Görgényszentimre, Rudolf pointed to Archduke Francis Ferdinand and said to Franz von Pausinger, the painter of hunting scenes: 'Not I, but the man walking towards us will become Emperor of Austria.' Rudolf was wrong, for Francis Ferdinand was murdered in Sarajevo two years and three months before Francis Joseph's death.

10

Rudolf at the Apex of his Career

Of the romantic figures of the 19th century none has been so misrepresented as Crown Prince Rudolf of Habsburg. Although perhaps the hardest worked prince of his time, the popular picture presented to the world has been one of an irresponsible playboy, who was a great trial to his father, with whom he quarrelled endlessly; a woman-chaser who led astray a girl of seventeen and killed her in a suicide pact. The facts are far different, and emerge from his writings and recorded actions, most clearly during the period May, 1881–February, 1886.

Enlightened and patriotic people in Austria as well as in Hungary looked to Crown Prince Rudolf as the one man who would transform and regenerate the Monarchy. Even Crown Princess Stephanie who—judging by her memoirs—neither loved nor understood him, admitted that: 'In the opinion of the Viennese he was at the head of all modern thought. More and more was the interest of intellectuals concentrated on him. This was perhaps the climax of his career. His health was still unimpaired by his exhausting occupations and his unwholesome way of life. He took delight in studying the problems of European politics and science, and the leading spirits of the western world regarded him as exemplifying the devotion of the dynasty to progress and liberal ideas.'[1]

Neither Rudolf nor Stephanie kept a systematic diary. Rudolf recorded daily events during his trip to Spain; in 1885 he kept an engagement diary with practically no comments. Stephanie had engagement books and of course the A.D.C.'s had to keep diaries. But the lives of Rudolf and Stephanie can be reconstructed from other sources. With Rudolf it is comparatively easy, for his political letters, especially those to Szeps, provide a vivid picture of his thoughts and aspirations when he was at the height of his powers both as a thinker and a writer. With Stephanie the fullest information is provided by her memoirs, *I Was To Be Empress*. Rudolf's letters, written at the time, and Stephanie's memoirs, reconstructed four and a half decades later in a bitter, frustrated spirit, are like two voices painfully out of tune, none the less complementing each other. Julia von Stockhausen, Stephanie's research secretary, says in her book *In The Shadow Of The Hofburg*: 'The Princess was full of hatred, which she had had to keep down for forty years; . . . hatred veritably burst forth from her' (p. 27). According to von Stockhausen, Stephanie was tactless, insecure and she lacked moral courage. Even at the age of sixty-five 'she did not have the courage to tell the full truth. She only talked around it'.

Rudolf worked very long hours. In many of his letters to Szeps he described his days, which started by being called at seven o'clock, however late he went to bed, and he was always at his military office before nine. Stephanie never stopped complaining that because of his military duties Rudolf neglected her, and that no one paid any attention to her wishes, the only important thing being that she should please him, defer to his desires, adapt herself to his habits. Yet one can almost hear Rudolf's deep voice telling Szeps: 'On top of all my work and obligations, I am plagued by relatives and friends, and for the last two days I accompanied the Emperor to Steiermark.'

He took profound interest in staff work, in drill, in the fire-power of weapons, in the views of his fellow officers. Most days he lunched in the officers' mess, and was personally acquainted with practically all of them. On February 4, 1884, he wrote to Szeps that he was making a point of frequently lunching with the officers and their wives at the Officers' Casino (Club) in Vienna.

He suggested once more that Szeps should publish an anonymous article by him about the food of the other ranks which he considered was unsatisfactory in quality. Again Szeps refused to take up the offer as it would have caused too much annoyance in the highest quarters.

Rudolf spent much time with his staff officers working out strategic problems, observing and assessing the armed forces of other countries. It was as a result of this steady work that he predicted in 1885 that, if it came to a show-down between the

Serbs and the Bulgars (and he thought that this war was inevitable), the Bulgars would win. Field-Marshal Archduke Albert, the Commander-in-Chief of the Austro-Hungarian armed forces, and his advisers scoffed at Rudolf's views, saying that the Serbs were much stronger than the Bulgars. But when the war between the two did break out on November 13, 1885, the Bulgars routed the Serbs at Slivnica and at this time Serbia owed her survival to Austria.

Military matters were the only subject in which the Emperor and his son had a mutual interest. Rudolf said, 'The Army is the only binding substance which in these chaotic days still represents the ideal of our times. It is greater Austrian. One ought to correct it, develop it, favour it—that should be the endeavour of all liberals.'[2]

According to many observers at the Hofburg, Francis Joseph not only distrusted Rudolf because of his liberal views, but was jealous of him. Archduke Leopold Ferdinand, who renounced his rank and wrote several books under the name of Leopold Wölfling, said in *Habsburger Unter Sich*: the Emperor, outwardly gallant and gentle, was in fact autocratic and brutal. As a child Leopold was so frightened of him that it kept him awake at night. Among his intimates Francis Joseph admitted that he could not bear the thought that after his death Rudolf should become emperor as he feared that Rudolf would wreck the Monarchy. His passion for power was so great that he refused even to consider relinquishing some of it to his son. As Rudolf grew to manhood, the Emperor became more and more envious of him. 'Francis Joseph—and I know this from first-hand observation,' wrote Leopold Wölfling, 'even envied Rudolf's conquest of women. To his confidants the Emperor used to lament that no woman had ever loved him for his own sake until he met Frau Schratt, whereas Rudolf had only to look at a woman and if he wished —quite regardless of his rank—he could make her fall for him at once. One quality in Rudolf in particular aroused Francis Joseph's ire. He could never forgive him for possessing such a quick statesmanlike grasp of international affairs. Rudolf's gift of imaginative vision was just what he himself lacked. The poor stolid monarch had but to converse with his son for half an hour on any topic of the day to be left limping behind. Immediately he discovered this quality in his son, he refused to discuss with him as much as a single State paper. Indeed whenever possible, he avoided talking to Rudolf at all.'[3]

Yet the Emperor did recognise Rudolf's military talents and his dedication to the Army; on September 9, 1878, he appointed him Commanding Officer of the 9th Infantry Regiment in Prague; and in 1883 (after Rudolf had applied for promotion[4]) he gave him the command of the 25th Infantry Division, with the rank of Lt.-General, (replacing Archduke Johann Salvator) which brought Rudolf and his family back to Vienna in December, 1883. This is how it came about that a month later Rudolf witnessed the workers' violent demonstrations in the streets of Vienna. The Government declared an emergency, and Rudolf was given the order to send a battalion to the West Station, keeping another in readiness at the barracks; two squadrons had been called out elsewhere. On January 9, 1884, he wrote to Szeps how amazed he was that this should be happening in Vienna—he had thought that uprisings were for Russians, not for Austrians. He added the news that the Prime Minister, Count Eduard Taaffe, had been sent a letter bomb which, thanks to a lucky chance, did not go off. Then he went on to say: 'In the fight against the sound Liberal bourgoisie, against the truly progressive but orderly principle in the State, this is the slogan of the so-called conservatives, of the feudal aristocracy here and in Hungary, now they incite the workers to fight. They want to play off these elements against each other, but thereby order, livelihood, trade and commerce, all the possibilities of regular development are endangered. It can reach the point in Vienna where the Army, which is a cultivated, liberal, State-supporting element, but is already in a bad mood, will take the matter in hand. And then not only anarchism, but the root of all evil will be purged in a most energetic and, I admit, not very gentle manner.'

Rudolf had a intuitive understanding of the situation, yet he was wrong in imagining that there would be an Army coup. With the ultra-conservative Archduke Albert as Commander-in-Chief, and fully trusted by the Emperor, a military coup was impossible.

While Rudolf was taken up with military affairs, Stephanie had her own problems with the move to Vienna. She was indignant over the 'gloomy and inhospitable quarters' assigned to them in the Hofburg; all the windows opened onto a courtyard; there was no gaslight, let alone electricity; they had to live with 'horrible paraffin lamps, which stank all the time, and were perpetually smoking, or their glass cylinders would break'. When they were taken out to be cleaned, Stephanie and her guests had to sit in darkness. There was no running water; she and Rudolf had to bath in rubber tubs, and pour hot water over themselves from two big wooden buckets; her pan of the closed stool (and Rudolf's) was carried through the passages under the eyes and nose of anyone around. The kitchen was on the same floor and the smell of onion and garlick, both freely used for popular Hungarian and Austrian dishes, was disgustingly penetrating.

Stephanie had cause for complaint, but she spoiled her case by her constant nagging, always comparing the discomfort and the antediluvian conditions of the Hofburg with the modern comfort of the Brussels palace, and all other Belgian royal residences. Her tearful moaning bored Rudolf so much that he practically ran away when Stephanie started on what he called her hobby-horse. Even the Camarilla, whose natural ally Stephanie should have been, could not swallow her constant criticism of Austrian backwardness compared to the modern elegance of Belgium. This explains why Stephanie did not become a centre of the people forming the imperial circle, whose views and feelings were infinitely more attractive to her than Rudolf's free-thinking, progressive ideas.

In the end Stephanie not only made their apartments very attractive, but put in two bathrooms at her own expense, and insisted on having a French chef. This caused consternation at the Hofburg; the imperial entourage thought it 'scandalous' that a good Austrian cook was not good enough for *das Trampeltier*. Finally Stephanie applied to the Emperor for permission to use beautiful furniture, tapestries and pictures stored in the cellars of the Hofburg; but her request was turned down. All this she has described in her memoirs[5] almost with venom; at the time her indignant account of the Emperor's lack of cultured taste made Rudolf very angry. Stephanie always lost sympathy by the tactless manner in which she told her side of a story; most unfortunately for herself, this was one of the things that drove Rudolf to other women who amused and flattered him, while Stephanie's complaints implied criticism of him because he did not resent the shortcomings of the Hofburg, which Stephanie pointed out—usually quite accurately.

Rudolf retained his modest bachelor flat, in which he had stayed when in Vienna during the Prague period. According to Stephanie this was the place where he entertained his 'unsatisfactory and dangerous friends'; and she had strict instructions never to come there. One day, driven by jealousy, she penetrated into the forbidden room—Rudolf shouted and ranted at her, almost losing control of himself. Later Stephanie was to say that Rudolf's intrigues against his father had been spun in this flat. She also implied—we know from Julia von Stockhausen that she deleted the full passage from her memoirs—that Rudolf was deeply involved in a plot with the Hungarians, whom he received in the forbidden room.

Both Rudolf and Stephanie regretted leaving Prague, and were sad to say good-bye to Empress Anna, who was indeed sorry to see them go. They assisted at the first performance of Anton Dvořak's *Dmitri* at the Czech National Theatre, where they were given a tumultuous ovation. Rudolf was later to change his views about the Czechs, not because they were determined to have their own king crowned in Prague and as much independence as the Hungarians, but because, unlike the Hungarians, they backed Taaffe's reactionary policy. At this time—November–December 1883—he was still their warm supporter, firmly believing that the future belonged to the Slavs and that Austria's future could only be assured if she made herself their leader and spokesman. He had faith in Austria's great cultural mission in the Balkans. In April, 1884, the Emperor sent Rudolf with Stephanie on a journey to the Balkan countries. The ostensible purpose was to invite their Governments to participate in an exhibition to be held in Budapest. Rudolf knew that the Balkan nations were no longer Austrophil,[6] and that Hungary had harmed the situation by her policy towards the Croat, Serbian and Rumanian minorities. But he was determined to overcome these obstacles, and create new friendships for Austria, thus smoothing the way for spreading western civilisation among the small nations carved out of the Turkish Empire.

On April 14, 1884, the young pair set out from Vienna. They had been carefully briefed for their task—Stephanie discussed even her wardrobe with Rudolf. Her observations of what they saw were shrewd and vivid. She noted the poverty of the Wallachians in Rumania, who lived in wattle and adobe huts. She and Rudolf crossed the Danube at Giorgiu where the charming yacht of Alexander of Battenberg, the Prince of Bulgaria, waited for them to transport them across the river. They spent only two days in Bulgaria, to the disappointment of Alexander; but it was known that the Russians were hostile to him, and a prolonged visit by the Austrian heir to the throne would have been too great an honour to him. The Sultan would also have been displeased if they had stayed with a mere prince before staying with him. Of Alexander Stephanie wrote: 'Prince Alexander devoted most of his attention to me and since he was a highly cultured man, I enjoyed myself exceedingly.' Meanwhile Rudolf was immersed in the report about Turkey sent by Baron Heinrich Calice, the Austrian Ambassador to the Sultan, the half-demented Abdul Hamid.

In Varna, Bulgaria's chief port, the entire population turned out to see Rudolf and Stephanie. *Miramar*, the Austrian imperial yacht, had to anchor some way off-shore as Varna had neither proper harbour, nor satisfactory anchorage for sea-going vessels. *Miramar* was reached by steam launch. General Saver Pasha, sent by the Sultan, greeted them aboard. Stephanie thought that his task was to keep an eye on them and to report to the Sultan. In the evening Varna was illuminated and a whole flotilla of flower-bedecked boats surrounded *Miramar*. A regular battle of flowers developed 'between ourselves and the boats' wrote Stephanie.

Next morning dolphins were playing around *Miramar*—she soon entered the Bosphorus and Rudolf and Stephanie admired the steep banks; Riva, the strong citadel guarding the entry to the Bosphorus, stood opposite the European fortress of Kilia. Both banks were beautifully terraced; villages embedded in gardens covered the slopes to the water's edge. There were marble palaces belonging to Turkish princes and foreign ambassadors. Stephanie thought that Constantinople was the most beautifully situated town in the world—the Byzantium of Antiquity, the Stambul of the Osmanlis, the Gate of Happiness of the Persians. The huge palaces of Ciragan and of Dolma Bahča had a magical effect.

Accompanied by warships and other vessels *Miramar* slowly steamed up to her anchorage. Baron Calice, aware that Yildiz Kiosk— Sultan Abdul Hamid's guest palace—left much to be desired in the way of comfort, suggested that the Crown Prince and his wife remained on *Miramar*, but the Sultan would not hear of this. He dreaded conspiracies—Rudolf might have plotted on the imperial yacht! In order to keep an eye on him, he assigned the most recently built and most comfortable pavilion of Yildiz Kiosk to Rudolf. Calice described the Sultan as an eccentric and ultra-suspicious personality, who suffered from persecution mania. There were huge crowds to watch Rudolf's and Stephanie's arrival—they were rowed by twelve Albanians in a golden barge to the imperial palace, Dolma Bahča. Members of the Austrian Embassy and the Belgian Legation were lined up on the quay from where a carriage drawn by six superb black Arab stallions drove them to Yildiz Kiosk where Janissaries stood at the gates. As soon as they had entered the palace, the Sultan hurried to meet them.

'My delicate white skin, my blue eyes and my golden hair, dressed so as to show it off to best advantage,' wrote Stephanie, 'seemed to impress the Sultan. While we were talking, his eyes continually turned towards me.[7] The conversation was in French, which the Sultan understood well enough, although he spoke it haltingly. Mumir Pasha acted as interpreter. The man about whom they had heard so many unfavourable reports overwhelmed them with kindness—he conferred on both of them the Grand Cross of the Osmanlis studded with brilliants. His anxiety and dread seemed to have disappeared.

There were very few officers among the courtiers; the Sultan was mistrustful of soldiers as both his predecessors—Abdul Aziz and Murad V had been deposed by officers; Abdul Aziz was also murdered by them.[8]

Next day Rudolf and Stephanie were invited to accompany the Sultan to his Mosque. In the evening there was a grand official dinner; then Stephanie was taken to visit the harem. She walked in on the Sultan's arm, and was greeted by the favourite Sultana. She was also welcomed by the Sultan's mother, his daughters and his chief Mistress of Ceremonies. The harem atmosphere was stifling with the scent of attar of roses. There were no chairs, only two divans. The Sultan, with his favourite and his mother, sat on one, Stephanie, with Baroness Calice and her ladies in waiting, on the other. Richly aromatic coffee was served in diamond-studded gold cups. The harem ladies wore gorgeous dresses and glittered with jewels. Next morning Stephanie received from the Sultan a magnificent tiara with red stones—*samtetni*, and felt that she had made a great impression on him.

That day they went sightseeing—in the St Sophia they saw treasures taken from Greek and Roman temples: pagan, Christian and Moslem elements all jumbled together in a strangely impressive magnificence. Green and pink porphyry, pink and white marble, the carpet on which Mohamed used to kneel—were all there. Every Friday the officiating imam entered the pulpit carrying a naked sword in memory of Mohamed II who, in 1453, had conquered Byzantium, sword in hand.

The Foreign Minister, Kálnoky, had entrusted Rudolf with the mission of raising the question of the building of the Orient railway across Turkish territory—the Sultan regarded this new-fangled means of communication as a threat to his country's independence, which would enable the Powers to bring their armies quickly to the gates of Constantinople.

It is in this connection that Rudolf first heard of Baron Maurice Hirsch.[9] In Vienna gossip had it that the Crown Prince was using his position to obtain the railway concession for a rich financier interested in Turkish railways, because he was heavily in debt, and that in return for the concession Hirsch would settle Rudolf's debts. There was not a shred of truth in this; in 1884, when he was trying to induce the prevaricating Abdul Hamid to make up his mind, Rudolf had only just heard Hirsch's name. Moreover, Kálnoky's instructions to Rudolf have been preserved. A month after Rudolf had left Constantinople, Baron Calice reported: 'The Sultan has, in fact, on account of the suggestion made by H.I.H. the Crown Prince, given orders to expedite the matter.'[10]

From Turkey, Rudolf and Stephanie went back to Bulgaria—in Varna Prince Alexander had a surprise in store for the Crown Prince; he took him to shoot birds of prey at Rustchuk—using his yacht as their base of operations. From Rustchuk Rudolf and Stephanie went on to Bucharest, and had a warm welcome. At this time relations between King Carol of Rumania and King

Milan of Serbia were strained, and each one wanted the exclusive favour of entertaining Rudolf and Stephanie. 'Our visits to both Courts were animated by a strong desire to build foundations for a thriving future,' wrote Stephanie in her memoirs.[11] 'Truly, both visits were a great success.'

Rudolf wrote a most competent report on his journey, with an economy of words and shrewd descriptions of all the people he had met. He analysed Abdul Hamid, Alexander of Battenberg, King Carol and Queen Elisabeth of Rumania and King Milan of Serbia with great astuteness. This report is an able document—summing up the position of the rulers, their popularity or lack of it, their knowledge of conditions, their relations with their ministers and their subjects. In his report Rudolf included a subtle appreciation of the personalities and knowledge of the Austrian diplomatic representatives in these countries; he especially commended Karl Count Khevenhüller, the Consul-General to Serbia.

Here is its concluding passage: 'We have, undeniably, great interests in the Balkans, and the destiny of the Balkan countries is a vital question for us. On the whole I found the soil better prepared than I had expected. The moment is now favourable. Austria, allied with Germany, makes a solemn impression on these peoples, and the thought must arise in everybody that, as the nearest cultured State, connected by a river which is above all an Austrian trade-route, Austria is destined by her geographical position to play a great part in the civilisation of the Balkan Peninsula.

'From Austria and through Austria Western and Central European culture penetrates to these still fallow regions. It must spread and find an outlet, which it rests with us to provide; financially, commercially, and through the dissemination of culture, we must bring these countries under our direct and dominating influence and win them over.

'In Constantinople, as well as in Rumania, Bulgaria and Serbia, one believes and feels that Austria, on account of her standing and her geographical position, is called upon to play a great part in the East. I think that people there realise this more than we in our modesty have ever dared to imagine. I have always considered Austria's mission in Eastern Europe in the light of a natural law, and now, after this visit, my belief in a great future for these regions is firmer than ever.

'The division of the sphere of work with another great Power—for instance Russia—was an idea which was formerly much discussed in Austria. I consider this a complete impossibility, since all the Balkan countries form one whole territory, and instead of furthering peace we would only lay the foundations of endless quarrelling and complications.

'One recoils from the possibility of a war with Russia, and means are sought whereby the Oriental question may be prolonged and peace bought by unnatural concessions on our part. But nothing can protect us from this struggle, except the complete renunciation of her present Eastern policy on Russia's part, a gesture which is scarcely within the bounds of likelihood.

'Eastern Europe is better prepared for us than people here think. If, by the establishment of rail and water communications, the reinforcement of the already large Austrian colonies, and by every other means at our disposal, particularly by the appointment of very efficient and energetic diplomats to the Balkan Courts, we are able unswervingly to work towards our goal, indifferent to what Russia may say, as anyhow, no matter what happens, we shall have to fight her some time, then that which, in the nature of things, must happen, will do so—and we shall be masters of Eastern Europe.'

Rudolf's report on his second Balkan trip—early in 1885 he went to Montenegro and Greece, from there to Syria, and on the way back coasted among the Greek Islands[12]—has unfortunately been lost. There is no reason to believe that it was written with less acute observation and crisp summing up than the first report. From then on, on Francis Joseph's orders, the Foreign Ministry showed its Balkan reports to Rudolf.

Stephanie has described this second journey in her memoirs: they drove up from the Bocche di Cattaro along an Austrian-built road to the Montenegrin border, where Nikita, the Prince of the Black Mountains (Montenegro), waited for them with his Ministers and State dignitaries, and took them to his capital, Cetinje. From there they could see the majestic peak of the Lovcen, and the green Lake of Scutari. But Nikita had pro-Russian leanings. As for King George of Greece, he postponed

Rudolf's visit because the Grand Duke Paul, brother of the Tsar, was still staying in Athens. When they eventually got to the Greek capital Rudolf and Stephanie had a poor reception. The anti-Austrian newspapers had reported that Northern Macedonia and Salonika would be annexed by Austria—and that this had been settled the previous year in Constantinople by Rudolf and the Sultan. By the end of their visit Rudolf's denials were believed, the atmosphere had improved, and there was genuine disappointment when he cancelled all plans and went off bear-hunting in Albania, a trip he hugely enjoyed. Stephanie was allowed to go alone to Corfu, where she was enthusiastically welcomed, and presented with olive, laurel, orange and oak plants for her garden in Lacroma. All her plants took and the oak can still be seen on Lokrum, as the island is now called.

As Rudolf could receive practically no information about political developments from official sources, he obtained it from his intellectual friends, primarily from Szeps and his two brilliant collaborators, Dr Frischauer and Gyula Futtaky. All three were Jews, liberals, Europeans. Szeps had excellent contacts in France—Leon Gambetta had been a close friend. Georges Clemenceau became one, and his twenty-years-younger brother, Paul, married Szeps' daughter Sophie on December 23, 1886; by then Georges Clemenceau was already a force in French politics. The Clemenceaus were aristocrats, who had given up their title in 1789; Georges Clemenceau had been a mayor during the 1870–71 Commune; he had trained as a doctor but was a wealthy man in his own right. By May, 1880 (when his interview with Szeps took place) he was treating only poor people free of charge. Clemenceau told Szeps that in France there was neither freedom of speech, nor of writing; once these were obtained, France would be able to do what was needed to regain Alsace-Lorraine. Clemenceau's conclusion was that Germany—the most disliked country in Europe—needed the alliance with Austria, and not the other way round. (See the full text as written by Szeps immediately after the conversation had taken place, in the Appendix.)

Szeps sent his notes of the Clemenceau interview to the Crown Prince on October 8, 1883. It must have made a very deep impression on Rudolf for three years later, on January 12, 1886, he sent

Szeps a long memorandum in which he said: '. . . Germany needs this alliance more than we do. This is a truth that can easily be proved if one only takes the trouble to study thoroughly the happenings of the last few years. And yet few people realized it, and this is one of the great successes of Bismarck's genius—to isolate Austria more and more from all other powers, and to make it dependent upon the help of Germany. Bismarck taught us to believe that Austria could not exist without an intimate Austro-German alliance; all the same, things in Germany are not going as smoothly as the rest of Europe feels obliged to believe.'[13]

11

Crown Prince and Iron Chancellor

The German Chancellor was deeply concerned by the quick recovery of France after her 1870 defeat. She paid off the last instalment of her heavy indemnity within two years. Moreover, Bismarck feared that one day, when Crown Prince Rudolf became Emperor, he would not only want an alliance with France, but—backed by his friend, the Prince of Wales—would try to expand it to Russia.

At this time Rudolf had little liking for reactionary, unprogressive Russia, but he was greatly impressed by Republican France. On June 2, 1882, he wrote to Szeps: 'The happy, healthy, powerful French Republic, which proved itself able to survive, scarcely twelve years after Sedan now stands as an undeniably obvious proof that European republics can perform great tasks. . . . We are indebted to France as the source of all liberal ideas and constitutions in Europe. And whenever great ideas begin to ferment, France will be looked to for an example. What is Germany compared to her? Nothing but an enormously enlarged Prussian regimental barbarism, a purely military state.'

Rudolf was sufficiently realistic to know that until he came to power, his father with his reactionary advisers would not make a single move in the direction of closer relations with France. In theory the Emperor of Austria and the Tsar of Russia, the two most conservative—not to say reactionary—rulers of Europe should have been close allies. But Francis Joseph had for ever antagonised the Tsar by not coming to his assistance during the Crimean War. And, as Rudolf has written with rare insight: 'Russia, lying in the convulsions of delirium tremens, is lost as a support for the Conservative principles of the Holy Alliance. It is that which brings the Conservative Courts of Vienna and Berlin together.' On May 20, 1882, Austria signed an alliance with

Germany—and Italy. It was a master-stroke of Bismarck that he had told the Italians that 'the way to Berlin leads over Vienna'. The French played into his hands when on April 12, 1881, they seized Tunis, on which Italy had set her heart. Indignant over the French action, that year the Italian King Humbert and his Queen twice came to Vienna, the second time on October 27, when Francis Joseph cleared up outstanding problems with the Italian King.

In view of what he had observed during his two Balken trips, Rudolf knew that Russia was determined to dominate the sphere in which he saw Austria's civilising mission. He did not believe in the possibility of dividing the Balkans between Russia and the Monarchy; therefore he was certain that sooner or later, Austria would have to go to war with Russia. This was the only reason why he accepted the necessity of an alliance with Bismarck's Germany.

When at the age of twenty he was sent to Berlin on a visit, Bismarck charmed him by treating him as an equal—which his father never did. Rudolf wrote to Latour: 'The crowning glory of my stay in Berlin was a visit to the Chancellor. It lasted more than an hour. We talked of everything which concerns Germany and Austria, about the most important and delicate circumstances of home and foreign policy. It was easy for me, as Bismarck spoke the whole time and would not let me put in a word. Anyhow as I was armed with instructions from Vienna, I knew what I ought to answer.'[1]

In 1882 Rudolf was three times in Berlin, and each time saw the Chancellor, but no letters or reports as to his impressions of the two other interviews have survived. However, Bertha Szeps, the confidential secretary of her father, who knew of all the letters and conversations that passed between Szeps and the Crown Prince, wrote in her diary: 'Although at this time there was an official alliance between Germany and Austria, Bismarck was very well aware that once Rudolf came to the throne, Austria would take her stand beside the western democracies. Because of the fundamentally different Prussian ideology, the ordinary Austrian and even the Emperor, did not feel happy that his country should be tied to Germany; he felt that Austria's many constituent races should be united in a free federation. So

Bismarck had his doubts about the durability of the 1878 agreement, and wanted it to be ratified by the parliaments of Berlin, Vienna and Budapest. A storm of protest against this proposal arose throughout the Monarchy. Perhaps the clearest insight into this situation can be given from my father's account of an interview with the Crown Prince.'[2]

This took place at 3 p.m., December 28, 1882, at the Hofburg and lasted three hours. Rudolf took up a lot of time by his complaints about Habsburg Day, when all the Habsburgs foregathered in Vienna. It had been shabby, colourless and dull; the whole of the old nobility had kept away, both from the church ceremony and the Court. Then Rudolf related to Szeps that he had asked Kálnoky to visit him that morning, as rumour had it that he was to be sent to Berlin once more. Rudolf forced Kálnoky to admit that he was to attend the silver wedding celebrations of the Crown Prince and Crown Princess, Queen Victoria's 'dear Vicky' —the Princess Royal. Then he drew from his pocket a letter from Prince William of Prussia, telling him that the silver wedding would be only an intimate family affair, and told Kálnoky that he understood very well what Bismarck wanted—the ratification of the Dual Alliance[3] by the Vienna and Budapest Parliaments. In 1879, when Bismarck came to Vienna, he had already tried for this, but to his intense annoyance the Emperor refused to discuss it. Now Bismarck revived the old plan.

Rudolf had also received a five-page letter from Archduke Albert, who warned him under no circumstances to act as an intermediary in the matter of the parliamentary ratification. Albert's reasons were very different: in his view, the position of the rulers had already been restricted; if treaties were to be ratified by parliaments, this would further curtail their powers.

Szeps—whose advice Rudolf sought—told him either not to go, or if he had to, go only on condition that the Prime Minister guaranteed that the Austrian Parliament would turn down the ratification of the German alliance. But as ratification might be regarded as an alteration of the constitution, and therefore require a two-thirds majority, this was an easy promise. Eventually all Rudolf's conditions were accepted and on the order of the Emperor, he and Stephanie prepared for this important Berlin trip. Both of them were carefully primed as to what to say and not to say. Then Emperor William's only surviving brother died and the visit was postponed until February 27, 1882.

The day after his arrival Rudolf had a long, outspoken talk with Bismarck,[4] who repeatedly stressed the importance of the Austro-German alliance, which would ensure peace in Europe. Austria could deal with Russia, the German Chancellor said, Germany with France, but if they were attacked by other countries simultaneously, they needed each other. Bismarck wanted a re-insurance treaty with Russia, the good will of England, and the Dual Alliance built up into a legally binding, offensive and defensive alliance.

Rudolf explained as tactfully as he could that Austria was not in a position to bind herself to such a degree. Bismarck realised for the first time that Rudolf was not only intelligent—this he had known after their first meeting—but that he had a political concept of his own, to which he would stubbornly hold.

Yet after the interview, Bismarck said: 'Your Crown Prince was pleasant, as indeed he always is. But as to the development of his mental powers and the maturity of his opinions and conceptions, these surpassed even my expectations. His comprehension of political matters, which proves that in spite of his youth he has reflected independently and seriously on many subjects, is no ordinary one, and really surprised me. We were not always of the same opinion, but he was able to argue his point of view excellently, and what struck me most about this was the cautious manner in which he did it.'

However, at their meeting in September, 1883, it nearly came to a row between the Chancellor and Rudolf, who stood his ground even more firmly than in February. Bismarck became convinced that the young Crown Prince was aiming at weakening the all-important Austro-German Alliance and would eventually establish closer relations with the French, the English and the Russians. His attitude to the 'charming heir to the Austrian throne' changed completely.

About the same time Rudolf also changed his mind about Bismarck. On February 17, 1884, he wrote to Szeps: 'I thought for a long time that Prince Bismarck was an honest man; now for some time I have great mistrust of Berlin and with good reason. Why is Count Taaffe's policy supported? Why do they flatter those of a conservative point of view? Why are they so pleased that here everyone blows the same absolutistic horn? Because Austria must be driven towards the Orient. It must be economically undermined, prove itself unviable in its present form, and then be gently pushed eastwards. That is why they were always so loving towards me in Berlin—they wanted to win me over to this line. But I have a good nose! The story has appeared foul to me for some time.'

In a strange way, Crown Prince Rudolf and Prince Bismarck, two such very different personalities, had certain qualities in common. First, both were political animals to their fingertips. Rudolf started writing about political questions at the age of eight—after the battle of Sadowa, for he understood very soon what the loss of Austria's leading position among the German states meant. For this he hated the Prussians, the upstart Hohenzollern and their 'evil genius'—Bismarck.

Otto von Bismarck was a little older than Rudolf when he began to dream about Prussian hegemony in Europe. He saw very clearly that the pre-condition for the creation of the German Empire was the destruction of Austria. The Iron Chancellor pursued this aim with icy determination.

Rudolf had not been allowed to argue out his views at a university with other young men of his own age as Otto von Bismarck did at Göttingen. Both Rudolf and Bismarck were ardent patriots—unfortunately Rudolf never had the chance to put his reform plans to the test, and modernise 'old Austria', while Bismarck tried and succeeded in creating the German Empire—with the utmost ruthlessness and lack of scruple.

In her memoirs, Stephanie described the warm feelings between the chivalrous old Emperor William and Rudolf; Rudolf's 'sense of oppression' when with Bismarck; and his intense dislike of 'little Willie'[5]. Stephanie had many intimate talks with the Crown Princess, who confided in her that she fully shared the ideas of her husband, and that this had created a great gulf between herself and her son, William. To her mother, Queen Victoria, she wrote: 'Crown Prince Rudolf spoke with wonderful clearness, shrewdness and a sound knowledge of men and things; he is thoroughly well informed as to the situation, and has been entrusted with a number of difficult missions to Prince Bismarck. He is assured that his views are more in accordance with ours than with those of the Emperor (William I) or of Wille.'[6]

As for Rudolf's feelings, Leopold Wölfling has written: 'He considered William a dull-witted, arrogant boor', whose strut and pomposity were ludicrous and his ideas so shallow and reactionary that Rudolf found him a colossal bore.[7]

In his memoirs, *My Early Life*, ex-Emperor William II wrote: 'I got to know the Crown Prince Rudolf at the time of the Vienna World Exhibition in 1873. He was inspiring and shrewd, and his fresh vivacity and fascinating disposition was full of sparkling humour. . . . To my regret I was forced to notice in the course of years that he did not take religion at all seriously, and it pained me when he poured out his mordant wit not only on the Church and clergy, but also on the simple faith of the country folk. . . . Nor could I help becoming aware of other faults of character, so as to destroy my original confidence and we drifted further and further apart.'[8]

It goes without saying that until his fall—eighteen months after Rudolf's death—Bismarck indoctrinated William II about the need of a strong alliance with a *submissive* Austria, and of a re-insurance treaty with Russia so that Germany should never have to fight a war on two fronts.

Bismarck was fully informed about Rudolf's life and activities. He knew that apart from his military duties, the Crown Prince liked best his work as a writer. He started contributing—of course anonymously—to Szeps' *Neues Wiener Tagblatt* in 1882, and kept this up to the end of his life. In one of his letters to Szeps he expressed the hope that, if need be, he could earn his living as a writer. Every journalist will recognise a kindred spirit in Rudolf's many suggestions to Szeps of articles he would like to write; his pride when one of his pieces was praised and published; his efforts to send items of news with admonitions that Szeps should on no account reveal their source, and so on. Szeps, a very experienced and talented editor, with a fantastic memory, was known for his skill and wit in circumventing the censor. He took excellent care of Rudolf's work. He copied all his articles—duly edited—in his own hand, and returned the originals to the Crown Prince. When Rudolf's devoted servant,

Nehammer, took an article to Szeps, he had to change trams several times, and use all kind of ruses to shake off the detectives who followed everyone of the prince's entourage.

Bismarck knew that Rudolf was aware of this, and of his letters being censored. The Crown Prince complained bitterly to Szeps about it. For instance on January 13, 1883, he wrote: 'I must draw your attention to a number of odd things today. They are becoming very watchful and suspicious of me, and I see more clearly every day by what a narrow circle of espionage, denunciation and supervision I am surrounded. Be very careful if ever you are asked about your relations with me. Even if you speak to Nehammer, or give him letters or messages, do not omit the slightest precaution. . . .

'I have already told you that I had good reasons to believe that our relations were known in high quarters; since then I have proof of it. Futtaky has told me that he was asked by Vodianer[9] a few days ago whether it was true that you often came to the Vienna Burg. Vodianer is a banker, as far as I can gather, the banker of Archduke Albert, he certainly sees him often.

'I know only too well the way in which my enemies work. First they send out scouts, then they advance under cover. Then they prepare an ambush by means of cross examinations, and finally when everything has been properly prepared, the general attack begins. I have already had to go through it all, in a shameful and unpleasant way. But we will talk about it some other time. The preliminaries are now beginning, the accounting has commenced.'

Rudolf had received a letter, dated January 5, 1883, from Archduke Albert. The Field Marshal knew all too well that Rudolf had friends among journalists, many of whom were Jews, and that his close friend, Szeps, was both a journalist and a Jew. Yet he wrote to him: 'Practically all journalists are Jews, baptised or unbaptised, Jews who stick together all over the world, and who are in addition Freemasons. The rulers of this most dangerous secret society, most dangerous because it is directed against the throne and the Church, oblige the world brotherhood to an absolute mutual help, from which none of them can be exempted. Originally, Jews were excluded from it, but nowadays all the literate rich are Jews, and zealous Freemasons who are often more numerous in the Lodges than are Christians. But the *Neues Wiener Tagblatt*, whose editor is Szeps (epithets must be deleted!), seems to me a dangerous paper, more dangerous even than the *Neue Freie Presse*, because it calls itself a democratic organ and unobtrusively works for the fostering of republican ideas, from time to time disguising its aims by some dynastic, loyal, patriotic leading article so that it misleads a lot of well-meaning peoples, and circulates widely amongst the lower classes. Thus it published recently an article about you which was overflowing with loyalty.'

Rudolf was so infuriated by Albert's impertinence that he copied the letter and—impetuously—enclosed it in his long one to Szeps.[10]

'. . . From these examples you can see their mode of attack, which this time has been a little altered,' he continued. 'Previously they began by cursing my acquaintance, as they are cursing you now. This was followed by a few weeks' peace. Then the epistle about the Freemasons arrived, which this time was launched at the start. Then peace again, and after some time the storm broke. Anonymous letters addressed to me, full of denunciations about the people with whom I am in contact, warnings and cries from the pious and the well-meaning. Then quite open accusations and denunciations of me in the highest quarters. All that I have been through already. I have been denounced as a Freemason, and complete proofs, with dates, have been supplied, whereas I do not even know the rules of the order.

'The source of attack from which the last letter comes [Archduke Albert] is not the only one. There is a big circle and an active committee who are continually brewing complaints and intrigues of this sort.

'For a long time they tried to bribe me, but when this did not work, they took to the technique of trying to terrorize me from time to time, and creating many difficulties and unpleasantnesses for me.'

This is only one of several letters in which Rudolf described to Szeps how he was being treated. The lamentable fact is that he was absolutely right. The secret papers of the Head of the Vienna Police, Franz Baron von Krauss, found accidentally in 1953 in Berlin, in the suitcase of a German actor who during World War II acted in Vienna, published in 1955 under the title: *Das Mayerling*

Original, bear out the spying and informing that went on. Every morning the police delivered to the Emperor's Private Office a report of every move Rudolf had made the previous day, whom he had seen, and when possible, what was talked about. Rudolf had no private life.

Bismarck admired the Crown Prince for the great literary work on which he had embarked: *The History of the Austro-Hungarian Monarchy in Words and Pictures*. In March, 1884,[11] Rudolf applied to the Emperor for permission to write the story of the Monarchy. He said that 'the literary and artistic circles among all the people of the Empire would be united in a common undertaking; well-known names would shed lustre on the work, and opportunity would be provided for the younger aspiring intellectuals to make themselves known and use their gifts. . . . This work shall show at home and abroad what a rich treasure of intellectual power this Monarchy possesses in the peoples of all her countries and how these co-operate in a splendid achievement, which is bound to serve to develop the consciousness and power of the common Fatherland.'

Rudolf was in constant touch with the two editors, Josef von Weilen for the German edition, and Maurice Jókai[12] for the Hungarian, but he reserved for himself the ultimate decisions as to content.

The Crown Prince—like Prince Albert in the 19th century, and Prince Philip now—took a great interest in scientific development. He agreed to open the electrical exhibition on August 16, 1883; he ended with these words:

'The ultilisation of a mighty force of nature through scientific knowledge and its exploitation to open new opportunities for daily life, is the purpose of this endeavour. The full success will not be felt overnight. A great and far-reaching future is in store for electricity; it will cause a transformation the effects of which are incalculable, and it will penetrate deeply into all aspects of human life.

'This is the third exhibition of this kind. Yet it is perhaps not an accident that, thanks to the unremitting work of the men of science and the application of many practical skills, Vienna can present within its hospitable walls the greatest electrical exhibition of all. Is it not from this our native city that Preschel's matches emanated in 1833, ousting the old flint, dating back to the Stone Age? and in 1838 did not the Stearin[13] candle start on its way from Vienna round the whole world?

'Yes, even the gaslight of the streets, this enormous change in town life, was invented by Mährer Winzer in Vienna and then taken to England.

'Now we are at the beginning of a new phase in the history of the development of illumination. . . . Mindful of the great importance of this exhibition we can say that it will bring honour to the Empire and to our capital and residential town of Vienna. . . . And a sea of light shall radiate from this town and new progress shall emanate from it.

'In the name of His Majesty, Our Lord and Emperor, I hereby declare this exhibition open.'

The audience was wildly enthusiastic; the sentence about 'the sea of light' became the slogan of the liberals, who used it on the banners of their party. More and more intellectuals and progressives gathered around Rudolf, saying quite openly that the Crown Prince was their only hope that old Austria should take on a new lease of life and once more become a leading power in Europe. Rudolf went out of his way to demonstrate that old Vienna could be a leader in the fields of science and medicine. Indeed at this time, Vienna was still the medical centre of the world.[14]

Rudolf's activities met with open ill-will on the part of Prime Minister Taaffe. He did not come to the opening of the Electrical Exhibition, nor did a single member of the old aristocratic families. This enraged Rudolf; next day (August 16, 1883) he suggested to Szeps that he should write an article about it. Wisely, Szeps discouraged Rudolf on this occasion, which was all the more fortunate as on January 10, 1884, Rudolf received an appreciative letter of thanks from the Emperor for all the work he had done to make the Electrical Exhibition a success.

Prince Bismarck watched Rudolf's growing popularity and his increasing self-confidence with concern. To his wife he confided that he would have preferred to have Rudolf as his pupil to Prince William, but he was far from happy at the prospect of Rudolf succeeding Francis Joseph as Emperor of the Austro-Hungarian Monarchy.

At this time Rudolf was looking forward eagerly to the day

when this would happen. His feelings were reflected in his New Year's wishes to Szeps: 'Out of the darkness which surrounds us —from the night of reaction—may we at last awake to the dawn of a better time in which our ideals will be victorious. First let us free ourselves from the grip of pessimism, which is tantamount to submission to fate and to loss of self-confidence. Let us always be aware that better times must come when we shall have to answer for those principles to which we have devoted our lives.'[15]

Rudolf was pleased to be in Vienna again; he believed in the future and in his ability, through hard work and the performance of public duties, to strengthen his position so as to create a new, modern, powerful Austria.

12

Rudolf and Women

Crown Prince Rudolf did not concentrate all his energies on politics—young and attractive, he liked the company of women, and of many women. He behaved to them lightheartedly—as he did to most things—discarding one for another, regardless of their feelings. He was both the engineer of his own misfortunes and the victim of circumstances beyond his control. That he was profligate—and he was very profligate—was but one aspect of the general weakness of character which became apparent from his early years. On the other hand he was the victim of circumstances in that his parents did not understand him. Saddest of all, in his marriage he wholly failed to find the warmth and understanding which could have been the stabilising factor in his erratic character and which his father and mother so significantly denied him. An illness at that time incurable was the final blow to his physique and his nervous system.

In 1877 when the Crown Prince was eighteen years old, General Beck wrote to his wife: 'Rudolf has an exuberant nature and wears his heart on his sleeve and his tongue, and has not digested the liberal doctrines of some of his teachers; for the rest love will soon become his chief occupation.' Beck, though a soldier of little distinction, read the character of the young Crown Prince like a book.

The official account of Rudolf's sex education makes extraordinary reading. On December 27, 1871, when the Crown Prince was thirteen years and four months old, Latour took him, accompanied by two doctors and several tutors to a fish-breeding establishment in Salzburg. There they explained to him the facts of life. The doctors wrote an official report which all his tutors had to sign and use as a guideline when their precocious pupil asked awkward questions. What Rudolf thought on discovering the workings of nature is unknown. When he first became interested in or experienced sex, is also uncertain.[1] It would have been consistent with Austrian moral views of the time if the task of initiating the Crown Prince into the pleasures of the flesh had been deliberately engineered by a trusted friend of the Emperor.

Gossip in Vienna had it that the task was accomplished by Captain Karl Karnauer who had saved the life of Francis Joseph[2] and was greatly trusted by the Emperor. Karnauer may well have arranged with the discreet proprietress of a brothel that the Crown Prince should be introduced to sexual relations by a carefully selected, healthy member of the establishment. Such a procedure was not uncommon for young men of aristocratic families—unless a peasant girl or housemaid had performed the service before the young man's father or guardian felt called upon to deal with the situation.

If Captain Karnauer was conniving at escapades to a brothel, it would have been perfectly practicable for Rudolf to slip out unbeknown to Latour or his parents. At this time the police had not started to keep the Crown Prince under surveillance—his radical political views were known to Latour but he kept his knowledge to himself—and the Emperor and Empress were astonishingly ignorant of what their only son thought or did. According to the diaries of Archduchess Valerie, Rudolf's younger sister, and Countess Marie Festetics, Rudolf behaved quite differently in the presence of his parents than he did with other people. They did not know what was an open secret in Vienna, that Rudolf enjoyed sexual indulgence from his early years.

One thing, however, is certain. Rudolf fell desperately in love with Maria Antonia, the sixteen-year-old daughter of the Grand Duke Ferdinand III of Tuscany and Anna Maria of Saxony, the niece of the man who was to become Rudolf's closest friend at the end of his life—Archduke Johann Salvator, better known to the world as Johann Orth. As Grand Duke Nando was a close friend of the Emperor, this love affair should have been a happy one, but Francis Joseph regarded Maria Antonia as not sufficiently grand to become Rudolf's wife and Empress; and rightly considered her health not satisfactory to assure the succession. Yet there were frequent visits, and in spite of Francis Joseph's disapproval,

Rudolf and Maria Antonia went on meeting each other. If Rudolf wrote to her, and if she answered, these letters have never been found. Like so many girls of that period, and like at least two other women in Rudolf's life, Maria Antonia suffered from consumption. At this time—in the late 1870's—there was no cure for tuberculosis. Maria Antonia grew thinner, paler and pathetically more beautiful. She began to spit blood—and fled to a convent. She died on April 13, 1883, in Cannes, of tuberculosis of the lungs, as Abbess of the Theresa Foundation of the Noble Ladies in Prague.

Rudolf was heartbroken over her decision to take the veil. This had been his first love, she was young and beautiful and he wanted to marry her, and was trying to get round his father—it is believed with the blessing of the Empress Elizabeth. Rudolf was admittedly six years younger than Francis Joseph had been when he married; but his father too had married the girl he loved, contrary to the wishes of his mother. And Francis Joseph had become Emperor at eighteen, just about Rudolf's age on meeting Maria Antonia. It was at this time that Rudolf developed an interest in suicide, and it is a matter for speculation whether or not Maria Antonia's sacrifice in becoming a nun had anything to do with it.

It is revealing of the gross misrepresentations about the Crown Prince current to this day that in 1974 a popular West German weekly, *Die Frau Im Spiegel*, published two articles by a Journalist called Birg Cassel[3] entitled *Kronjuwelen*. In these the author tells an entirely fictitious story about Rudolf having secretly married Maria Antonia, stating the date, the place, the name of the priest who performed the ceremony and the address of the flat in which the Princess is alleged to have lived. There is a description of the scene when Rudolf told his father that he would not marry Stephanie of the Belgians and Francis Joseph boxed his ears; of the advice of his mother that Rudolf should go through with the Belgian marriage as it would not be valid anyhow and he could discard Stephanie as soon as he came to the throne. According to Birg Cassel, Rudolf disappeared from Laxenburg on the wedding day and at midnight Archduke Johann Salvator went to tell the mortally offended Stephanie that 'your husband is otherwise engaged'. There is not one word of truth in all this, and even less in the story of Maria Antonia's son, for whose education Rudolf is alleged to have made arrangements after her death from tuberculosis. In spite of these blatant lies, the two articles were avidly read by Germans, Austrians and Swiss.

After Maria Antonia had taken her vows, Rudolf was inconsolable, but Bombelles went into action and found distractions. He knew Court society, the theatrical world, the women of the *cafés chantants*, the *Heurigen*, and the 'establishments'. The Crown Prince would have had little difficulty in charming any Austrian girl even if he had been very ordinary, but he was highly intelligent, witty, full of charm and handsome. It did not take long for him to forget his short, tender love affair and to learn to appreciate attractive women of all classes and backgrounds. Soon Vienna was full of gossip; men in coffee houses told each other who Rudolf's latest favourite was; women heard of it at the hairdressers and the dressmakers; and of course the coachmen of the un-numbered *Fiakkers*[4] and jockeys who drank with them added embellishments.

It was a new game in Vienna to bet how long Rudolf's 'latest' would last. The stories were usually greatly exaggerated, as though it had been someone's intention to undermine Rudolf's reputation and inevitably there was talk of beautiful Jewish girls who had acquired influence over him. One such story was true. Rudolf himself told it to a nerve specialist, Dr Moritz Benedikt, whose daughter recorded it. So did Szeps' daughter, Bertha, in her memoirs:[5] 'At the time when the Crown Prince was still residing in Prague, he paid an official visit to the "ghetto", the Jewish quarter there. During this visit he met a young Jewish girl of great beauty. They fell in love. Her parents (her father was the cantor of the Staronova synagogue), however, made it impossible for them to meet, by hiding her away in the country. But in the hope of seeing her beloved again, she ran away, and secretly returned to Prague, where she fell ill of fever the day of her arrival, and subsequently died.'

Another version is that after her secret return, the girl stood under Rudolf's window in very inclement weather, caught pneumonia and died of it.

Bertha Szeps concluded: 'Ever since then the Crown Prince has often visited the Jewish cemetery secretly at night, bringing flowers to place on her grave. He could not forget her.' This was the romantic side of Rudolf's character, which came to the fore when least expected, and it remained part of him to the end of his life.

When Rudolf threw himself into night life, he did exactly what his shrewd teacher, Walterskirchen, had advised him *not* to do—he gorged himself with love affairs with unseemly haste. And in this Bombelles was a very useful mentor. When Rudolf went to England in 1878 and met the Prince of Wales for the first time, that *bon vivant* took Rudolf around London. Subsequently he remarked to his A.D.C.: 'For a young man of his age, it is surprising how much Rudolf knows about sexual matters. There is nothing I could teach him.'[6]

In his book, *My Life Story*,[7] Wölfling said about Rudolf: 'He had magnetism which won him the friendship and loyalty of all people whom he wanted to win over, I would say that Rudolf had a greater hold on people than even Napoleon.' Some of his gestures were original as well as endearing. When his sister Gisela married, Rudolf gave her a box with a hundred sheets of paper in it. On the top of each sheet it said: 'Please will you . . .' and signed 'Granted. Rudolf.' Gisela used about half-a-dozen, and on each she wrote, 'Please will you come to see us? We are waiting for you with love.'

Leopold Wölfling went on: 'Rudolf was mad about women. . . . What can be said in his defence? If what he mistook for love was in reality its loathsome travesty, lust, you will perhaps forgive him for this error when you consider how love in its higher manifestations had been rigorously withheld from him from his earliest years. Never was there a lad with more unnatural parents. . . . Until her death, when too late she was stricken with remorse, his mother, the Empress Elizabeth, had no time for him, while his father, Emperor Francis Joseph, could not tolerate the idea that at his death Rudolf would be Emperor.'[8]

Elizabeth worried a lot about Rudolf—only she seldom did anything about it. Two predictions frightened her. One was that a Rudolf had been the first Habsburg Emperor, another Rudolf would be the last. Even Rudolf half-believed this. The second prophecy was that the year 1886 would bring disaster to the Habsburg dynasty—this originated with a monk of the Middle Ages. And this prophesy was to be fulfilled.

But in his young days, Rudolf enjoyed himself wildly. In his will, drawn up in 1879, he sent 'a last kiss of farewell to all the beautiful women of Vienna, whom I loved so much'.[9] Rudolf liked to mix with the ordinary Viennese; he enjoyed the noise and *brouhaha* of the *cafés chantants*, where the girls jumped on the tables to do some crazy dance; where everyone knew his identity, and where he shouted coarse jokes in as good a Viennese accent as anyone. He did his best to prove to the Viennese that he loved them—and they adored him. For them he could do no wrong, and there was many a woman, high or low born, who would gladly have had an affair with him.

Legend has it that Rudolf was a demon lover—the Rudolf Valentino of his day. But Lónyay,[10] who knew well not only Crown Princess Stephanie, but two of Rudolf's former equerries, and also some of the former Austrian society beauties, who in their old age were willing to talk about the past, reported that 'it was literally painful with what little success Rudolf's greatest efforts were crowned'. He never blamed his poor performance on his weakness and overwrought nerves, but on the lady in question. He was consequently always hoping that the next one would have a better reaction on him and he went on experimenting.[11]

General Wilhelm von Gradl, another former A.D.C. of Rudolf, related to Count Lónyay that Rudolf kept a 'Register of Conquests', with entries in red and black ink. In red ink were entered all the ladies who had been innocent before meeting him; his ministrations to Stephanie; and references to 'a lady of doubtful reputation'—Mizzi Caspar. In the police reports to the Controller of the Imperial Household, Mizzi was also referred to as 'the woman invited by H.I.H.'; or 'the said woman', or 'Miss Mizzi' (only Mizzi spelt her name with a C, the family with a K).

All the women who figured in the 'Register of Conquests' received as a souvenir a silver cigarette box, differing only as to the engraved inscription or emblem; each noting the rank or birth of the recipient. It is extraordinary that in this one field Rudolf kept in line with Spanish Etiquette!

Ladies of princely families equal in rank with the Habsburgs were given a cigarette box bearing an engraved facsimile of Rudolf's signature. Ladies of high nobility but not of equal birth, received a silverbox with the inscription: 'EH. R. GM.'—meaning

Erzherzog Rudolf, General Major, that is Archduke Rudolf, Major-General. Ladies belonging to ancient noble families, but not admissible to Court balls (probably because they had one great-grandmother who was a commoner) even if their families were older than the Habsburgs, were given a box with the inscription 'Rudolf', with an archducal crown; ladies of the lesser ancient nobility a box with only an archducal crown; finally ladies of the lesser aristocracy, or commoners, a box with an archducal coat of arms only.[12] The A.D.C.'s were responsible for no mistake being made in precedence.

Lónyay maintains that women were not of great importance in Rudolf's life; as soon as a woman had been entered in the 'Register' and presented with her silver box, she was forgotten. For Rudolf yearned not for conquests or easy successes, but for loving kindness and understanding. This neither the ladies of the Austrian aristocracy, nor the women of easy virtue of Vienna could provide for him.

And it is because of this that only one woman captured his heart and shared his life (as far as anyone could share it) for nine years. She was a simple girl, born in Graz, Steiermark, on September 9, 1864. She came to Vienna in 1879, her name was Maria Caspar.[13] In view of the role she played in Rudolf's life, it is astonishing how little is known about her. Someone must have brought her to Frau Wolff, the most notorious *madame* of Vienna, who introduced her to the Crown Prince. At first she discussed with Frau Wolff Rudolf's sexual habits but from the moment she had fallen in love with him she became completely devoted and discreet. Princess Louise of the Belgians, Crown Princess Stephanie's sister, in her book, *My Own Affairs*, has written.

'I told him—get married. . . . I have a sister who looks very much like me, marry her! The first time he replied "How could I? I have sweet Mizzi." Mizzi was a pretty lovable girl, the perfect Viennese type, a Parisienne of East Europe, by whom Rudolf had two children.'[14]

The latter is untrue, unless both children died in infancy. Professor Walter Hummelberger, a historian who made a special study of Viennese characters,[15] was helped by Mizzi's step-sister, Frau Anna Krüzner, born Kaspar, who is still alive in Vienna. Mizzi's mother, Frau Anna Kaspar, in her will dated April 14,

1909, left 'all the photographs of my daughter Maria to my step-daughter, Anna Krüzner'; as well as the few letters Mizzi had not destroyed. Professor Hummelberger is the only historian to whom Frau Krüzner has shown Mizzi's photographs and letters.

Mizzi was neither an actress, nor a dancer, nor a model. She was a striking woman, handsome rather than beautiful, with a dusky complexion, and an easy, natural manner. With her Rudolf found a haven of rest and relaxation; and with her he shared his ideas open heartedly. Mizzi had no social ambitions with which others importuned the Crown Prince; she repeated no tittle-tattle, she had no complaints; she never wanted anything except his love—or as much of it he could spare for her. She amused him, soothed him, made him laugh, and fortified him with her love and affection. She was for Rudolf not only a mistress but a mother with whom he could seek refuge when hard-pressed and of heavy heart. Once Mizzi had restored his spirits, for an hour or so he was his old self.

Mizzi only had a rudimentary education;[16] she was gentle and witty in a typically Viennese way—the *süsses Wiener Mädel* par excellence that Rudolf so often praised and so greatly enjoyed. She filled a very special place in Rudolf's life because she realised that a man is most likely to be true to a woman who least pesters him. But probably what captivated him was Mizzi's modesty and understanding devotion. It seems safe to conclude that she was the type of woman Rudolf yearned for—simple, gay, uncomplicated, with whom he could relax and just be like any ordinary man.

Rudolf was most generous to her. Hirsch,[17] his banker friend, lent the money Rudolf thought Mizzi should have. She lived comfortably and unostentatiously at Heumühlgasse 10, later she moved to a house in the Wieden district (one of the smartest and most expensive parts of Vienna) for which she paid 60,000 Gulden.[18] Clearly, a penniless lower-middle class girl could not have spent this kind of money unless she had received it from the Crown Prince—she had no other 'protector'. Maximilian Major Count Orsini und Rosenberg, Rudolf's A.D.C. from 1885 until the end, stated before the Commission of Enquiry that in the last two years of Rudolf's life Mizzi travelled with him everywhere, even to Army manœuvres.

Yet Mizzi never talked about Rudolf, or his generosity to her. The only exception was the day on which she heard of his death, when she broke down in the presence of the police informer, Florian Meissner. But apart from this one emotional outburst, when she was hardly in control of herself, Mizzi never told anyone anything about her private life with Rudolf. She never gave an interview; never wrote her memoirs; never published any one of Rudolf's letters, yet she could have earned a great deal of money with them.

One popular legend can be eliminated: Rudolf did not marry Stephanie on the Emperor's orders, against his own wishes or inclinations. He went to Brussels in quest of a wife, and it is true that Francis Joseph was keen to see him settled. By then Rudolf's wild goings-on had become known to the Hofburg; to put a stop to these and also to make sure of the succession, his parents—principally his father—were anxious to marry him off. They realised how limited the choice was—especially as Francis Joseph insisted on a suitable bride. It is also true that Rudolf was accompanied to Brussels by Mizzi, whom according to Mary Larisch[19] Queen Henriette met by chance in Rudolf's quarters. Unfortunately Stephanie got to hear about it (not from her tactful mother) for Rudolf's enemies among the reactionary Hofburg clique missed no opportunity to cause trouble for him. Stephanie of course was livid—as she says in her memoirs.

Another fact is indisputable: Rudolf, incredible as it may seem in retrospect, fell in love with Stephanie. We know this not only from eye-witnesses in Brussels, but from his own letters to Latour. One of these is reproduced on p. 69; the second, written to King Ludwig of Bavaria on March 13, 1880, read: 'In Stephanie I have found a real angel, a faithful good being who loves me; a very clever, well-educated, cultivated and able companion for this life who will stand by my side well and successfully in all my difficult tasks. I am also convinced that she will soon love her beautiful new country and as a good Austrian and a loyal subject of her Lord and Emperor will become an ornament of my dear fatherland.' Reading this, one would almost believe that Rudolf had been bewitched. The Stephanie who emerges from her own memoirs and from the recollections of people who knew her or worked for her, is so utterly different from the person described by Rudolf that one wonders how he could have misjudged her so completely. On top of all her other shortcomings, Stephanie was a bigoted Roman Catholic, who was bound to disagree with Rudolf's anti-clerical attitude at every point.

As for Stephanie's side of the marriage, she told it in her memoirs very frankly.[20] On March 5, 1880—a Friday—her parents called her in and her father told her: 'The Crown Prince of Austria-Hungary has come here to ask for your hand in marriage. Your mother and I are very much in favour of this marriage. We have chosen you to be the future Empress of Austria and Queen of Hungary. Withdraw now and give us your answer tomorrow.' She rushed to her room and threw herself into the arms of her maid, Toni Schariry, who was her only trusted friend, and then jumped about with joy at the thought of the great position she would hold. Her mother dressed Stephanie and did what she could to improve her red, chapped hands. What Stephanie felt about Rudolf is revealed if we compare her views of him with those of her sister, Louise of the Belgians.

This is how Louise sketched Rudolf's portrait: 'He was more than handsome. He was fascinating. He had a slight figure, but it was well proportioned. Notwithstanding his delicate appearance he possessed a strong constitution. He reminded one of a thoroughbred. He had the shape, the light build and the temper of one. His nervous force equalled his sensitiveness. His pale face reflected his thoughts. His eyes, the iris of which was brown and brilliant, assumed varying shades and changed in shape. A caressing look would change into a glare of hatred, yet in an instant be transformed into a caress again. . . . Like his mother, the Empress Elizabeth, Rudolf had a way of talking that held everybody, and these traits, added to his winning and mysterious personality, charmed all with whom Rudolf came into contact.'[21]

Stephanie in her memoirs described Rudolf in the following terms: 'The Crown Prince could not be called handsome, but I found his appearance by no means displeasing. His small light brown eyes had an intelligent expression, but there was something unfrank and hard about his gaze. He could not bear to be looked directly in the face. About his wide mouth, which was half-hidden by a small moustache, there was a queer expression which was difficult to read.'[22] This is hardly the description of a young woman passionately in love.

After listing her usual complaints, Stephanie went on about Rudolf: 'The Crown Prince had neither taste nor understanding of a kind that would have enabled him, if only for the sake of setting a good example and to prepare me for my future position as mother of the country, to lead the affectionate existence of a young married couple. Speaking generally, it was the fashion at that day to despise the joys of family life; and I know now that I was not the only wife to suffer as the result of these perverted views and habits. The seductions of such a capital as Vienna then was could not fail to extend their lure upon the Crown Prince, who was the centre of general interest and a leader of rank and fashion.'[23]

And yet, Stephanie also complained of Rudolf's jealousy: 'My husband was of an extremely suspicious temperament. When at home, he would not let me out of his sight for a single moment, and I had to remain in his room, even when he was receiving officers or various other persons many of whom were uncongenial to me. He would not allow me to write letters. While I was thus dancing attendance on him, the letters I wrote to my parents were read by him before they were posted. . . . The Crown Prince gave orders that during his absence no one except my ladies-in-waiting be admitted to my presence.'[24]

Stephanie liked to deputise for the Empress—for her position and rank were all-important. She was delighted with the stiff ceremonial of the Spanish Etiquette and resented Rudolf's contacts with intellectuals and ordinary people. Yet according to Szeps, until 1886 Stephanie often sat in the room blue with smoke, while he was talking to Rudolf, or she came in to remind Rudolf that he had to change and keep some appointment. To Szeps Stephanie did not seem unhappy at this time; he had the feeling that the Crown Prince and his wife were leading the satisfied life of a young couple. Rudolf's own warm letters to Stephanie indicate this for instance, the following which is one of a great many which have been preserved. It is dated December 28, 1884, Mürzsteg.

Dearest Angel,

Sincerest thanks for your telegrams. I am so glad to learn that you and the little one are well. Take great care of yourself these days. I am continually thinking about you, and long so much for the afternoon of the 31st.

Sport was very poor today. I brought down only three beasts, although I did not miss any. The cold has let up since yesterday, and it is much warmer today. I think there is going to be a thaw.

The Emperor wants us to give a dinner for Leopold and Uncle Nando.[25] It is to be at half-past five on the 31st. If you like, you can ask Louise and Philip. A very good menu please: soup, oysters, *langouste*, etc. As wine, the new white sparkling burgundy; but if that has not yet arrived, then ordinary burgundy. Besides, whatever happens you must have claret, sherry, champagne, cognac, and Turkish coffee. The Emperor is not coming, so we shall be only six, even if Philip and Louise come. Tell Buk that when I arrive I want a hot bath, and that the barber must be on hand. I shall wear my military uniform.

I hope you have not forgotten to send condolences to the Mopey family.

Let Spindler[26] know that I should like to find C. E. Franzos' books, which I ordered, awaiting me on my table.

With warmest love to you and the little one.

Your own
Coco.

A second is that written from Kremzier and dated August 24, 1883.

Dearest Angel!

At last I can write to you; since leaving you I was in an uninterrupted rush, and had not one moment free time. From Laxenburg I drove directly to my chancellery; then into the Burg where I met Weilen. At 11 o'clock we left from the North Station. Here we arrived in rain and cold; our reception by the people was wonderful; from the station to the castle the mounted contingents (*Banderien*) of the Hannaken[27] in their remarkable costumes were very interesting. After dinner there was a torchlight procession and a very nice illumination. The castle is magnificent; colossally big and well suited for furniture —which is however in very bad taste. In the evening I had a chance to have a good look at my accommodation; I am staying with Uncle Charles (Archduke Charles) in a newly built therefore damp house hitherto uninhabited. It is very cold and uncosy, and we are afraid of catching cold.

I got home a few minutes ago—at last—it is 11 o'clock and I am now going to bed with Lord. Tomorrow there is a shoot, then lunch in the forest; in the evening dinner; at 11 the Russians are leaving; immediately afterwards our Emperor goes to Bohemia; Uncle Charles and myself to Vienna.

Be careful about everything you do, I worry about you. I long terribly for you and I count the days while we are still parted.

Embracing you with all my heart,

I am your faithful

Coco.

Most of Rudolf's letters to his wife were signed Coco, a nickname Stephanie must have given him. In her memoirs she said that he wrote her such lovely letters to keep her quiet while he was going out with other women.

Stephanie herself was furiously jealous. One evening she drove in a Court equipage to the 'house' where Rudolf was spending his time. She changed into his un-numbered *flakker*, driven by Josef Bratfisch, the coachman whose whistling and singing were well-known, and had herself driven home. When Rudolf came out in the early morning hours, he had to return to the Hofburg in a style he certainly did not want on that occasion. Of course there was a scene. And there was an even more bitter one when Stephanie induced a Jesuit, Father Berthold[28] to talk to Rudolf and tell him that if he did not live with her more frequently, she could not become pregnant, and would never produce the much-wanted heir. In view of Rudolf's anti-clerical and anti-Jesuit prejudices, a Jesuit father was the last person to intervene in such a delicate matter. Had Stephanie had any diplomatic sense, she would have chosen someone like Hans Wilczek or Count Samuel Teleki, close friends of Rudolf, who cared for him and for the dynasty—and would have known how to talk to him to make an impression without giving offence.

Stephanie admitted Rudolf's intellectual talents. In her memoirs she said, 'His original and shrewd contributions to the newspapers, and the huge work *Die Österreichisch-Ungarischa Monarchie in Wort und Bild*, which he had inspired, and of which he was the editor-in-chief, brought him into contact with distinguished and worthy authors and pressmen, but unfortunately likewise with so-called "friends" whom he picked up here and there—the sort of people who would never be received at Court! I already had an intuitive fear of these people, although in my seclusion I was not able to judge their quality or their merit.'

No woman could have been further removed from Rudolf's aims and ideals. One final quotation from Stephanie's memoirs shows her attitude. 'Myself—young, good-looking, and greatly admired—I wondered whether this world which was so attractive to the Crown Prince might not offer me similar charms. Probably it was nothing more than curiosity or jealousy which led me, on one occasion, to kick over the traces. The fancy seized me to dress up as a smart middle-class girl, in order to accompany him on one of his outings. The idea was piquante. But, surprised as I was to note how little the Crown Prince troubled to preserve his incognito, I was yet more disillusioned when we visited various *cafés chantants*, and other places of dubious reputation in and outside the city [Vienna]. The air everywhere was stifling. There was a stench of garlic, burned fat, wine and tobacco, which I found nauseating. We sat until dawn at dirty tables, with no tablecloths on them, playing with greasy cards, whistling and singing. People danced; girls jumped upon the tables and benches, singing again and again the same commonplace sentimental ditties, to the accompaniment of an atrocious orchestra. I would have amused myself had it been possible, but I was bored to death and repelled by my experience in the smoke-laden bars. I simply could not understand what pleasure the Crown Prince could take in them.'[29]

For his part Rudolf understood Stephanie all too well. When he first saw through her is difficult to tell; it may have been in July, 1880, when he went to Brussels for the 50th anniversary celebrations of Belgian Independence. Marie Festetich and others observed that during the period of the two postponements of the wedding he became more and more depressed; he lost his gaiety and sense of fun. When he spoke, his remarks were biting or cynical. Marie Festetics suspected that he did not know how to extricate himself from his situation, and went through with a marriage he knew could not lead to a happy life.

For once Marie Festetics was wrong. For the first four years Rudolf was surprisingly happy with Stephanie, and this state of affairs might have continued had she not nagged and pushed him, always wanting worldly goods or social distinctions for which he cared very little. In other words, had Stephanie had any understanding of the real Rudolf, had she genuinely loved him, he would have reciprocated her feelings with all his heart.

Lónyay described her as: 'a bully, a bore, a nagger and a fool, who asked nonsensical questions when Rudolf's nerves were most frayed; if Rudolf had a headache [he suffered from migraine] Stephanie would continue with her singing lessons and her voice was usually compared to a foghorn. Her tactless remarks were the jokes of all European Courts.[30]

Rudolf certainly sought and found consolation with many women. Princess Stephanie told her friends that he had at least thirty illegitimate children. That he had ruined her health—her life—that he had plotted against his father—and so on. Rudolf had a few illegitimate children; with his delicate nerves and weak character, the life he led was bound to undermine his health. Often up all night, he none the less was always at his military office on time. He never neglected his military duties, and carried out political tasks entrusted to him very conscientiously. But due to fatigue, he began to drink a good deal, and woke up after a few hours' sleep more tired than when he had turned in.

The girl he had thought would stand by his side 'well and successfully in all my difficult tasks' had proved not only useless, but a burden to him. Leopold Wölfling described Stephanie as 'a volcano covered with snow', her character did not suit Rudolf; he would have been much happier with a neutral woman 'not one driven by endless ambition—always dissatisfied, both sexually and socially'. There were many all too anxious to console Rudolf. But that is not what he wanted; strange to say Rudolf wanted a home, with an understanding wife, the partner he had sought since his childhood, and who had always eluded him. He found peace with Mizzi Caspar, but for a few fleeting hours only. And then another catastrophe befell him which ruined his life.

13

First Signs of Decline

During 1885 Rudolf kept a diary.[1] The personality that emerges from its entries is suffering from nervous strain, and poor health. Rudolf had probably been infected with gonorrheoa in 1876; from his 1885 record it appears that instead of having shaken it off, as his father had done, he repeatedly re-infected himself, and began to suffer from its unpleasant side-effects.

From Rudolf's diary we learn of the various stages of his second Balkan journey, and of his visit with Stephanie to Brussels, to participate in the celebrations in honour of Leopold's 50th birthday. On April 15 they drove to a military parade in the carriage with the Queen of the Belgians and the Count of Flanders, heir to the Belgian throne. Suddenly a young man threw himself on their carriage and with his bare fists smashed one of its windows. His name was Omer Cude, he was twenty-five years old, an architect employed by the Ministry of Public Works. He readily confessed to his crime because he believed that the Queen had intrigued with God to have him sent to hell. The medical authorities declared Omer Cude 'irresponsible—incapable of judgement'. Unfortunately Rudolf does not say what became of him—presumably he lived out his days in a criminal lunatic asylum. At the time the incident was hushed up.

Rudolf had a lot to say about the Hungarian exhibition in Budapest which had been expected to be a failure, but which turned out to be quite successful. For two days he had to look after his unloved Prussian cousin, Prince William, who had come to Budapest specially to see it, and borrowed 3,000 Gulden from Rudolf to be repaid at an indefinite date in the future. Francis Joseph was much amused by this episode.

Rudolf described one of his days—May 31, 1885—as follows: '6 a.m. arrive in Budapest. I drive to the Castle, then to the

Exhibition; from there to the meeting of the Academy of Sciences; then back to the Exhibition. Lunch at the Hungarian National Club.[2] Departure at 2 o'clock; Vienna 6.30; Laxenburg 7.30.' During his visits to the Budapest Exhibition, the names of his friends, Pista Károlyi and Samuel Teleki, occur several times.

Rudolf also gave a graphic description of the fire in Laxenburg, when—according to Stephanie's memoirs—he helped the fire brigade with great courage and saved the lives of several people. This was on June 9, and it took quite a while to put the Castle into good order again.

On August 4 Rudolf wrote to his friend, Szeps, that Francis Joseph and Czar Alexander III were to meet at the end of August. 'No one will come from Germany.[3] There is a great fear that there might be attempts on the lives of the Russians, that is why the whole thing must be kept a secret. While the Monarchs will embrace each other, the Russians are sending masses of rifles and ammunition to Serbia, and even to Bosnia, to prepare a rising. We can see how useful the policy of our statesmen at the Ballhausplatz is. I am sending you an article which you might publish at the time of the meeting.'

This article,[4] is revealing of Rudolf's understanding of the political situation, and also of the fact that in matters requiring judgement, he could be rash and unsound. Had Francis Joseph allowed him to participate in any capacity in the policy making of the Monarchy, and had Rudolf worked with some of the excellent officials of the Ballhausplatz, he would have known better. He correctly spelt out the political factors of the situation, but in a manner suited to a confidential intelligence report, not a newspaper article at a time of delicate negotiations. No wonder Szeps refused to print it and tartly wrote to the Crown Prince: 'Not on account of a single sentence, but on account of every sentence, would this article be suppressed; it was therefore impossible to make it acceptable by curtailment or any other means.[5]

Rudolf's lack of judgement made him oblivious of the fact that his sarcastic comments would have greatly upset the Emperor, who was trying to establish a *modus vivendi* with the young Czar. Francis Joesph still felt remorse over having let down Czar Nicholas I (who had rescued him in 1849 from the Hungarian insurgents) during the Crimean war; also he wanted at all costs to avoid an armed conflict with the Russians which at this time Rudolf regarded as inevitable.

On August 21, 1885, Rudolf celebrated his 27th birthday. He saw the future in very dark colours. and was deeply concerned over the fate of the Monarchy. Then came the Kremzier meeting. Alexander III, who after the murder of his father had become extremely suspicious, had at last decided to return the visit Francis Joseph had paid him two years earlier at Skiernevice. The Emperor welcomed the suggested meeting on condition that the Germans would be included. After a lot of correspondence and diplomatic negotiation, Alexander accepted the Germans and Francis Joseph was determined to make his stay as agreeable as possible.

On August 24 Rudolf wrote to Stephanie from Kremzier:

Dearest Angel,

At last I can write to you and tell you that this morning there was a parade, the troops looked very fit. Then I drove with Papa to Hullein to meet the Russians. At twelve we arrived with them here; the Russian Emperor has grown very fat: Grand Duke Wladimir and his wife as well as the Czarina look old and worn by life. The suites and staff are terrible; with their new uniforms they again look completely Asiatic. At the time of the late Emperor the Russians were at least elegant, and some gentlemen of the entourage looked distinguished. Now they all seem a dreadfully common lot. Tomorrow there is a shoot, then lunch in the forest; in the evening dinner; at 11 the Russians are leaving; immediately afterwards our Emperor goes to Bohemia; Uncle Charles and myself to Vienna.

Embracing you with all my heart, I am your faithful

Coco.

In his letter, Rudolf did not mention the tremendous security precautions taken to please the Czar. Every window along the road he drove from Hullein to the Palace of the Archbishop of Olmütz, where the Monarchs were staying at Kremzier, was tightly closed and not a soul was to be seen in the streets. The Czar was very frugal, his entourage consisted of only forty eight persons.

The first meeting took place after breakfast on August 25.

Bismarck, who represented the aged German Emperor, opened the proceedings by suggesting an alliance between the three emperors. The Czar got extremely cross and agitated, and flatly refused to have anything to do with this idea. 'We want war with no one, but we are being constantly threatened,' he shouted. 'We will act according to circumstances.' Alexander accused Austria of wanting to create a second Slav Empire; Germany of wanting to occupy the Black Sea and drive Russia from its shores. At last the Czar calmed down, but the Kremzier meeting ended without any palpable result from a political point of view.

However, one odd incident occurred, which had unexpected and lasting consequences. As already stated, Francis Joseph had done everything he could to please Alexander, he had even invited the Burg Theatre company to come to Kremzier from Vienna and to stage a gala performance for the Czar. To quote Rudolf's letter to Stephanie once more: 'At six there was a big dinner, at eight a theatrical performance, then supper with Charlotte Wolter, Kati Schratt and Paula Wessely in the same room with their Majesties. After supper there was a reception, from which suddenly the Czar disappeared. The consternation—mounting to panic—of his entourage was extreme, and the Austrian security police were also alarmed. But then word went round that Alexander was safe—and with a knowing smile it was added, "It is only a small matter of *Galanterie*." '

The Lord of all the Russians, the firm believer in his autocratic powers, had lost his heart, temporarily, to one of the pretty actresses of the Burg Theatre, by name Katherina Schratt, and set out with an enormous bouquet and a sizeable emerald brooch to woo the lady, not doubting for one moment that he would spend the night with her. But it did not work out that way. Kati Schratt was a spirited and determined *Wienerin*, who had no intention of going to bed with the Czar. She entertained him, she made him laugh, she accepted his flowers—and his emerald—but he had to go back to his magnificent quarters in the Archbishop's Palace without as much as a proper kiss.

When the incident was reported to Francis Joseph, he laughed with delight and decided to have a good look at the virtuous and clever Austrian girl who had handled his tempestuous guest with such diplomatic skill. The Empress had seen Kati Schratt on the stage several times. Now she took one of those imaginative decisions which endeared her so much to those close to her.

Back in Vienna, she went to visit the fashionable painter, Heinrich von Angeli, and persuaded him to paint Kati Schratt. At the second sitting, Elizabeth walked into the studio and had a friendly chat with the young actress. In her diary, after the record of her weight (which was invariably her first entry), she wrote: 'Today I got to know Frau Kiss, Katherina Schratt, I am so pleased to have met her. There are few such natural and uncomplicated human beings in the world as she is.'

Then Elizabeth invited Kati Schratt to tea, and after a pleasant conversation she confided 'I want to travel again, but before I leave Vienna I hope we will get to know each other—in fact that we will become friends.' Suddenly she added: 'Could you trust me—trust me fully? You will never regret it if you will trust me. I can assure you of my gratitude. . . . Before I go off to distant parts, I have to settle something very important in which you can help me . . .'[6]

Then Elizabeth invited Kati Schratt to her castle in Lainz, and asked her to read Heine's poems to her.[7] 'I love the aching and disillusioned tone which emanates from his works. I have had a similar experience to his, that is why I understand him so well . . .'

And looking Kati straight in the eyes, Elizabeth said, 'You are my exact opposite. Therefore you may succeed in what I failed to achieve. It is my firm conviction that you will have a very good influence on the Emperor. You will be able to draw him away from the eternal reading of official papers, and to free him from the rigidity of his surroundings. The Emperor needs light—bright light—so that he should be able to breathe in the Spanish semi-darkness of the Hofburg. I have tried with all my might to change this situation, but I could achieve nothing.'

Later in the conversation, Elizabeth told the amazed Kati Schratt: 'Do you realise what my sincerity with people has achieved? The Viennese police are watching me! There is a gentleman in the *Evidenzbureau*, a certain Dr Zeicher, also a Herr Erz and a Herr Huber, who have chosen as their profession to control my mail and anything with which I am connected. Charming occupation,' Elizabeth said bitterly, 'to be a police informer. You have no idea what humiliations I have to endure—

this is one reason which prompts me to leave Vienna as soon as possible.[8]

'I am counting on you, dear Fräulein Schratt. I have got to like you and I seek your friendship. Give me your hand that you will not let me down—whatever will happen . . . I fear very much that which will follow . . .'

A year later, from Ischl, the Empress with the Emperor drove to Castle Frauenstein, where Kati Schratt was staying with friends. That was the occasion when the fifty-eight-year-old Emperor and the thirty-three-year-old actress first stood face to face. And at the tea party on Kati's balcony she did exactly what Elizabeth had hoped she would do—she enchanted Francis Joseph. In spite of his worries over the Bulgarian situation—it was the year 1885—he not only participated in the conversation, but actually laughed twice.

Many similar parties *à trois* took place—Elizabeth worked at it hard until the Emperor got to like the young woman sufficiently to promise to see her also in Elizabeth's absence.

As can be imagined, the 'Camarilla' was indignant and furious. Especially Alfred Prince Montenuovo, the *Oberhofmarschall*, who disliked Schratt intensely—but no one dared to be impertinent or nasty to her in public. However gossip about her was disgraceful. In secret they now referred to the Emperor as 'Herr Schratt'. Only one person defended Kati Schratt publicly as well as in private: the Crown Prince. He approved wholeheartedly of his father's new friend, and through his mother sent her warm messages.

As far as Rudolf was concerned, various incidents took place in 1885, indicating his declining health.

On September 5, while driving from Penzing to Laxenburg, his horses shied, got completely out of hand and the carriage overturned. Rudolf was unconscious for a while, he had hurt his right hand badly, there was a gaping wound in it, which had to be dressed, but the accident itself was hushed up. Furthermore, against doctor's orders, next day he went out stalking although he could not shoot. He simply could not keep quiet in his rooms.

What strongly emerges from the 1885 diaries is Rudolf's restlessness. His days were either overfull with appointments, interviews, and military work from 9 a.m. to 6 p.m. without a break; or he went shooting, walking miles, or stalking for miles, sometimes two and three days in succession. Rudolf, who in his young days only wanted to observe game, by 1885 had become a passionate, not to say a fanatical, shot, who spent 200 of the year's 365 days either shooting or stalking. Even reading his laconic engagements diary, one has the impression that he could barely wait to get into the forest and collect as large a bag as possible.

But what is not been hinted at in the diary is Rudolf's experience at a bear hunt in Transylvania. Sitting on a mountain-side, he sighted a bear approaching and stood up to take aim. The bear also saw him; Rudolf let off four shots from two guns and the bear collapsed-only to get up almost immediately. Instead of promptly re-loading, Rudolf fumbled for cartridges while the bear, snarling with rage, rushed towards him. Rudolf was shaking with nerves. His devoted imperial note-bearer, Rudolf Püchel, fortunately stood behind him. Püchel threw himself between Rudolf and the bear, stuck the muzzle of his gun into the animal's mouth which closed on it: simultaneously he fired and the bear collapsed backwards. Rudolf was saved from almost certain death. After a few moments, having collected himself, he came up to Püchel, grasped his hand and said warmly: 'That was a bad half-minute.'

Clearly in the autumn of 1885 Rudolf's nerves were already in a worse condition than was generally realised; perhaps even more indicative, his reactions had slowed down.

Another shooting episode of 1885 also throws light on Rudolf's deteriorating condition. On February 3 he wrote in his diary: 'I went with the artist Pausinger over to Lobau. We admired the magnificent view and saw several eagles and some very fine stags. I got a great 18-pointer illicitly; the temptation was too great for me to let him go.' For a keen and experienced sportsman, as the Crown Prince certainly was, wantonly to shoot a stag during the closed season, indicates that he was no longer bound by ingrained discipline.[9]

Also in September 1885 Rudolf had to go to Germany to attend the Prussian manœuvres. With his intense dislike of Prince William, this was a real penance, although the efficiency of the Prussian armed forces impressed him. In view of Rudolf's ambitions in the Balkans, and the Czar's efforts to stir up trouble in Serbia, Bosnia, Herzegovina, Montenegro—thus crossing Rudolf's plan for Austria's cultural mission—the Crown Prince was certain that Austro-Russian relations would inevitably come to a show down, hence the Monarchy had to rely on the much-disliked German ally. The only pleasant aspect of the visit were his conversations with Crown Prince Frederick and Crown Princess Frederick (Princess Royal) who sympathised with Rudolf, and were themselves very unhappy about the politics and the behaviour of their son, Prince William.

A happy interlude in an otherwise unhappy year was the mission on which Francis Joseph sent Stephanie: she was to counteract the irredenta in Trieste. She went to Miramar via Trieste, ostensibly 'because bathing is good for her health'. At first she was greeted by shouts, 'Abbasso Austria!' She paid endless visits to institutions; she made real efforts to talk to the population. She bought flowers and fish in the open market; she even put out to sea with the fishermen. Gradually the mood changed; towards the end of her stay, crowds gathered round her, gave her flowers and cheered her: *Stephania benedetta, Stephania carissima* . . . When she returned to Vienna on October 5, 1885, to her amazement and joy the Emperor and Rudolf were waiting for her on the platform and both complimented her on her success. This is almost the only occasion when these three personalties spent an evening in relaxed, friendly conversation.

This was memorable for one more reason: Stephanie noticed with concern the changes in Rudolf's appearance. His eyes were inflamed, he looked drawn and aged; he was extremely nervous; chain-smoked and drank a good deal. His restlessness was only too evident, and Stephanie's feelings that there was some trouble with his health, were well-founded. Although forbidden to set foot in his former bachelor quarters she knew—as pretty well every Viennese knew—what a dissolute life he led. This time her feelings were not just jealousy, she was profoundly perturbed, for she sensed that Rudolf was ill, though she had no idea what kind of illness was affiicting him.

It was also in 1885 that Rudolf's great friend, Szeps, had to serve one month's imprisonment for having libelled Georg Ritter von Schönerer, the anti-Semitic leader of the German nationalists, the *Deutsch Nationale Partei* was its official name, whose main aim was that the Austrian Monarchy should disappear and Austria be incorporated into the German Reich. Of course Rudolf hated von Schönerer, and so did Szeps. But Szeps also had enemies within Government circles, and with the support of the reactionary Prime Minister, Taaffe, they managed to get the *Neues Wiener Tagblatt* banned from street circulation, which meant that it was only obtainable in bookshops. This was a great financial blow for Szeps. There were questions in Parliament by members of the United Left, and also demonstrations at the Vienna City Council, and the ban was eventually lifted.

Then Szeps got involved in a newspaper controversy with the reprehensible Schönerer, who sued him for libel; a Viennese jury found Szeps guilty and a severe penalty was inflicted. Through imperial intervention the punishment was mitigated to one month's light imprisonment. What Szeps' imprisonment was like is described by his daughter Bertha in her diary on October 25, 1885: 'This is the first time I have written anything since Father went to prison. Of course, it is very sad for us to be parted from him, but really his imprisonment, instead of being a triumph for Schönerer, is a triumph for Father. Every day visitors crowd to see him. Flowers, fruit and gifts are sent to him, and even private letters reach him unopened. In fact, he is hardly guarded, or put under any surveillance at all. . . . It was even possible to get a letter from the Crown Prince slipped to him.'[10]

This is what Rudolf wrote to his friend: 'Many thanks for your interesting letter. I am extremely sorry to hear that you are behind bars. For in spite of all the special favours that you receive, and in spite of all the philosophical consolation of the "welcome peacefulness" of your surroundings, the confinement is an unpleasant thing—for it has been forced upon you and not chosen by your own free will. My feelings are roused against all compulsion, and I really cannot understand how you can take things so calmly.

'Our times and manner are becoming savage, there is no doubt about it, and Austria has gone a long way back since we began our parliamentary life. There will soon be sticks and revolvers (in Parliament). And worst of all, the reactionaries, not excluding those in the highest circles, are exploiting it by saying that people who are not even house-trained want to rule, and that they should themselves be properly brought up before they try to improve the country. That's what they say about the Right and the Left parties, and they thoroughly enjoy the spectacle of Parliamentarianism making itself ridiculous.' Then Rudolf wrote about his concern over the German alliance, about the trouble in Spain which would become 'a second European Republic'. And finally about the desire of Bismarck to start another war because the Germans 'need new glory. Isn't that—except for a few nuances —the same attitude that actuated Napoleon III? . . . As far as diplomacy is concerned the time of complete success is at an end. Things have happened that were against Bismarck's will and because of them the magic of his Almightiness has disappeared . . .'[11]

Morally his imprisonment had done Szeps no harm, but just because of this, his enemies were all the more determined to ruin him. Through a clever manœuvre they brought down the value of the shares of his own publishing firm, and he was forced to give up the editorship of the great daily. Rudolf stepped in and provided Szeps with the means of founding his own paper, the *Wiener Tagblatt* which first appeared in October, 1887. Thanks to Rudolf Szeps overcame great difficulties, but to the end of his life he regretted the loss of his beloved *Neues Wiener Tagblatt*.[12]

But as far as Schönerer was concerned, Szeps had the last laugh, if laugh is the right expression. In 1888 the *Wiener Tagblatt* published a premature report of the death of the German Emperor, William I. Schönerer, with some of his followers, entered its offices and assaulted members of its staff. For this and for publicly toasting Kaiser William I as 'our glorious Emperor', he was deprived of his parliamentary mandate, sentenced to six months imprisonment and Francis Joseph took away his patent of nobility. 'Francis Joseph was especially wounded by Schönerer's having voted against the Army estimates on the ground that world power position was a luxury a rotten edifice like Austria could not afford.'[13]

The last significant event of 1885 was the publication of the first instalment of Rudolf's impressive work, *The Austro-Hungarian Monarchy In Word and Picture*. The Crown Prince may have got the idea for his work from W. H. Rihel, who between 1859 and 1867 wrote a similar opus on *Bavaria*. He also discussed it with Archduke Johann Salvator, who can be regarded as the spiritual godfather of Rudolf's enterprise. But without Rudolf's youthful enthusiasm and determination, the obstacles put in the way of his work could not have been overcome. The Minister of Finance, Julius Ritter von Dunajevski,[14] agreed only on June 30, 1884, that the Court and State Printing Works, which fell within the competence of his ministry, should print it. He added the mean rider that, as the work was bound to be a financial failure, expenses should be kept to a minimum. Rudolf was convinced that Dunajevski wanted to drive him into the arms of a private publisher, and would not give in. But Rudolf had also to struggle against other mainly political obstacles. He had to resign himself to change his original plan to deal with each nationality in turn and separately, to bring out his thesis that the Monarchy must try to work along with all the national groups. By the legal position and the official status of Austria-Hungary, he was forced to formulate his book in two parts, and this form of presentation greatly reduced the effectiveness of the Liberal political message which Rudolf was trying to convey. On top of this he had to put up with innumerable chicaneries thought up by Taaffe.

The Press also caused him a lot of annoyance. While the liberal *Neues Wiener Tagblatt* greeted his enterprise enthusiastically in an editorial called 'Let Us Get To Know Ourselves', the feudalist *Das Vaterland* met it with deafening silence, and the conservative *Narodny Listy* warned its readers against subscribing to it; the German Nationalists were also critical; as for the Southern Slavs, they were furious that the book was based on the Dualism of 1867, which they so strongly resented.

It was a triumph for Rudolf that not only had he written the very able introduction to the work as a whole, but also the chapter on *The Agricultural Position Of Vienna* (*Die Landwirtschaftliche Lage Wien*), the geographical descriptions in the chapter on Lower Austria, the introduction to the sections on Natural Sciences and on Hungary.

Although Rudolf could not be called a lover of the arts—once he had let slip the phrase: 'Why spend money on State Museums?' —yet he collected notable artists to illustrate *The Austro-Hungarian Monarchy In Word And Picture*. He was a patron of Franz von

Pausinger, who contributed literally hundreds of sketches to Rudolf's writings on wild life and the chase, and whose pictures still adorn the former imperial residences.[15]

For once Rudolf was vigorously backed by his father; Francis Joseph was genuinely pleased to receive the first volume of *The Austro-Hungarian Monarchy In the Word And Picture* on December 1, 1885. At last father and son seemed to have come near to each other. Unfortunately Francis Joseph noticed none of the symptoms of deterioration in Rudolf's health to which Stephanie had drawn his attention, and he ignored her warnings.

14

The Crown Prince's Illness

The year 1886 began in the traditional way—the Crown Prince and the Crown Princess received New Year congratulations on behalf of the Emperor. This and what followed are known from an unimpeachable source: the diary kept by Rudolf's A.D.C. It has been preserved in the *Haus, Hof und Staatsarchiv*, and is a chronicle of restless activity.

On January 2nd and 3rd Rudolf arrived at his office at Divisional Headquarters at 9.45 a.m.; on January 4th he visited a school at Neuberg, and returned only next evening at 9.45; on January 6th he was at his military office at the usual time; on January 7th he went out to shoot, leaving the Hofburg at 4 a.m., and had dinner with Bombelles; on January 8th he arrived punctually at his military office; on the following day there was a large dinner for military notabilities; on the 10th a Habsburg family dinner; on the 11th, 12th, 13th and 14th large dinners, judging by the poor handwriting of the A.D.C., probably for members of the aristocracy. January 15th: Rudolf went shooting; on the 16th he was at his office; in the evening at the military dinner in his honour; on the 17th Rudolf went shooting, but returned for a family dinner; on the 18th he started shooting early in the morning, then dinner with 28 officers; on the 19th a shoot with the Emperor, dinner in Vienna at 6p.m.; onthe 20th a shoot, then dinner at the Military Club; 21st—shoot—dinner; 22nd and 23rd—office in the morning—shoot later in the day; 26th—Rudolf went to mass with the Emperor; then together they received a long list of aristocrats; on the 27th, 28th 29th and 30th of January he was at his military office at the usual time; there were two Court Balls, and on the 30th he attended the exhibition of Hans Canon, known as the Austrian Rubens. On February 1st, 2nd, 3rd and 4th Rudolf went to his military office in the morning, on the

2nd he also visited Latour, on the 3rd he attended a Ball at Court and on the 4th some military ceremonies.

On February 5th Rudolf stayed at home; the A.D.C. did not record any reason; February 6th and 7th ditto. On February 8th there was an official announcement that the Crown Prince had been ordered to rest until February 17th; there was no entry by the A.D.C. until March 4th except one line: 'The Crown Prince is ill.'

At last it was officially stated that Rudolf had been suffering from peritonitis and inflammation of the bladder. The prescription book of the Vienna Court Pharmacy records that Rudolf was treated with 0·5 g. *Natrium Salucylicum*, and 'diuretic tea'. He also received suppositories with 0·003 g. morphia in coconut butter. On February 16th he was prescribed *Copaiva Balsam* in capsules; on February 28th *Zincum Salfuricum* 1·0 Aq. dest. 300·0. On March 3 he was put on a milk diet; throughout he received copious doses of morphia as 'pain killer'. Rudolf was also treated with *Zinc Sulphate* irrigations. In the 1880's these were standard therapy for gonorrhea.

On March 5th Rudolf and Stephanie departed from the *Südbahn* (the Southern Railway Station) for Pola; Bombelles and Silva Taruca, Dr Franz von Auchenthaler and twelve domestics travelled with them. On March 6th they arrived in Pola, where Admiral Maximilian Freiherr von Pitner had organised a reception in their honour, but they could not have attended it, for the A.D.C. records: 'Immediate departure by S.S. *Greif* (the imperial yacht). There is a strong *Bora*' (the hot, enervating wind of the Adriatic). On March 7th: 'The *Bora* continues.' March 8th: 'We cross the Calamota Canal. We arrive at 4 p.m. at Gravosa, the port of Lacroma. We go to the Monastery of St Giacomo and settle in.' March 9th: 'The luggage, etc., brought up to the Monastery.' March 10th: 'Less *Bora*. The Crown Prince in bed.'

In her memoirs Stephanie had this to say: '1886 had hardly begun when Rudolf was taken ill—he could not attend the marriage of the Archduke Charles Steven to Archduchess Maria Teresa, or participate in the customary festivities of the winter season, where I had to represent the Empress at the Emperor's side.'[1]

It was officially announced that Rudolf went to Lacroma, the island opposite Ragusa (now Dubrovnik) on medical advice to recuperate from his illness. So fascinating was the beauty of Lacroma that in 1859 the Archduke Maximilian bought the island and transformed its ancient abbey, which was founded by Richard Coeur de Lion, into a residence. After Maximilian's execution in Mexico the island became the property of a health officer who wanted to turn it into a resort. But Rudolf was equally smitten with Lacroma and he took it over.

Stephanie in her memoirs wrote:[2] 'I likewise was so enthusiastic about Lacroma that I published a book on it, finely illustrated, which appeared in Vienna in the year 1894, and was subsequently translated into French.' And she went on, 'We had hardly reached Lacroma when I, too, fell ill. For weeks I was in bed suffering intolerable pain. The doctors who were summoned from Vienna and Trieste announced that the trouble was peritonitis. By order of the Emperor this was kept secret. I received the best care and attention. My sister Louise hastened to my bedside. She and my attendants did everything to promote my recovery.'[3]

The A.D.C. reports that Prince and Princess Philip of Coburg—Stephanie's sister and her husband—arrived on March 25th, that is thirteen days after Rudolf's and Stephanie's arrival, and her being taken ill. Stephanie does not mention that she was up when Professor Egyd Valponer, an eminent Belgian gynaeocologist, arrived with them from Brussels, and ordered her back to bed. According to the A.D.C., the professor 'informed Dr Max Braun of her condition'. Dr—later Professor—Braun was specially called in from Bavaria.[4]

On January 29, 1968, Julia von Stockhausen wrote to Dr Fritz Judtmann: 'One afternoon very soon after our arrival in Oroszvár,[5] the Princess told my husband and me that Rudolf had infected her! If I recall correctly, she was torn between a desire to tell the truth (in which, no doubt, certain motives played a part) and a reluctance to make these matters public.'

On October 10, 1976, Julia von Stockhausen[6] wrote to me: 'My husband had the difficult task of preparing the memoirs for publication, to be precise, to make a properly written book out of the available material and notes. . . . Rudolf's illness? very probably gonorrhoea. I remember clearly how she talked to us about it. She was not clear about the difference in these illnesses. . . .

After a lot of backwards and forwards, changes, my husband completed the editing. . . . The princess certainly had no moral courage. She wanted to tell the truth, talked to us, put at our disposal letters and other material dictated to my husband, and when the book had been published and the Austrian aristocracy reacted with indignation, she lost courage. She had not only read, but signed each corrected page after having studied it, yet she now blamed us!'

Princess Stephanie told many of her friends that Rudolf had infected her, and that it was his fault that her Fallopian tubes had been destroyed and she could have no more children. All people she chose to befriend were given a tearful account of this terrible wrong Rudolf had inflicted on her.[7]

It was no surprise to the Viennese in particular that Rudolf had caught venereal disease; with his dissipated life, Austrian doctors actually expected this to happen. To quote the remarkably well-informed, anonymous article in the *Berliner Börzen Courier*[7] of February 24, 1889: 'His blood, his inclination, his too great mental efforts, and to a lesser degree too many fleeting acquaintances with women made it inevitable—it was merely a question "when?" '[8] He then added, 'Rudolf suffered great pains in his joints; he used morphia in increasing quantities without the knowledge of his doctors.'

According to accepted opinion, gonorrhoea is 'the preventer of life', while syphilis is 'the destroyer of life'. The mortality rate from gonorrhoea is negligible, but indirect effects by its not infrequent sterilization of both sexes, particularly women, are incalculable. The incubation period of gonorrhoea is usually three to five, but occasionally two to ten days. The signs, symptoms and outcome in male and female differ.

With men the first symptoms are burning on urination and purulent urethral discharge that may be severe or so mild as to go unnoticed. In the absence of treatment, the infection usually expands deeper to involve the posterior part of the urethra, the neck of the bladder and complications are abscess of the prostate or seminal vescicles and inflammation of the spermatic cord and epidydimis (which lies next to the testicles in the scrotal sac).

Complications of the disease are extremely painful; pain alone would have kept Rudolf in bed for a whole month in Vienna, and for eight days in Lacroma. It is not known if he got up willingly, or whether Archduke Ludvig Victor, who came uninvited and whom Rudolf did not like, had challenged him.

For Stephanie the realisation of her illness was an appalling shock. Elizabeth, although she had adored Francis Joseph, fell out of love with him because of the gonorrhoea he had passed on to her, but she never mentioned it to anyone. Fortunately she overcame it. Stephanie was not so lucky, and paid the full consequences. To quote Ambrose King[9]; 'Many women recover spontaneously from gonorrhoeal infections that extend no farther than the cervix. In many, however, there is extension through the uterus to involve the Fallopian tubes and ovaries. Fever usually accompanies these extensions to the pelvic organs, and lower abdominal pain is a prominent symptom. Pelvic abscess or peritonitis may result.' This is obviously what happened to Stephanie. Furthermore, Dr R. D. Catterall[10] says that in seventy per cent of women gonorrhoea does not produce any symptoms at all for weeks or months, and that a high proportion of women can be carriers of the bacteria and not know that they are infected.

From 1884 onwards Rudolf's eyes were constantly in a state of inflammation; he had severe pains in his joints; he suffered from headaches which became worse whenever he had a minor accident such as a fall from his horse. He looked much aged; he was not in control of himself—screamed at people, even cursed them, only to apologise afterwards; in February 1886 he felt so ill that he took to his bed, and stayed there for practically four and a half weeks.[11]

As to why Rudolf had this attack if he first contracted gonorrhoea ten years earlier, Dr Catterall says that there are three possible explanations: either he became re-infected with gonorrhoea, or his symptoms were due to syphilis, or they were due to some totally unrelated condition. The latter is most unlikely, for had Rudolf suffered from an ordinary disease, this would have been officially announced.

When Rudolf was infected with syphilis on top of gonorrhoea, can only be conjectured. According to psycho-graphologist Klára Ács, it happened some time in 1886–87. Syphilis remains alive in the tissues for a lifetime, unless destroyed by treatment, and in the 1880's there was not yet any effective treatment. Massage with mercury—*unguentum cynererum*—was the only medication until 1909, when Paul Ehrlich discovered *Salversan*, also known as 606, as it was at the 606th experiment that Ehrlich succeeded.

I learnt about Rudolf's affliction by syphilis quite accidentally from an eminent Austrian venereologist who said that his professor, Dr Gustav Scherber, had been the pupil of Professor Stephan Wolfram, whose head-nurse had massaged the Crown Prince with *unguentum cynererum* on the first floor of a house in the IVth district in Vienna. The head-nurse, very efficient in her profession, had one weakness: she liked to drink, and when under the influence, she talked, naming the Crown Prince and many well-known Austrian aristocrats among her 'mercury patients'.

What Stephanie could not know—and in the 1880's even few doctors were aware of it—was that anyone who suffered from syphilis and gonorrhoea was in mortal danger, for syphilis can destroy the brain, cause blindness and heart disease, and much pain in the loins; gonorrhoea adds to the danger for it weakens the body's resistance. In other words, by the end of the 1880's, Rudolf's health was thoroughly undermined, and there was no way to cure him. He sensed it and it was this belief that he was incurable that caused his desperate frame of mind. In 1886 he had not yet reached this stage.

Gradually Rudolf recovered, and Stephanie also seemed well on the mend. Although all medical reports on the two patients at Lacroma were destroyed on the Emperor's orders, it seems very probable that Rudolf believed Stephanie, with her robust health, had overcome the worst effects of gonorrhoea. It is extroardinary that he does not appear to have infected Mizzi Caspar.

The report of Professor Egyd Valponer, sent out from Brussels to treat Stephanie in Lacroma, has not come to light. Yet the opinion of this Belgian gynaeocologist would be invaluable assessing Rudolf's condition as well as Stephanie's. At all events on March 14, 1886, Rudolf got out of bed for the first time in order to greet Archduke Ludvig Victor, who persuaded him to go sightseeing, first to Ragusa, then further south, to Cattaro. When his brother-in-law, Philip of Coburg, arrived on March 25, Rudolf went out shooting with him and enjoyed it; on April 1st another very close friend, Samuel Teleki, turned up accompanied by six people. He was on his way to Zanzibar and the African mainland to explore the areas north of Bagamoyo, where he heard that a big lake existed.[12]

On April 27, Rudolf and Stephanie returned to Vienna, to the Hofburg. Both were allegedly cured and in excellent health, but in fact both were scarred for ever. One person noticed that all was not well: Archduchess Marie Valarie, Rudolf's young sister. She wrote in her diary: 'Rudolf has much changed, he has become cold and cynical.' Forty years later, with hindsight, Stephanie wrote: 'How distressing it was in these days when the trouble was in the making, no one recognised or was willing to recognise, what was amiss. Not until the Crown Prince's condition seemed to make it more and more improbable that he would ever procreate an heir to the throne, were attempts made to induce him to lead a more orderly life. For the same reason very great care was taken of me. I was sent to Franzesbad, and then to Switzerland. Afterwards I went to Jersey, and from the Channel Islands to stay with my parents. There had been no improvement in the Crown Prince, matters having gone from bad to worse. The hopes of an heir being born became more and more remote. At length things reached such a pass that the Crown Prince never returned home until the small hours and then in a most disagreeable frame of mind. In such circumstances conjugal life had become impossible; my whole nature rose in revolt. Since respect and confidence were at an end, nothing but compassion could build a bridge between myself and him. Nevertheless, I had to conceal my sentiments from the eyes of the world, for no one must know about our private distresses'.[13]

For Rudolf the realization of his own condition and that he had infected his wife were not factors calculated to soothe his already shattered nervous system.

15

Rudolf's Assessment of the Future

The pressures and tensions which drove the Crown Prince to want to end his life in 1889 were building up inexorably during the two preceding years. Despite the effects of syphilis and morphia addiction, which were destroying his body, Rudolf's mind was not yet affected: indeed he seemed stimulated in his thinking and writing, and during these years he produced a long analysis of the Monarchy's domestic and foreign policy, which was remarkably penetrating. Unhappily at the Hofburg and at the Ballhausplatz, Rudolf's advice fell on deaf ears, and this indifference took further toll of his unstable nervous system.

The Crown Prince clearly understood the anxious problem facing Europe during the close of the 19th century, namely who would replace the moribund Turkish Empire in the Balkans. Would it be Austria or Russia, or would the two divide the Balkans between them? At the end of December 1885 Rudolf addressed a long letter on this subject to the Foreign Minister, Kálnoky. He re-iterated his belief that war with Russia was inevitable, and that the Monarchy had to prepare for it under the most favourable circumstances. With his instinctive understanding of what the young men of the renascent countries wanted, Rudolf said that, apart from Montenegro, which was beholden to Russia, the Monarchy's aim could be achieved by gaining the good will of the Balkan peoples. The Monarchy, he argued, should support an independent Bulgaria, and prevail on Prince Alexander of Battenberg, Bulgaria's ruler, to cede the Widdin area to Serbia; Austria should promise Greece an extension of territory if she attacked Turkey at 'Vienna's nod', and should promise Bessarabia to Rumania if she made an alliance with Vienna against Russia. Thus the Monarchy could play the part of the saviour in the Balkans, instead of the oppressor as she had done hitherto, and her Army would remain intact for the war with Russia.

In his prompt answer Kálnoky countered that relations with Russia were friendly again. He agreed that preparations for war against Russia had to continue and a favourable situation created. But in his view the Balkan people had only one aim: their own independence; they showed little gratitude for help for anything else. From Austria–Hungary's point of view the most important thing was that Germany should back her 'with body and soul'. If the Monarchy wooed the Balkan people without German approval, Bismarck might withdraw his support and leave Austria to face Russia alone.

Kálnoky rightly stressed that religious and racial ties between Russia and Bulgaria would not be broken for ever. Serbia would get rid of the pro-Austrian King Milan; the Rumanian alliance was important, but should Austria fight for Bessarabia? Austria had survived 'the loss of her Italian provinces, for her position among the German States, and defeat by the Prussians'. Of one thing Kálnoky was certain: the Monarchy could not survive defeat at the hands of a Slav State. It was therefore imperative that Austria should not become embroiled in the Balkans if there was any danger of her being on the wrong side.

Rudolf was not convinced by Kálnoky's arguments: on the contrary, he was convinced that a stronger line should be taken against Russia. He decided that the time had come to elaborate his thoughts about the domestic and the foreign policy of the Monarchy, in the form of an essay called: *Sketches Of Austrian Policy In The Last Years, 1886.* He hoped by this document to impress on Kálnoky and through him on the Emperor, that their policy *vis-à-vis* Russia was wrong.

This essay has survived in two curious forms. The first is a handwritten draft, with every page crossed with a red pencil, a method Rudolf used on drafts that he had copied. The second was a printed copy by an unknown printer. Both were found among Rudolf's effects after his death. This document, unfortunately too long to be published in this book, is a shrewd analysis of the position of the Monarchy.

Rudolf started from the fact that after the many disasters of the years 1849–66, Andrássy—former revolutionary and then Liberal politician—breathed new life into the Monarchy when he became Foreign Minister in 1867. But there was one fact Andrássy had

1 The Emperor Francis Joseph

2 The Empress Elizabeth

3 Prince Max and Princess Ludovika zu Bayern

4 The Empress Elizabeth with Rudolf in her arms and Archduchess Gisela

5 Rudolf as a small boy

6 The Emperor Francis Joseph and Rudolf

7 Rudolf's Hungarian history teacher,
Father J. J. Rónay

8 The Hofburg

9 Rudolf aged 20

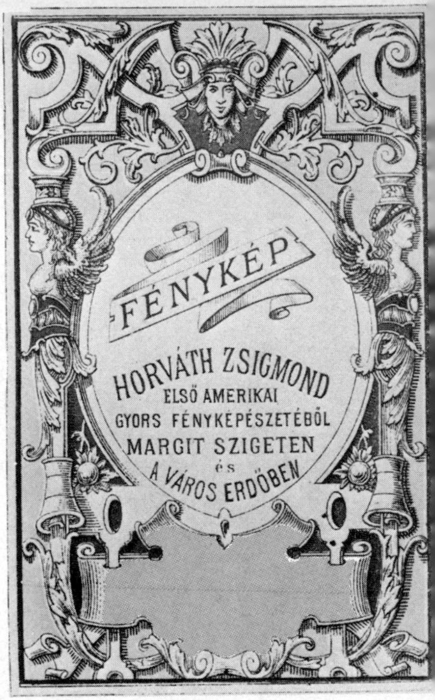

10 Mitzi Caspar

11 Mitzi Caspar's gravestone

12 Princess Stephanie of the Belgians

13 Rudolf

Mayerling. Altes Jagdschloss des Kronprinzen Rudolf
vor dem Jahre 1889

14 Rudolf's shooting lodge at Mayerling

15 Rudolf in 1888

16 Mary Vecsera

not faced up to: that Austria had lost the leadership of the German States.[1] Without their backing, she was numerically dominated by Slavs, and therefore she should have followed a completely new policy. In the geographical area of Hungary Slav and Rumanian nationals were in an even greater majority. Rudolf's proposition was to defeat Russia in a war as soon as possible and thus bring culture, order, and well-being to the Balkans. This was Austria's mission; only Russia's defeat would restore to the Monarchy her former position as a first class power.

Of the German Empire he said: 'After the colossal successes of the years 1866 to 1871, it seemed that little Prussia had brought about the unification of Germany, and thus became the leading power in Europe. But the German *Reich* has not become a unified state; despite their victories, their power, and the nimbus of their Emperor, the Prussians have not had the courage to transform the German States into Provinces and totally break with historic traditions. After fourteen years' work, no further progress can be registered. . . . Thus Germany is only held together by the imposing, ruthless power of Prussian bayonets. The Prussian Army is what Europe respects under the name of Germany.[2]

'A German Empire under Hohenzollern leadership is inconceivable; the intellectual, cultured and wealthy population does not live in Prussia; the Prussians are brutal, ruthless, though very efficient in war. . . . I believe that Germany will retain her power only as long as the Prussian Army exists. . . . One unlucky war would bring about her end. . . . Only a Republic can achieve the unification of Germany, and she will never be a unified Republic like France, but a confederation on the lines of North America.[3]. . .

'It is with this Germany that Austria has formed the closest possible alliance. . . . Austria has often had the ill-luck of allying herself with declining empires. Should this be the case once more? . . . Undeniably Germany and the Monarchy have many common interests, such as the maintenance of the monarchical principle and preparation for a war (with Russia) which must come, as it lies in the nature of future events that it should come. For us it is therefore vital at that moment to have the support of the German armed forces.'

Rudolf then turned his attention to the Monarchy's domestic

policy, which he regarded as a 'transition'. Austria had survived a series of disasters; only if the foreign policy he advocated was put into effect, could a mighty development in domestic affairs take place. The agreement with Hungary in 1867 had been carried out too quickly, with the result that the Monarchy was now divided into two countries, neither of them viable. The German elements in Austria were beginning to think of joining the forty million Germans of the Hohenzollern Empire. While the close alliance with Germany lasted, this constituted no danger, but should that change, the consequences might be catastrophic. Therefore a different domestic policy had to be worked out. To do this, the dreams of the Slavs of Austria had to be considered.

According to Rudolf, hopes of a restored Polish kingdom had to be dismissed because the Poles lacked the ability to administer their country. Rudolf even suggested pushing further back Russia's frontiers in the north, by uniting 'Russian Poland' with Germany. He held very different views about the Czechs, whom he knew and liked. There were dreamers among them, he wrote, who wanted to unify all the Slavs; others wanted to get rid of all German—i.e. Austrian—influence and culture; yet others sympathised with the Russians and were connected with the Pan Slav Committee. But the great majority in Bohemia, Moravia and Silesia wanted to unite the three provinces (some wanted to add Slovakia, tearing her away from Hungary), and obtain for the subjects of St Wenceslaus' Crown the same advantages as the subjects of St Stephen's Crown had obtained. These responsible Czechs wanted to be ruled not by the Emperor of Austria, but by Francis Joseph in his capacity of King of Bohemia. With this aim Rudolf fully sympathised.

The best-written pages of Rudolf's *Sketches of Austrian Policy* are those dealing with Hungary. With enthusiasm he described how the Hungarians had developed their country since 1849—how industry and commerce had flourished, railways and roads had been built, the ancient but dirty 'Turkish style' capital, Pest, linked by a modern chainbridge with its neighbour across the Danube. Buda had, by 1873, not only grown into an attractive capital, but into a town westerners found civilised. Rudolf gladly paid tribute to the Hungarian liberal achievements, but had harsh words for the Hungarian treatment of the ethnic minorities.

He had always deprecated the backward civil service[4] of Hungary, which was stupid, uneducated and arrogant.

'It is probably a misfortune that there are so few Hungarians,' Rudolf concluded. 'If all the territories of St Stephen's Crown were inhabited by Hungarians, many things would be different, but we must deal with facts. And here it is very regrettable that the Hungarian nation, instead of keeping itself close to Austria, so as to increase their joint strength, instead of supporting the common Army as much as possible, indulges in suicidal chauvinism and unlimited *folie de grandeur*, of a "Hungarian Mission in Europe", and of ruling over all other nationalities.'

Rudolf expressed deep concern over the fate of Hungary unless her policy towards the nationalities took a radical change. It did not and this led to the Treaty of Trianon of 1919, which not only chopped off all areas inhabited by non-Hungarians, but also placed three million Hungarians under alien rule. This was the unhappy outcome of the conditions so clearly discerned by Rudolf.

As far as can be ascertained, there was no reaction either from the Emperor, or from the Foreign Minister to Rudolf's penetrating study. Of course his basic principle—the need for a victorious war against Russia—ran counter to the Emperor's policy, but Rudolf's analyses of various parts of the Monarchy were remarkably accurate. *Sketches of Austrian Policy* is a thoughtful document on any rating; it was probably owing to the influence of Taaffe that the Crown Prince's work was ignored.[5] Taaffe was the only person who was allowed to call the Emperor by his Christian name in view of their childhood friendship, and Francis Joseph deferred to his opinions. Unfortunately it was also through Taaffe's influence that the liberal era of the 1870's was replaced by an extremely conservative régime which Rudolf hated. If there was truth in the rumours that the Crown Prince was involved in conspiratorial talks with the Hungarians, of which no concrete proof has ever been found, this may have been the point at which Rudolf decided that he had to use force to save the Monarchy.

What the rebuff of his efforts at statesmanship did to Rudolf's pride and self-confidence is not difficult to imagine. Even had he been a healthy man, he would have felt frustrated and slighted, but

Rudolf was far from healthy—his alleged recovery after the Lacroma convalescence was a myth. Illness had affected his tense nerves, which became tenser with every upset, every real or imagined offence. Add to this his private habits, his very disorganised way of life (to borrow an expression Stephanie often used) and it is clear why Rudolf was constantly exhausted and near the end of his endurance. To alleviate his fatigue, he drank heavily and also took morphine to relieve a cough which plagued him for years. On March 21, 1887, he wrote to Stephanie from Berlin: 'I can't get rid of my cough. Sometimes I am free from it for hours, then I have downright spasms of coughing, which are a great nuisance, especially at dinner parties and on other ceremonial occasions. I am keeping the cough under with morphine, although it is an injurious drug. In Abbazia I shall be able to wean myself from it.'[6] Rudolf in fact never gave up morphine; there are indications that he increased the doses. Without realising it, he had become an addict. According to Professor T. Sollmann 'it takes only ten days' use of the drug to convert an unstable personality into an addict, and twenty to twenty-five days' use is enough to make a similar conversion of the stable and well-adjusted'.[7]

After Rudolf's death, the Crown Prince's prescription book was on imperial orders removed from the *Hofapotheke* (the Court Pharmacy), as Frau Magister Lichal told the author in 1974. Several double pages have been taken out of it, and replaced with innocuous sounding prescriptions. The thus doctored prescription book is now in the Vienna Archives.'[8]

Princess Stephanie reported in her memoirs that after their return from Lacroma Rudolf turned with renewed energy to the writing of his essay on the foreign and domestic policy of Austria-Hungary. Actually, that work had been finished weeks before Lacroma. Szeps commented on it most favourably in a letter dated January 15, 1886. He also said that, having weighed up Rudolf's latest work, he had many more ideas which he had not told the Crown Prince during their last conversation.

Stephanie had no real idea what her husband was doing, yet she did realise that 'a whole epoch is basing its hopes upon him and his liberal principles; being of an impatient passionate nature, it is inevitable that he will try to fulfil these expectations in a manner peculiar to himself and in conflict with actualities'.[9] What she meant by the last half-sentence is not clear, unless it was just an expression of her disapproval of Rudolf's way of life.

Rudolf's correspondence with Stephanie at this time provides abundant evidence that the way of life he had chosen for himself was making him more and more restless. For instance, in August, 1885, he wrote from Bruck: 'Dear Stephanie! Warmest thanks for the photographs and the two letters, which gave me the greatest pleasure.' He had had no chance to write because for four days 'I have been rushing all over the place'. On Friday they had manœuvres. 'I changed horses several times since one mount could not stick it out. After Uncle Albert [Field Marshal Archduke Albert] left, I rode at full gallop to Schwandorf, changed horses and continued my ride to Vienna—twenty-five miles in all. Had business in Vienna, ordering the prizes for the athletic sports I am organizing here. On Saturday he had a day off.' Rudolf had a report for General Arthur Graf Lichtenberg: this he delivered personally in a gallop to Bruck, and then went off to shoot. 'Then I took a train to Vienna. Early this morning I returned here, partly driving, partly on horseback. . . . In the evening in absolute incognito, Ferdinand Coburg[10] is driving over in a cab. Do not say a word about this to the suite, for he lays great stress upon the secrecy of the visit. . . . With warmest love your most devoted Coco.'

On July 27 1886 he wrote to Stephanie that Weilen,[11] who had visited him, 'was gasping with heat and foaming at the mouth as he talked, so that he looked like an old pointer. . . . He only comes to Vienna once a week, to look me up and greet me with a damp handshake. As soon as I have finished this, I shall get into a bath where I shall smoke, doze and sing. . . .'

At their face value these letters, and there were two to three a week, seem like those of a considerate husband, keeping his wife informed of his day-to-day life. Stephanie, however, was to write in her memoirs: 'It is difficult to reconcile their affectionate tone with the irreparable breach that has occurred in our family life. They were written in an endeavour to repair this breach; but they conveyed no true sense of warmth. They are all alike, all commonplace; they breathe nothing but perpetual unrest.'[12]

16

Mounting Tensions

With his nervous curiosity, Rudolf took up every contemporary issue. In 1886 three problems aroused his special interest: the position of France; an unhappy incident in Hungary known as the Jansky affair; and sinister developments in Prussia. In 1887 both his anxieties and his restlessness grew; during his visit to Germany he had a disturbing interview with Bismarck; only his visit to England formed a delightful interlude. At the end of the year two incidents showed up the most unattractive side of Rudolf's character.

Through his correspondence with Szeps, Rudolf kept himself abreast of developments in France. Szeps provided the Crown Prince with information even while he was in Lacroma; through his daughter, Mrs Paul Clemenceau,[1] he had a real insight into French affairs. In May 1886 in Zurich Szeps met Georges Clemenceau, who was 'much more reassured than formerly on the subject of Germany. The French appear to have counted their number and found them to be fairly strong. They seem to have resolved upon a vigorous resistance to hold out for a very long time. They are worried that during the probable socialist disturbances in Belgium in June, Bismarck may plan to let German troops advance into Belgium, in which case a *casus belli* could easily arise.'

Rudolf was indeed well informed about the military strength and political attitude of France, even if his views were influenced by Szeps' presentation. He loyally passed on all he knew to Kálnoky, and this was very useful to the Ballhausplatz for its political assessments. But there is no indication that he reported to the Foreign Minister his interview—organised by Szeps—with Georges Clemenceau, probably on December 26, 1886. Unfortunately no notes or comments have come to light either by the

Crown Prince, or by the future 'Tiger', who was to be chiefly responsible for the destruction of the Monarchy after World War I.

That same year an incident in Hungary, known as the 'Jansky Affair' caused Rudolf great annoyance. In retrospect it seems so trivial that most history books deal with it in a few sentences, or even in a footnote. At the time it appeared crucially important. On May 21, 1886, the anniversary of the storming of Buda by Hungarian patriots during the 1848–49 War of Liberation, Major-General Ludwig Jansky and Austrian officers of the Budapest garrison, put flowers on the graves of General Heinrich Hentzi Edler von Arthurm and his fellow officers who had defended Buda. This caused immense indignation in Hungary. The Prime Minister, Kálmán Tisza, condemned Jansky's action in Parliament, whereupon the general resigned, but his resignation was not accepted. This led to counter-demonstrations in the Austrian Upper House, a vituperative speech by Archduke Albert, and it was Tisza's turn to resign, but his resignation was not accepted either. Throughout the Hungarian press poured furious attacks on the Austrians.

Rudolf was indignant over 'the Hungarian ineptitude', and wrote to Szeps that Tisza had committed a real blunder and that the Austrian military authorities were bitter against him. 'No nation of the Monarchy needs a strong Army as badly as the Hungarians, who can only maintain themselves in the midst of attacks by the other nationalities against them while Austria and her Army stand by them unweakened.'[2]

Francis Joseph summoned Tisza, who—according to Rudolf—'left the Presence broken'—and told Szögyényi (Rudolf's friend at the Ballhausplatz) that there would be a full apology in the *Pester Lloyd*. The editor, Miksa Falk, published one (drafted in Vienna) which proved satisfactory to Jansky. Rudolf was placated; he regarded the affair as closed, but it left a bitter taste in the mouth of the protagonists on both sides. It caused Hungarian extremists to wish to break away from Austria—forgetting the consequences this would have in connection with the nationalities.

During this same month of May, 1886, Rudolf paid another visit to Berlin, and saw Bismarck riding through the streets, wildly cheered by the population. Everyone talked of war, officers toasted the coming war. It was a disturbing atmosphere; Rudolf had the impression that Clemenceau's judgement was right: Bismarck would use some convenient excuse to have another show-down with France; he was deeply worried about the possibility of a Franco-Russian alliance.

This time Bismarck's opinion of Rudolf was much less favourable than on the previous occasions—or, he felt it no longer opportune to pay compliments to a man he regarded as dangerous to the German Reich. He was aware not only of Rudolf's friendship with the Prince of Wales, but of his indirect association with French politicians. Bismarck wrote: 'We must be anxiously impressed by the fact that the Crown Prince not only associates with *literati* and journalists but also allows himself to be imposed upon by editors who formerly were in receipt of French money, and now maintain intimate intercourse with Paris. If the Crown Prince continues to pursue this path, it will fill us with apprehension for the future and oblige us to be doubly prudent in our political decisions.'

For his part Rudolf was also wary of the German Chancellor. He was to see him again in August, when Emperor William I, accompanied by Bismarck, came to visit Francis Joseph in Gastein. Rudolf wrote to Szeps that Bismarck considered another war with France inevitable; he was also preparing for war against Russia, to be fought together with Austria. He insisted that Germany and the Monarchy should coordinate all their military preparations; 'there must be unity in our armies from the Baltic to the Black Sea'.[3] He also planned to turn Prussian Poland into a German territory, but after a victorious war, he intended to create a Polish State to act as a buffer between Russia and Germany. Bismarck also wanted an independent ruler in Bulgaria, free from Russian influence; a strong Turkey which could be used against Russia, and the Balkans to be dominated by Austria, not divided between Austria and Russia. Obviously the last points suited Rudolf's book.

The rest of 1886 was filled with military work—a series of manœuvres, in which Rudolf played an energetic part and he continued with his work on *The Austro-Hungarian Monarchy In Word And Picture*.[4] It is an interesting side-light on his character that he firmly refused to let his sister Valerie write the chapter on

Gödöllö; as a woman he was certain she could not do it adequately. With all his liberalism and progressiveness, he was certainly no feminist.

During 1887 Rudolf became even more restless than he had been in 1886; his nerves were constantly on edge. For the first time some members of his entourage noticed that his mental faculties had slowed down; he no longer enjoyed as much as before his scientific interests and the outstanding men whose company used to give him so much pleasure. But with his remarkable faculty of hiding his feelings, and his almost schizophrenic change of attitudes, outsiders were completely unaware of the deterioration that was going on in him.

In March, 1887, Rudolf went again to Berlin for the celebrations in honour of Kaiser William's nintieth birthday, and had another long interview with Bismarck.[5] His report, found after his death, was marked *secretissimum* (top secret); reading it is like looking into a witch's cauldron. These were Rudolf's highlights: Bismarck received him cordially and assured him that he was above all and everything, 'in favour of peace'. He thought it very regrettable 'that the whole Army talks of war and the necessity for it'. He told Rudolf specifically: 'They want to push me into war and I want peace; to seize the first opportunity of war would be frivolous; we are not a pirate State making war just to oblige a few.' Should the Orleans Party or the Boulangists come to power in France, there would be war, for they needed military successes. In that case Germany would need a very great number of troops for France's military strength was vast. Bismarck wanted a firm alliance with Austria, because there might be a 'dual war'—against France and Russia. He wanted to come to terms with England and Italy, and returned repeatedly to the question of an Austrian-English-Italian alliance.

Bismarck said that Russia would use any favourable opportunity to make progress in the Balkans, to occupy Bulgaria and eventually march on Constantinople. Austria should stay neutral at first, let the Turks and the English, who must intervene because of the route to India, fire the first shots. Italy must be bribed, with offers of Nice, Corsica, Albania and the north coast of Africa. He believed that a revolution could break out in Russia at any time;

in the case of an unsuccessful war the dynasty would be deposed and a republic set up.

Bismarck asked Rudolf many questions about the domestic situation of Austria; in case of war, would the Slavs—especially the Orthodox—be loyal? Would the Slav territorials[6] do their duty? At the close of Rudolf's visit Bismarck repeated that there would be peace during 1887; the advanced age of the Emperor obliged him to do everything to maintain peace. Yet Austria must be in a state of readiness, for 'there is always danger'. In conclusion Rudolf added: 'During that hour and a half's conversation I had the opportunity of noticing that Prince Bismarck was less sprightly than usual, he seemed to me in a very serious mood, and at the same time uneasy and rather excitable. I missed the serenity and firm purpose which I had cause to admire in him on previous occasions.'

Even Taaffe could not have found fault with Rudolf's report, it was sound, calm and concise. There is no evidence of how the Emperor reacted to it—in fact whether he reacted at all. What Rudolf did not tell the Foreign Minister was that he felt uncomfortable about Bismarck's attitude; he had a suspicion shared by Szeps that something unfavourable to the Monarchy was happening.

As it transpired five years later, he was right. Bismarck did not tell his Austrian allies that the *Drei Kaiser Bund*, the 'Alliance of the Three Emperors', having expired, he had substituted for it a dual arrangement between Germany and Russia. This became known as the 'Re-insurance Treaty', which had a very secret protocol. Its third clause was that Germany recognised the preponderant influence of Russia in the Balkans, especially in Bulgaria, and agreed to prevent the restoration of Prince Alexander of Battenberg to the Bulgarian throne. This was a clear betrayal of Bismarck's promise, given in so many words to Rudolf in their March 17 interview that Germany wanted Austria to dominate the Balkans on her own without any sharing with Russia.

Rudolf was no longer alive when the 'Re-Insurance Treaty' was revealed; had he known about it, it would have given him great satisfaction that his intuitive suspicion of Bismarck had been right.

It is probable that it was at this time that Rudolf faced up to the fact that Stephanie could not have any more children, and he must have begun to think of 'making an end of it all'. On March 3, 1887, he made his second will, given in the Appendix. It is a very different document from the almost gay will of 1878, when he sent kisses to Vienna's lovely women.

A month later Rudolf was ill again, which was not mentioned in any official statement, therefore presumably it was connected with his venereal disease. Perhaps he suffered from another re-infection. This is why Rudolf could not accompany Stephanie to Pola, where a new battleship with gun turrets was christened *Crown Princess Stephanie*. This was the sort of event Rudolf enjoyed, and he was proud when Stephanie was *feted*, as she was on this occasion.

Then Stephanie spelt out very clearly her views about Rudolf. His health had further deteriorated, his restlessness increased, his passion for shooting assumed unnatural intensity. 'It was plain to me that the Crown Prince had completely withdrawn from me, had moved into a different world. Everyone knows now that the changed demeanour of the Crown Prince was merely the outcome of the severe moral and political conflicts from which he could not free himself. These were the days which decided the fate of Crown Prince Rudolf.'[7]

This means—according to Stephanie—that it was at this time that Rudolf enmeshed himself in some kind of conspiracy with his Hungarian friends.[8] Despite thorough, patient research by many experienced historians, not a scrap of solid evidence to bear out this allegation has ever been unearthed. Before World War II. I often heard the subject discussed in Hungary, yet it was always conjecture. This does not mean that there was not irresponsible talk among Rudolf's Hungarian friends, talk about Hungary becoming really independent, Rudolf becoming King of Independent Hungary, and that Rudolf did not participate in this talk, especially when he had drunk a lot of champagne. However, careless talk and conspiracy are two very different propositions.

Much more serious is what Stephanie wrote about their private life. 'Subsequently conditions improved to outward appearances, but really during these months, I felt at the end of my tether. . . . Fortunately the demands for our joint presence in public were so frequent as to leave me little time for brooding, and for the time being I failed to realise the full misery of my lot.'[9]

Stephanie's bitter complaint against Rudolf referred to the spring of 1887, but Rudolf's 'disorganised' life had started much earlier.[10] To this innumerable contemporaries bear witness; an exceptionally important one is that of Rudolf's A.D.C., Orsini und Rosenberg. The *Fiakker* coachmen and prostitutes of Vienna could have testified (had anyone asked them to) to Rudolf's frequent visits to their *Weinstuben*.[11]

In 1887 Rudolf went to England for the celebrations in honour of Queen Victoria's fifty years' reign. This visit was a happy occasion, but one aspect of it received practically no attention: Rudolf went without his wife. The Viennese promptly inferred that Stephanie, who was not very popular with them, had refused to go out of sheer contrariness, although Francis Joseph and her own parents attached great importance to both Rudolf and Stephanie attending the English festivities. The facts, were, however, different.

In her conversation with von Küremberg, Fräulein Schratt told him of an unexpected invitation which Crown Princess Stephanie had sent her in 1888. The Crown Princess received Fräulein Schratt in her small boudoir, its walls covered in pale blue brocade, its furniture white Empire and a piano lacquered white. At first the conversation went slowly and awkwardly, but Fräulein Schratt seems to have made such a favourable impression that Stephanie gradually became quite natural and human. When at the end of half-an-hour, the usual time for an audience with a member of the imperial family, Fräulein Schratt was to be dismissed, Stephanie asked her to remain a little longer. After the lackeys had brought in chandeliers with lighted candles, and they were again alone, Stephanie drew out of a drawer of her writing desk a clipping from an English newspaper, which said that Baroness Mary Vecsera was coming to London in order to meet Crown Prince Rudolf.

When Fräulein Schratt asked who had sent her the article, Stephanie replied: 'Marie Larisch.' 'Surely Your Imperial Highness does not take this seriously,' Kati Schratt asked alarmed. 'As far as I know Mary Vecsera has not met the Crown Prince.' Stephanie started weeping and told Fräulein Schratt in obvious distress that she had refused to go to London because she could not face the humiliation of having her husband run after a girl who should still be at school[12] before the eyes of so many of her royal relatives.

Fräulein Schratt tried to cheer up Stephanie by telling her that journalists were incredibly ill-informed and told the most appalling lies. Stephanie wiped her eyes and said, 'When I hear you talk like this, I feel as though my heart had become lighter. But Marie Larisch has also told me that Rudolf is meeting the Vecsera girl even here in Vienna . . .'[13]

Fräulein Schratt assured Stephanie that this was yet another vicious lie. She was too tactful to point out that Marie Larisch was not only an inveterate liar, but a notorious mischief-maker; nor could she explain to the Crown Princess how unwise she had been by refusing to accompany her husband to London.

Mary Vecsera did go to London both in 1886 and 1887; William Henry Waddington, the French Ambassador to London, reported to the Quay d'Orsay that he and his wife had met Baroness Vecsera and her daughters several times during the 1887 jubilee celebrations; and that the Austrian Ambassadress, Countess Lajos Károlyi, had complained that she had to receive 'such people'.[14] Marie Larisch's wicked gossip was all the more reprehensible as she knew perfectly well that Helen Vecsera's sixteen year old daughter had never met the Crown Prince. But Marie, who in her young days dreamt of marrying Rudolf, loathed Stephanie and invented these tales to upset her, and provoke her to make scenes that would distress Rudolf and worsen relations between him and his wife. Her ugly calculations worked out correctly.

But to return to Rudolf's visit to England in 1887: he thoroughly enjoyed himself; his friend, the Prince of Wales, saw to it that every minute of his time was filled and he missed nothing. Rudolf made an excellent impression on the Queen and everyone else. The whole of London talked of his charm and courtesy, and the dinner at which the Queen walked in on his arm, ahead of several crowned heads. And she gave him the Order of the Garter, which was a special honour, as among foreigners it was usually only granted to crowned heads. As for the great occasion, Rudolf wrote to Stephanie: 'The old Queen came today, she was most friendly, and bestowed on me the Order of the Garter, pinning it on herself and fondling me as she did so, so that I could hardly refrain from laughing.'[15]

Count Charles Kinsky,[16] Secretary of the Austrian Embassy in London, whom the Ballhausplatz had detailed to look after Rudolf, wrote an amusing report to Kálnoky. He said it had been a terrible rush, from early morning until next day's early morning. On the first evening Rudolf went with the Prince of Wales to the Marlborough Club and stayed until 4 a.m., up again after hardly any sleep. Kinsky organised a luncheon for Rudolf at the New Club in Richmond, and a supper with such respectable ladies as the Duchess of Manchester. This surprised Rudolf as this was not customary in Austria. There was gipsy music and an Austrian quartet. It was all very gay, and yet after supper Rudolf went with his English friends to see Buffalo Bill at a music hall.

On the day the Queen returned from Windsor, she expected Rudolf and his companions at 1 o'clock. No sign of them! Rudolf had taken them to a private performance of a man eater who was the sensation of London. Rudolf and his friends arrived at 1.30—half an hour later—but were graciously forgiven by the Queen. Kinsky was much impressed by Rudolf's humility and simplicity, and by the extremely respectful way in which he talked about his father. But: 'I am sorry to have to say, the Crown Prince has tense nerves. There is no mistaking it. I was aware of it before and cannot help noticing it again. That is his misfortune. It particularly struck me during a traffic stoppage. He fights against it, but it is obviously there.'[17]

The rest of 1887, like the year before, was taken up with manœuvres, and work on *The Austro-Hungarian Monarchy in Word and Picture*. But there were also wild entertainments, and further evidence of Rudolf's disorganised life. He began to complain of sleeplesness. There was no more time to write articles for Szeps, even when he asked for them. Nor did Rudolf send him news as frequently as he had done before.

The late autumn of 1887 witnessed one of the most disreputable incidents in which Rudolf was involved. Archdukes Francis Ferdinand and Otto, with their A.D.C.'s, and some friends were riding outside Vienna. Suddenly they saw a funeral passing; they madly spurred on their horses, and jumped over the coffin. The A.D.C.'s immediately realised the indignation of the villagers and tried to soothe their feelings. But news of this scandal spread: soon the whole country had heard about it. In the Vienna Parliament a

Member, Engelbert Pernerstorfer, then the German National leader, drew attention to it. 'People,' he declared, 'often talk of the sowing of wild oats. Well, now, I have something to say about the sowing of wild oats. A tale has come to my ears about a young gentleman in an extremely exalted position who after drinking with his comrades, wished to bring them back with him to his wife's bedroom. A very well-known gentleman indeed.'[18] Then Pernerstorfer told the House that there was another tale of an exalted personage who, with his comrades, all of princely blood, was out galloping in the fields. 'From a distance, they caught sight of a funeral procession. They made it halt. Then all those noble princes amused themselves by jumping their horses over the coffin.'[19]

Everyone knew to whom Pernerstorfer was referring; the matter was even taken up in the international Press, and outside Austria Rudolf was certainly thought to have been the culprit although he had not been of the party. For his part he was infuriated that an M.P. should have dared to criticise members of the Imperial House. With his increasing moroseness came a strong reversion to the overpowering arrogance which typified the Habsburgs. He ordered Major-General Koloman von Bolla, Commander of the Infantry Brigade stationed in Vienna, to have Pernerstorfer horsewhipped by officers in mufti. Stephanie wrote in her diary: 'A few days afterwards Pernerstorfer was called upon by two gentlemen who on some pretext entered his house, and then gave him a savage thrashing with riding whips.'[20]

That an M.P. should have been horsewhipped without interference by the authorities naturally created a further scandal. Although it was officially denied that officers had been responsible for the whipping, Rudolf wrote to Stephanie and admitted that the culprits involved belonged to a regiment stationed in Vienna.

'On the whole I am leading a quiet bachelor life, sleeping a lot and seeing a lot of people in the morning. The police have given me some cause for anxiety. They have been on the trail and have discovered the regiment from which the riding whips came. They could not get hold of the "guilty parties" for we spirited away the two sergeants in good time, one to Southern Hungary, the other to Herzegovina. Still it needed all my cheek and ingenuity to save myself and Bolla from trouble. Now we are quite safe again.'[21]

This was Rudolf's nature at its most irresponsible. And worse was to come in the New Year.

Rudolf began 1888 with a sense of deep depression and fear of what the Czar might do. But he was determined to carry on according to his best ability. However, on January 3, 1888, he committed yet another irresponsible action that nearly had terrible consequences. Francis Joseph held a shoot at Mürzsteg, and both father and son had already quite a good bag and the drive was practically over, when Rudolf sighted another herd of deer. He fired; when the quarry dashed away out of reach, he left his place, and just as he was approaching the Emperor's stand, he fired again.

Martin Veitschberger, who was standing by the Emperor's side, stepped forward raising his arm in protest—thus preventing the shot hitting the Emperor. The bullet that narrowly missed Francis Joseph, shattered the bones of Veitschberger's forearm. His career as one of the Emperor's huntsmen was over.[22] He received 50 *Gulden* and a handsome pension.

Rudolf was forbidden to take part in the shoot the next day; the incident was the cause for serious estrangement between father and son. From then on Francis Joseph refused to see Rudolf alone; in fact he saw him as seldom as possible. He also had him watched, and this is how Rudolf's frequent conversations with Archduke Johann Salvator and the latter's contacts with extreme Hungarian nationalists came to the Emperor's ears.

Had Rudolf killed his father, it would at best have been the result of the grossest carelessness, but in view of his publicly known resentment that his father had never given him any responsible position, many people would have put an even more sinister interpretation on the tragedy.

Thus ended two eventful years in the Crown Prince's life, during which he had to face illness for which there was no cure, the fact that he had infected his wife with the additional possibility that he had rendered her sterile; and the depressing realisation that the Emperor would not allow him to play any responsible part in the political life of the Monarchy. His serious contributions were unknown to the general public, because they took the shape of reports and analyses that could not be published at that time; while his irresponsible and dissolute actions, especially the Pernerstorfer scandal and the Mürzsteg near-catastrophe, were the talk not only of Vienna but of the whole of Austria.[23] It did not need the knowledge of a psychologist to predict that unless the Emperor Francis Joseph—or the Empress Elisabeth—changed their attitudes, Rudolf would have a nervous collapse. Stephanie, with all her faults, was profoundly concerned over her husband, and at least noticed the deterioration in his physical and mental condition, but she never had a chance to open the eyes—let alone influence the attitude—of the Emperor. In her memoirs she says that she began what turned out to be Rudolf's last year in life with a dark premonition of some dreadful event which she could neither name, nor even conceive. The distraught life of the Crown Prince was indeed fast-moving towards a point of no return.[24]

17

Rudolf's Nerves at Breaking Point

The Emperor was incensed about the Mürzsteg incident not so much because Rudolf had endangered his life—he was no physical coward—but because it was yet further evidence in his view that Rudolf was totally lacking any sense of responsibility. He also considered that his son was temperamentally unqualified for the immensely difficult task of administering and keeping together the heterogeneous Monarchy. To Francis Joseph, Rudolf's determination to provoke war with Russia appeared madness: victory in such a war depended on Germany's support, and clearly Bismarck would only do what was in Germany's best interest; there was no certainty that he would back the Monarchy. From the Austrian point of view, the best policy was to work out (if possible) an accommodation with the Tsar. Rudolf's dream of starting a war, the outcome of which could not be foreseen, was utterly unacceptable. Francis Joseph had had to face the consequences of too many lost wars to enter lightly upon a dubious adventure.

Francis Joseph was also furious because of the gossip the Mürzsteg incident had engendered not only in Austria, but at every Court and Chancellery in Europe. Deep down he knew that Rudolf had the sympathy of many because he had not appointed him to a responsible position; but he was convinced that Rudolf was far from ready for holding such a position. The Emperor was at one with Queen Victoria who took the same line towards her son, Rudolf's close friend. Highly placed informers kept Francis Joseph up to date on how the heirs of the two most important thrones of Europe talked about their parents. But there is no evidence that anyone advised the Emperor on the damage he was inflicting to the mind, and even to the health, of his son by totally excluding him from any participation in power.

For weeks after Mürzsteg the Emperor would not speak to Rudolf. Fortunately the Empress was in Vienna for the whole of that winter and, rising to the occasion of what she realised was a critical situation, she played her part admirably. She interceded for Rudolf with her husband, well aware that if she exercised her charms he would give way—Francis Joseph always had, and she was certain that he always would grant her her wishes. And she proved right, for not only did she bring about a reconciliation, she even induced the Emperor to promise to give Rudolf an important promotion—a promotion that would show Austria and the world that all was well between father and son.

Marie Festetics, Elizabeth's observant lady-in-waiting, recorded in her diary that the Empress was extremely worried over Rudolf; she realised that his marriage was a disaster, and his health poor. Elizabeth certainly noticed his changed appearance and his constantly inflamed eyes, though she had no idea what illness was plaguing Rudolf. Yet, as had happened so often before, she could not bring herself to have a heart-to-heart talk with her son. This would have been probably her last opportunity to help him, by finding out the cause of his distress. She would have been horrified had she known Rudolf's despair—his sense of utter failure. After the promotion she had obtained for him turned into another bitter disappointment, it would have been most unlikely that she could have pulled him back into the main stream of life.

On February 4, 1888, Bismarck published the Treaty of Alliance between Germany and the Monarchy. The ostensible reason he gave for this was to prove to Russia that Francis Joseph would not stand alone were the Czar Alexander III to attack him. In fact, as Rudolf and Szeps guessed right away, this was a manœuvre to impress the Russians and to draw them into the German orbit. On March 9, Emperor William I of Germany died in his ninety-first year. Francis Joseph—by now again on reasonable terms with his son—wanted Rudolf to go to the funeral, but without Stephanie. Rudolf wrote her an amusing letter about the announcement of the German Emperor's death, which turned out to be premature; after black bordered papers were being sold in the streets of Vienna, telegrams poured in that Emperor William had had a good supper and drank champagne. This amused the Viennese. But when the following day he really did die, they received the news with indifference. 'They were much more interested in the fire at the *Bauernmarkt*,' Rudolf wrote, 'as soon as Berlin is finished, I shall come to Abbazia. Fondest love as ever from your devoted Coco.'

On this visit Rudolf had no political conversation with Bismarck; it was hardly the occasion for that, with ninety kings and princes in Berlin for the funeral. Besides, the Chancellor had his own problems: he knew that Emperor Frederick, practically mute because of his throat cancer, could not last more than a few months, if that, and then would come William II, at the age of twenty-nine full of his own importance and invariably imagining that he was right, as he considered himself a political genius. Emperor Frederick would wish to introduce liberal reforms and was moreover devoted to the Austrian Crown Prince. Fortunately from Bismarck's point of view, William II thoroughly disliked his cousin. He despised Rudolf's bookishness, his ambition to write, to keep the company of men of science, of writers and poets, and of Jewish journalists.

With his first-class intelligence service, Bismarck knew about Rudolf's venereal disease; he had at his disposal doctors who would have told him about the physical consequences of Rudolf's illness, and his spies no doubt reported about the Crown Prince's tense nerves, lack of self-control and moodiness. For anyone anxious that Rudolf should not come to power, he all too clearly suffered from weaknesses which could be easily exploited; he might even be driven to desperate actions. Bismarck realised, moreover, that he had allies in Austria, especially in the Prime Minister, Taaffe, and the Field Marshal, Archduke Albert, who also resented Rudolf's liberal political views. Bismarck was much less worried about Rudolf's progressive ideas than about his determination to provoke a preventive war against Russia, and the plans he and the Prince of Wales were hatching for an alliance between Austria and France, which England and Russia would eventually join. This meant the encirclement of the German Empire he, Bismarck, had put together. He was not going to let this happen without fighting with every means at his disposal. One clearly feasible strategem was to play on Rudolf's tattered nerves and his poor health.

After Rudolf's return from Emperor William's funeral, Francis

Joseph lived up to his promise to Elizabeth: he did promote Rudolf to a position specially created for him: that of Inspector-General of the Infantry. He was however still determined not to allow his son any influence on policy-making; a new military position had to be specially invented for him and was subordinated to the Ministry of War; none the less it gave Rudolf scope to work on the main body of the Armed Forces.

Rudolf was delighted by the appointment, and by having been forgiven for Mürzsteg. He hoped to play an important part in modernizing the Army, all the more so as he was convinced that Bismarck was preparing for war. It was almost impossible to guess what Czar Alexander III really wanted. *Nord*, an official Russian periodical printed in Belgium, stated that Russia was prepared for concessions—even sacrifices—if the agreements of the Congress of Berlin, 1878, were to be restored. Clearly the Czar did not want Ferdinand of Coburg on the Bulgarian throne; for Russia still wanted to control Bulgaria, and through this to expand her influence in the Balkans. In the Re-Insurance Treaty Bismarck had conceded that this was a legitimate aim of Russian policy.

This policy, now blessed by Bismarck, ran directly counter to Rudolf's belief in Austria's civilising mission in the Balkans, and strengthened his conviction that war between the Monarchy and Russia was inevitable. He was delighted that he would now be in a position to introduce the much needed reforms to prepare the Monarchy's armed forces for this all-important conflict.

As though some evil spirit were pursuing Rudolf, the day after his promotion an incident occurred which again damaged his standing with the Emperor. Easter was early in 1888, and for March 19 Rudolf had invited Archduke Otto and several friends to spend Holy Week on the imperial yacht *Greif* on a cruise down the Dalmatian coast, where the weather would be balmy.

When they set out, the captain wanted to steer a course out to sea because it was pitch dark; there was not a single lighthouse in the Quarnero, and under such conditions it was dangerous to sail among its innumerable islands. Rudolf insisted on an island course. The captain had no alternative but to obey. Much champagne was consumed, and the ladies retired soon after eleven o'clock. At midnight there was a tremendous crash, and the whole ship was convulsed. There was panic in the saloon; on deck the captain told

Stephanie, who had thrown on a wrap and rushed upstairs, that *Greif* had struck a rock and knocked a big hole in her bottom. The leak was considerable, but the sea being calm, there was no immediate danger of sinking.

'With ladders and ropes we were able to get the Crown Prince, Otto and other guests who had not slept off their potations, ashore,' Stephanie has written. 'I stayed on board till morning among the greatly distressed officers. The entire Navy was upset —the Admiral, Maximilian Freiherr von Daublevsky—Sternbeck, wanted the captain and the officers of the watch immediately to be dismissed the service, but I was able to persuade him to retain them at their posts.'[1] It was Stephanie who intervened for the captain who had unwillingly carried out Rudolf's thoughtless order, though it was clearly Rudolf who should have done so, and admitted that the fault was his. Apart from the costly damage to *Greif*, Francis Joseph and his Commanding Admiral were greatly embarrassed by Rudolf's conduct because of its injurious effect on the Crown Prince's image with serious men.

On Rudolf's new appointment Stephanie's comments were unenthusiastic. 'The new post of Inspector-General of the Infantry had been specially created for Rudolf; it involved much work which in conjunction with the perpetual rush and disorder of his private life, impaired his health. Even a man with a much stronger constitution than he would have been broken by such a mode of existence.'[2]

But Rudolf was pleased; indeed for a time very pleased. On March 21, thanking Szeps for his congratulations on his promotion, he wrote: 'I vow and hope to be able to carry out my vow, in my new position to act in the right way and in the Greater Austrian tradition.'[3] Illustrative of what military inspection by Rudolf amounted to and of his deteriorating physical condition at this time is the following passage from the memoirs of General Wilhelm Hirsch Edler von Stronstorff: 'At the end of July [1888] Crown Prince Rudolf came to inspect the regiment [at Jaroslau] and ate in our officers' mess. The whole thing was only a formality, there was no real interest. For the rest the Crown Prince was very gracious. One incident on this occasion, which did not lack a comic side, seems to me worth mentioning. The day before his arrival, an A.D.C. of the Crown Prince appeared to choose a horse for His Highness. For this six lamb-like animals were produced by the nearest cavalry regiment; but none proved completely satisfactory. Then I proposed the Regimental A.D.C.'s horse, an older animal, familiar with all eventualities and surprises, which would not be frightened by anything. It was declared to be a suitable mount. After the *defillée* of the regiment and reception of gracious praise, I turned my horse and started out in a canter to reach the front of the regiment. That was when I realised that the Crown Prince was cantering behind me, but not of his own volition. The A.D.C.'s horse, as it was used to, followed me. I had to stop so as to enable the High Gentleman to stop too. The Crown Prince was already then in a pitiful physical condition.'[4] Rudolf had never been a great horseman, but by now something seemed to have gone wrong with his balance. He fell off his horse on several occasions.

In spite of such *contretemps*, Rudolf threw himself into his work with fervour. On May 18 he wrote to Stephanie: 'Today I went to Znaim where we had a route march and a drill for the 3rd Regiment and one battalion of the 99th. Certainly it is not agreeable to ride different horses every day, often sorry screws. In other respects, however, I like my new post, it brings movement into my life, and suits me well.'

Rudolf's first shock came when he heard through Szeps and the Austrian military attaché in Berlin that Bismarck by no means approved of his promotion. As for William II who became Kaiser on his father's death on June 15, 1888, he said openly that Rudolf was not the right man for such a big job; he knew about Rudolf's illness, but at least he did not refer to it in public. Yet Rudolf's health was getting worse. In his letters to Szeps he complained that his eyes were 'somewhat better, but by no means well'.[5] His constantly inflamed eyes and his deteriorating eyesight were indications of the virulence of his venereal disease. It would have been a simple matter of deduction for Bismarck to conclude that Rudolf, in view of his incurable disease, might well not survive his father and that the next in line, Archduke Otto—who was known to the Viennese as *der fesche Otto*[6] and was not interested in politics—would be no threat to the German Empire. Rudolf, on the other hand, with his penetrating if unstable understanding of the political situation, with his friendship with the Prince of

Wales and the extremely well informed Jewish journalists in Vienna, might create a very difficult situation were he to realise his plans for encircling Hohenzollern Germany. Owing to Rudolf's death, this danger was averted; but that it had been real was evidenced by the conclusion in 1904 of the *Entente Cordiale* but without Austria.

During June, 1888, an important journey was planned for the Crown Prince and his wife to Croatia, Bosnia, Herzegovina and golden Sarajevo. On this trip Rudolf was at his most charming; he made a number of admirable speeches, almost invariably saying the things which won people over. The one exception was Sarajevo. Stephanie described the occasion as follows: 'Before proposing the toast to the Emperor's health, Rudolf remarked that it was the mission of Austria-Hungary to introduce western civilisation to the East. These words attracted a good deal of attention, above all in Russia, where they were regarded as giving expression to the intention of the Crown Prince (already regarded as an adversary of Russia) to strengthen this policy in the future. The greatest excitement of all, however, was aroused in the Viennese Foreign Ministry, where the policy of extending Austro-Hungarian influence throughout the Balkan countries was in vogue, but where these designs were kept secret.[7]

Yet on this trip Rudolf made himself popular both as a man, as a Crown Prince, and as their future ruler. The journey was a great success.

Back in Vienna, Rudolf continued with his restless life, inspecting regiments from seven in the morning to five in the afternoon. In answer to Szeps' good wishes on his thirtieth birthday, August 21, 1888, he wrote:[8] 'Thirty years is a long time—I have filled the years more or less usefully, but they are years empty of deeds and successes. Every year I become less energetic, less fresh. I still have great hopes, but will they come true? They can only be realised if we wage a successful war, after which a transformed Austria must achieve great things. However things will go, one must believe in the future—I hope and count on the next ten years.'

By then, however, Rudolf had come to realise that his position as Inspector-General of the Infantry was not taken seriously by the Emperor, and even less by his old enemy, Field Marshal

Archduke Albert. Rudolf was not regularly summoned to the Military Councils which were presided over by the Emperor. He was never asked when weighty matters were being discussed. Vienna gossip had it that this was partly because of Rudolf's cantankerous attitude sometimes on unimportant matters, which held up discussions.

In Berlin it was put about that Rudolf had chosen the faulty repeating rifle that had been issued to the Austrian Army. The Kaiser in particular was extremely rude in his personal criticism of Rudolf. Had the Crown Prince been healthy, and a stronger character, he could have put his enemies in Germany and at home in their place, for he was in no way responsible for this decision. Although it had not been published, the Ministry of War had taken it *before* Rudolf's appointment as Inspector General. In order to utilise existing stocks of ammunition originally intended for the larger caliber single loading rifle, the same caliber was specified for the new repeater. Many formations had already been equipped with the new weapon when it was realised that the quantity of ammunition needed for it was too heavy for the soldier to carry. Its replacement by the new smaller 8 mm. Mannlicher repeater involved heavy, unnecessary expenditure. As both Archduke Albert and Beck-Rzikowsky disliked Rudolf, they were only too glad to saddle him with the blame and to inform the Emperor, who consequently also held Rudolf responsible.

Various officers who came into contact with Rudolf during this dispute remarked on his irritable manner, and lack of self-control. Churlish, offensive, even unjust, were the words they used about him. In view of these strong personal feelings, Rudolf's sound efforts to modernise the Austro-Hungarian Army, which was not keeping step with other armies, could be frustrated by Albert and Beck.[9]

The deterioration in Rudolf's manners and temper were borne out by Stephanie, who wrote of this period: 'During the few days of this summer of 1888 when I had the opportunity of seeing the Crown Prince in the intervals between journeys of military inspection, I could not fail to notice that . . . he had become prone to outbursts of fierce anger upon the most trifling occasions. I had long become accustomed to the fact that the conventionalities of our life together as husband and wife, especially as our relationship found expression in his letters, contrasted glaringly with Rudolf's actual everyday behaviour. Now however he was often quite unrecognizable.

'His inward disorganisation led to terrible attacks of wrath, to intolerable and undignified scenes. It was as if, with the loss of inward stability, he had also lost any sense of good form. On such occasions he would not hesitate to talk to me openly about his distasteful *amours*. At length matters came to such a pass that he threatened to finish things off by shooting me and then himself. I was seized with horror.'[10]

Stephanie was greatly relieved when in September 1888 the Emperor allowed her to make a voyage alone to Greece. For his part Rudolf had the pleasure of entertaining his friend, the Prince of Wales, and of paying a short visit to his cousin, Archduke Johann Salvator.

Rudolf and Johann Salvator were the two stormy petrels of the House of Habsburg. They had much in common—early maturity, thirst for activity, progressive ideas, contempt for the Austrian nobility, mistrust of Prussia. Both detested Archduke Albert for his reactionary ideas. Perhaps because they were so much alike, there were many ups and downs in their relationship. Both were excellent soldiers and both talented writers. Archduke John Salvator was not yet twenty-four years old when he wrote a dissertation called *Observations Concerning The Austrian Army*, which dealt not only with technical matters, but also recommended the fortification of the Austrian border with Prussia. The dissertation caused such a sensation that Andrássy, then Foreign Minister of the Monarchy, had a discussion with Bismarck about it. As subsequently, however, he offered Johann Salvator the governorship of Bosnia, he probably did not disapprove too much of his views.

It was far different with the Emperor and Field-Marshal Archduke Albert. Francis Joseph not only gave a severe reprimand to Johann Salvator in the presence of Archdukes Albert and William, but he wrote Rudolf a letter informing him of the punishment meted out to the archduke; he was transferred from his artillery regiment to the Infantry Regiment Prince William No. 12. But six months later Johann Salvator was appointed Commander of another artillery regiment! He proceeded to compound his earlier offence by publishing a second article entitled:

Drill or Education? which not only caused another sensation, but was met with a flood of polemical essays, one of which was believed—rightly—to have been written by Rudolf. Although Rudolf's article ended with the complimentary statement that only 'from competition of thought, from the flaring up of mental sparks can result what is good, what is great', his censures chilled relations between the cousins; then came the Bulgarian crisis, which really strained them.

In 1879 Alexander of Battenberg had become Prince of Bulgaria. He was a nephew of Czar Alexander III, inexperienced in dealing with subjects and subservient to Russia. A Russian General became Prime Minister and another Minister of War of Bulgaria. They tried to dragoon the country and aroused the bitter resentment of the Bulgarians. In 1885 a conspiracy burst out in Eastern Rumelia, and the rebel Bulgarians expelled their Turkish Governor and proclaimed a union of 'The Two Bulgarias', and invited Prince Alexander to be their ruler. Russia was furious, but Stambuloff, the strong man of Bulgaria, persuaded Alexander to accept the union. The Czar in his rage withdrew all the Russian officers from the Bulgarian Army, and the Bulgarians were glad to see them go.

At this point Archduke Johann Salvator offered Prince Alexander his services as a soldier, without telling or asking the permission of the Emperor or his military superiors. When Rudolf heard of this, he was indignant, and wrote an angry letter to Kálnoky demanding that Johann Salvator should be severely punished.

However, Francis Joseph's draconian reaction to Johann Salavator's second offence had a devastating effect on Rudolf. The Emperor insisted that the Crown Prince should inform Johann Salvator that, not only had he nothing further to expect, but that the fateful decree exiling him from the Imperial Family had been invoked. It was indeed a savage decision on the part of Francis Joseph to order Rudolf to inform his friend—for the cousins had made it up completely since 1885—of the punishment which meant the end of Johann Salvator's career, almost the end of his life. Again one cannot but wonder what effect it had on Rudolf to be used as the spiritual executioner of the man to whom, in spite of periodical quarrels, he was deeply attached. Had he not been the

Crown Prince, the same sort of punishment would have been meted out to him too. This was not lost on Rudolf, and he suspected that Taaffe, Albert and Beck would have liked to do just that.

This incident brought the cousins closer together than they had ever been, and many contemporaries believed that it was Johann Salvator who drew Rudolf into his plotting with the Hungarians, although of this there is no firm evidence.

In their commonly shared frustration it is not surprising that it was to Johann Salvator that Rudolf went on September 16, 1888, when he was approaching despair and he tried to cheer himself with a romantic adventure. Archduke Johann Salvator, in the Habsburg family chronicle already demoted to Johann Orth, could be trusted never to betray the Crown Prince's two days' disappearance.[11]

18

The Kaiser Humiliates Rudolf

On September 10, 1888, the Prince of Wales arrived in Vienna in time for breakfast. Rudolf was delighted; here was one man with whom he was in complete agreement both politically and in his way of life. Only while the Englishman was philosophical and imbued with common sense, Rudolf, with his tense nerves and sick body, was driven to extremes and reacted with excessive anger or fell into deep depression.

The Prince of Wales's presence pleased and cheered Rudolf. As he wrote to his friend Szeps in an undated letter (probably September 12): 'Wales is here on a visit. I could not see you as I am in attendance on him all the time, and he wants something different every five minutes. So my service is strenuous. But we are having an enjoyable time.'

In his next letter Rudolf told Szeps in scathing terms of his views about the new Kaiser, presumably the outcome of his talks with the Prince of Wales: 'William II is coming on. He ought soon to be able to engineer a great crisis in old Europe. That is my feeling. He is just the man to do it. He is supremely narrow-minded; and at the same time as vigorous and obstinate as a steer; he considers himself the greatest political genius of all time. What more do you want? In the course of a few years, "little Willie" ought to bring Hohenzollern Germany to the plight she deserves. There are strong indications that Bismarck's position has weakened.' In this Rudolf's intuition was correct, but by being right he exposed himself to personal hostility from Berlin: Bismarck's suspicions of Rudolf's pro-French sentiments became coupled with William's intense personal dislike of Rudolf. And Bismarck was intent on influencing his Emperor to take the kind of action that would further undermine Rudolf's unsteady balance of mind.

The Prince of Wales had chosen to stay at the Grand Hotel, so as to be free to see those of his friends, like the Rothschilds, and Hirsch, who were not acceptable to the Hofburg. When informed that Francis Joseph and Rudolf were coming to pay an official visit, he promptly put on a gay Hungarian hussar uniform. The Emperor asked him how he would like to be entertained. A programme was worked out which absented the prince from Vienna on October 3. When he agreed to these arrangements, Francis Joseph casually remarked that the Kaiser was due to arrive on October 3. The Prince of Wales immediately said that he would return for the occasion; he would send for his uniform as Colonel of the Blücher Hussars and assist the Emperor and the Crown Prince in receiving his nephew. The Prince of Wales dined that night at the Hofburg, and Rudolf was forbidden to tell him that the Kaiser had stipulated that during his visit he should be the only foreign royalty in Vienna, and explicitly stated that he did not want his Uncle Bertie to be present.

Next day, September 11, 1888, the prince had himself photographed in his Hungarian uniform and expected the English Ambassador, Sir Augustus Paget, and his wife, for luncheon. Sir Augustus arrived straight from the Ballhausplatz in a state of some agitation, for Kálnoky had just informed him of the Kaiser's condition for his visit. Sir Augustus told the senior equerry, Major-General Arthur Ellis, that the Prince of Wales' presence was not acceptable to William II during his visit—hence it was embarrassing to the Emperor Francis Joseph. So would the Prince of Wales be sure to be absent from Vienna for ten days as of October 3?

When the Prince of Wales heard of the Kaiser's conditions, he was naturally amazed and indignant. He had written twice, on August 14 and on September 2, to William to ask the exact date of his arrival in Vienna, saying he was prepared to interrupt his shooting to be with Francis Joseph and Rudolf when he arrived but he had received no reply to either one of his letters. He now proceeded to discuss William's incredible behaviour with Rudolf, whose comments were even more derogatory than his own. Rudolf told the Prince of Wales that German agents had spread around the rumour that he wanted to interfere with the forthcoming conversations between Francis Joseph and William, and to embroil both with the Czar, so as to make mischief for the benefit of France:[2] that is why his presence was undesirable! There was no truth whatsoever in any of this. Sir Augustus carefully reported everything to the Prime Minister, Lord Salisbury, who put it to the Queen, and together they were planning their policy to Germany. They had no intention of allowing the Kaiser to get away with such insulting conduct.

It was decided that the Prince of Wales should go, with Rudolf, to shoot near Bjelovar in Croatia, and then attend manœuvres also in Croatia. From there the two princes went to Budapest and then on to Keszthely, to Count (in 1911 created Prince) Tassilo Festetics, who in 1880 had married a Scot, Lady Mary Douglas Hamilton, daughter of the Duke of Hamilton. The Prince of Wales and Rudolf and their host gave free reign to their feelings about the Kaiser; the Prince was heard to say loudly: 'William the Great needs to learn that he is living at the end of the 19th century and not in the Middle Ages.' Rudolf and Festetics made equally indiscreet remarks, all of which were reported to Bismarck, who had well-paid informers in the Hofburg and particularly in Rudolf's entourage.[3]

On October 2 the Prince of Wales went from Budapest by steamer down the Danube to Bucharest, to stay with King Carol and Queen Elizabeth, known as Carmen Sylva, the writer. His hosts did everything possible to make his stay amusing, and he greatly appreciated their efforts during his three days in Rumania at their castle in Sinaia.

Rudolf wrote to Stephanie on September 12: 'We left Vienna this morning. Great receptions here and a frightful racket, all just as it was in Agram, and no end of bustle. Tomorrow and the day after manœuvres, then I am going back to Vienna and immediagely afterwards to Orth. Wales is going to Rumania, then to Görgény. He is in great fettle, wants to see everything and will not allow himself to be left in the cold. Nothing seems to tire the old boy. I long for a rest. Your loving Coco.'[4]

There could have been no greater contrast than the respective arrivals in Vienna of the Prince of Wales and the Kaiser. For the latter the whole of Vienna was bedecked with flags (on orders by the authorities), military uniforms were in evidence everywhere; yards and yards of red carpet were rolled out, and the most luxurious quarters in the Hofburg were prepared for him.

What the Viennese public felt about all this, is indicated by a letter Szeps wrote to Rudolf on October 6, 1888: 'It was a lovely autumn day, and it has been obvious that the Kaiser is not liked in Vienna—I heard various people remark how curious it was for the Kaiser to travel via Stuttgart and Munich to Vienna just as if he intended to continue his tour of the South German Courts. There is a rumour abroad that the Kaiser expounded to Kálnoky his views on the relations between Austria and Russia, and that he especially suggested a compromise in Eastern affairs, including Bulgaria. This augurs no particular good for us. I do not much believe in that report although I think that here in Vienna some light may presently be thrown on the results of the St Petersburg interview and the arrangements made between the Tsar and the Kaiser.'[5]

Even the Emperor Francis Joseph had reservations about William's visit; for instance on the day of his arrival he ordered Taaffe to countermand the torchlight procession which had been arranged in William's honour for that evening, and 'to keep your eyes open'. Rudolf wrote to Kálnoky on the same morning, saying: 'The Emperor ordered me today to let you know that he is agreeable to my being present at the luncheon given by the German Ambassador, but he thinks the function should be conducted with the greatest discretion so that the real motive for it, i.e. to prevent the German Emperor from going about Vienna alone—shall not transpire.'[6]

From the tone of this letter it is clear that Rudolf was pleased to play a part, even a modest one, in the political preparations for the reception of the Kaiser. It cannot have escaped Rudolf's attention that the German Ambassador's invitation was only answered at the last moment. But this was the last pleasure Rudolf had in connection with the Kaiser's visit. For William was accompanied not by old Bismarck, but by his son, Herbert, whose detestation of the Monarchy was no secret. From the moment of the Kaiser's arrival Herbert sought out every possible occasion to be disagreeable to Rudolf and, no doubt coached by his father, pinpricked him where it would upset him most. For his part the Kaiser, under the cloak of the German-Austrian alliance, not only inspected troops, but criticised adversely the appearance of all the infantry regiments he reviewed. He broadly hinted that the

Inspector-General of the Infantry—Rudolf—should be replaced by a competent man.[7] Soon after the Duke of Aumale informed the Head of the Russian Ministry of Foreign Affairs, Count Lamsdorff, that the Kaiser had protested to Francis Joseph both verbally and in writing over the slovenly bearing of the troops which he had seen during his visit, and repeated each time the need for a competent Inspector-General for the Infantry.[8]

William II's visit lasted ten days; the humiliations that were inflicted on Rudolf during these ten days were enough to undo all the good his secret Swiss visit had done to him.[9] The whole of Vienna began to talk about how poorly Rudolf looked.

But the worst blow was as yet to fall: Francis Joseph received the Kaiser's letter, drafted by Bismarck, actually demanding 'for the sake of our alliance' that Rudolf should be demoted from his post of Inspector-General of the Infantry.[10] Instead of firmly refusing, the Emperor invited Rudolf to come to see him for an official interview. He told him of the complaints and criticisms of the Kaiser, and asked Rudolf whether he did not think that, for the sake of the German alliance so vital to the Monarchy, he should resign of his own accord. This insult hit Rudolf like a bolt from the blue: he was so angry that, in spite of the absolute obedience to his father drilled into him since boyhood, he flatly refused to resign. He said he was carrying out his duties conscientiously, and was working on a report how to improve the drill programme. Later on the Prince of Wales was to tell Queen Victoria that this interview 'led directly to the catastrophe'.[11] It was not, however, the only reason that drove Rudolf to his desperate solution; it took one more blow to bring about his utter demoralisation. That was to take place in December.

And during this crucial time the Empress Elizabeth was in Greece, visiting Missolonghi, dreaming about Byron and listening to the poems of Heine. She also called at several Greek islands, sailing in the worst possible weather, having herself tied to the mast in order to watch the storm. This was the final occasion when she let her son down.

Meanwhile Rudolf went to Transylvania, to Görgényszentimre, where the Prince of Wales met him on October 8 for a bear hunt. As though fate were determined to embitter every step Rudolf was taking, his plans to provide his friend with an exciting shoot came to nought because, on account of the drought of the summer of 1888, the bears had gone up high into the mountains, and there were none to shoot. Rudolf was mortified, but nothing could be done about it.

From Görgény the princes went to Budapest for two days of fun; by October 14 they were back in Vienna as that day there was a dinner in honour of the Prince of Wales at the Hofburg. Next day he went with Rudolf to Neuburg in Styria, and from there to France. The Prince enjoyed everything, including visits to *Heurigen*,[12] and was temperamentally capable of ignoring mishaps such as the Kaiser's arrogance. Rudolf had a completely different disposition; quite unable to shake off the distress caused by his father's treatment of him, he was slipping further and further into despondency.

It was in October, 1888, that he wrote in an undated letter to Latour: 'From time to time I look for an opportunity of seeing a dying person and trying to enter into his sensation as he draws his last breath. To me it is always a remarkable spectacle, and among all the people whom I have seen die, each one died in a different way. I also make a practice of intently observing dying animals, and am trying to accustom my wife to such a sight, for one must learn to reckon with the last necessities of life.'[13] In his *Life of Crown Prince Rudolf*, Mitis reports that the saying went round Vienna: 'Out of a young but faded face stare two lustreless eyes, exhaustion being betrayed in every feature.'[14] But his father, the Emperor, appears to have noticed nothing wrong.

Also in October, 1888, Rudolf wrote to Latour: 'I no longer find it within me to worry about anything, least of all about matters concerning myself.' Then to Szeps on November 8, 1888: 'The pursuit and struggle for high ideals—all that is dead and finished with. I am certainly not tired, yet I feel that some rest is necessary. Every year leaves me older, less fresh and less capable of the necessity and useful daily work which in the long run becomes exhausting, the external preparation and perpetual expectation of more specious times weaken one's capacity for work.'

For the first time Rudolf's entourage became worried about his state of mind. His health was deteriorating from week to week. He seemed to have taken a turn for the worse after a bad fall from his horse in October, hushed up at the time. Rudolf refused to consult a physician; he was no longer coherent in his arguments, though the military report he was drafting at this time was completely lucid and hard hitting. 'The Crown Prince just argued for argument's sake; when it seemed that his opponent was winning, he changed the subject saying: "Every question has two sides." He blamed Taaffe in violent terms for the coming downfall of the Monarchy. He had become a different person, in marked contrast to his brilliant self of earlier days.'[15] Rudolf had lost interest in serious books and no longer invited interesting people; he frittered away his time reading trashy novels. He only skimmed the papers in a perfunctory manner; the only items that excited him were reports about suicides, especially suicide pacts. When he heard of the suicide on May 11, 1888, in Budapest, of Steven Kegl,[16] the Hungarian sportsman and big game hunter in Africa, he rushed there on May 16, on the excuse of a military engagement, and insisted on being shown how Kegl had done it. He had used a hand mirror.

At the end of the last century, there were innumerable suicides in Vienna; Walburga Lady Paget has written: 'There was again an epidemic of suicides in Vienna. Servants kill themselves because they break a plate, children of seven and eight hang themselves because they can not do a lesson; soldiers because they do not like the Army, girls because they cannot marry their first love; the mania is such that I was warned not to ride in the *Prater* in the morning before the patrol which takes the corpses off the trees has gone around.'[17] 'At the slightest difficulties these people meet, they at once resort to suicide. There must be something in the air of Vienna which makes people do this.'[18]

In this distraught, abnormal state of mind, Rudolf saw his morganatic cousin, Marie Larisch, several times. She told him of a lovely girl called Mary Vecsera, who was madly in love with him. Normally Rudolf would have laughed away this 'great admirer', but in his depression, with angry scenes made by the unfortunate Stephanie, and with the fear that his military career was moving towards disaster, Rudolf agreed to meet the pretty girl whom he already knew by sight. Little did he suspect that for her activities as a procuress Marie Larisch was planning to use the seventeen-year-old Mary Vecsera to extract money from him.

19

Who was Mary Vecsera?

Mary Vecsera became known to the Viennese public for the last three weeks of her short life. Since her death, reams and reams have been written about her, films made, plays produced. It is necessary to de-glamorise the image of this ill-fated girl whose origins were very mixed. She was indeed descended from workmen and from noblemen of many nationalities, and she had relations all over Europe, from the Levant to England.

The Vecseras were Slovaks.[1] The spelling of the name is not Slav, but Hungarian, and it is known that a Josef Vecsera came to Pozsony,[2] at that time the Hungarian capital, sometime in the 18th century. He was born in Uzsor, a purely Hungarian village, and appears to have been a shoemaker, for in Pozsony he married a German girl called Elizabeth Killner, whose father was a master-shoemaker, and an eminent member of the Pozsony shoemakers' guild, which Josef Vecsera joined. There were ten children of the marriage; the youngest son, Georg Vecsera, married Karoline Ullmann, daughter of another master-shoemaker, Johannes Ullmann, whose wife was also German.

Georg Vecsera, Mary's grandfather, was born in Pozsony, on April 24, 1796. He was ambitious and when he was twenty-four years old got himself engaged as assistant town clerk by the Town Council of Pozsony. A year later he was promoted to Town Clerk and in 1839 to Town Captain—City Commandant—in charge of the city police and security.[3]

During the 1848–49 Hungarian Revolution Georg Vecsera took a strong stand against the Hungarian insurgents; for instance he had the Protestant preacher, Paul Rézga, arrested for his patriotic sermons and hanged on June 18, 1849. This incensed the inhabitants of Pozsony to such an extent that he had to resign as Town Captain, but it made him all the more popular with the Viennese regime. In 1858 he was appointed Assistant Director of the Imperial and Royal Court of Appeal, and on January 1, 1870, he was pensioned off as Director of the Subsidiary Offices of the Imperial and Royal County Court. A week later he died in his own house, Promenade 4.[4]

Francis Joseph did not forget people loyal to him; at the end of 1849 he offered to raise Georg Vecsera to the rank of nobleman.[5] But Vecsera was afraid that such a sign of favour by the Emperor would enrage the people of Pozsony so much that they would run him out of the town. He therefore petitioned the Emperor not to give him this new rank, but instead to enable his son, Albin, a bright young man, to study at the Oriental Akademie in Vienna, and then join the Austrian diplomatic service. This request was granted, and that is how Albin Vecsera, the father of Mary Vecsera, began his career on November 27, 1849.

He seems to have been a quiet, industrious young man. Obviously, the Director knew of Albin's family background. When he had completed his studies, his file was sent to the Ballhausplatz, where they also knew that the All-Highest took an interest in him. At the end of 1850 Albin was already in Bucharest as Assistant Interpreter (dragoman); on April 22, 1855, he was appointed Hon. Secretary of the Austrian Embassy in Constantinople; on May 23, 1858, he was confirmed as Legation Secretary; on April 14, 1868, Counsellor of the Austrian Embassy in St Petersburg, and soon after that Chargé d'Affaires. On December 10, 1869, he was transferred to Lisbon as Minister Extraordinary; on June 7, 1870, as Minister to the Grand Duke of Hesse Darmstadt—this position came to an end in 1872—so Albin, by now Baron Albin Vecsera,[6] was retired on a handsome pension. In 1880, however, Albin was brought out of retirement and appointed Austrian Commissioner to the Egyptian '*dette publique*' to establish the Austro-Hungarian share in it. In Cairo he lived very comfortably until November 4, 1887, when he died and was buried there.

In Constantinople Albin Vecsera had come to know the family of the immensely wealthy Italian banker, Theodor Baltazzi, who was to become the maternal grandfather of Mary Vecsera. His daughter Helen, born in Marseilles in 1847, was seventeen years old when, to the surprise of her friends, she married Albin

Vecsera in Pera. Albin's petition to the Emperor for permission to marry Helen Baltazzi[7] is in existence; Francis Joseph signed the agreement on February 17, 1864.[8]

The Baltazzis were an old Italian trading family. They are mentioned in documents of the 15th, 16th and 17th centuries in Northern Italian towns, in Venice and in Dalmatia. They were neither powerful, nor rich, but their reputation was that of reliable merchants. By the time Helen married Albin in 1864, her many Baltazzi relations were well-known throughout Eastern Europe and the Levant as merchants and diplomats. They had made a great deal of money, and, assisted by a series of judicious marriages, they came to move in good social circles. That young Mary Vecsera was able to enter the world of Crown Prince Rudolf, owed much not only to the fact that she had, in Helen, a highly ambitious mother, but that in Helen's brothers and sisters she had a bevy of dashing uncles and well-connected aunts.

Theodore Baltazzi and his wife, Eliza, the daughter of Richard Sarrel (an English county gentleman turned Levantine merchant who became Vice-Consul in Constantinople), had eight children: four daughters and four sons. Their four daughters were: Helen, Mary Vecsera's mother; Marie Virginie, who first married Count von Wallsee, and having divorced him, Count Georg von Stockau, with whom she lived in London; Elizabeth who married the third Lord Nugent and lived in Beacon Lodge, Christchurch, Hants.; and Charlotte, who had married the Hungarian Count George Erdödy. The four sons—Mary Vecsera's four dashing uncles—were all excellent horsemen, horse-breeders and gamblers.

Alexander Baltazzi, the eldest dashing uncle, was born on May 15, 1850.[9] He never did a day's work, but he was mad about horses and riding, and became the owner of *Kisbér*, one of the most famous Hungarian racehorses, which won the Derby in 1876. It was he, with his brother-in-law, Georg Count von Stockau, who had to take Mary Vecsera's body from Mayerling to Heiligenkreutz.

Uncle Hector Baltazzi was a wild, brave sportsman, who met with quite a few accidents, but his amazing physique invariably recovered. Between 1881 and 1886 he was five times Austrian champion gentleman jockey. In 1874 he married Anna Countess of

Central Library

020 8303 7777

Thank you for using the Self Service facility. If any items have been returned late, overdue charges may be payable. Please enquire at counter.

Account Status 26/10/2009 13:33

XXXXXXXXXX9582

Item Title	Due Date
A Habsburg tragedy : Crown	16/11/2009

Ugarte,[10] but the marriage ended in divorce. About 1900 Hector Baltazzi moved to Paris; in 1914 he returned to Vienna where he died in 1916.

Aristide Baltazzi, 1853–1914, was also an excellent horseman as well as being an outstanding horse-breeder. He married Maria Theresa, Countess of Stockau, and through her he came into possession of the famous Nepajedl stud, which he made known the world over. He was elected member of the Jockey Club.[11]

Theodore's fourth son, Heinrich Baltazzi, born on August 5, 1858, served with the 5th Hussaren Regiment, and like his brothers, was a splendid horseman. He married Paula Freiin von Scharschmid von Adelstreu, and they had two daughters and one son. It so happened that in the 1880's his regiment was stationed near Pardubitz, where Heinrich built stables and a practice course for jumping horses. Countess Marie Larisch practiced on it while her husband was busy re-building their house in the neighbourhood. Helen Vecsera often came to stay with her two brothers; she already knew Marie Larisch from Gödöllö, where she and her brothers Aristide and Hector had been staying with Prince Nicholas Esterházy. Gradually Marie and Helen became close friends.

It is something of a mystery why Albin Vecsera never took his wife Helen with him to his various postings—St Petersburg, Lisbon, Hesse-Darmstadt, Cairo. Helen had the money, the talent, and the ambition to entertain in proper style. Yet he settled her and the children—they had four in due course—in Vienna, in 11 Schüttelstrasse, the house in which Mary Vecsera was born on March 11, 1871, and which stands to this day.

Mary was baptised at the church of St Nepomuk, her Aunt Marie-Virginie (at that time Countess von Wallsee) acting as godmother. Helen later rented the Castle of Schwarzau, to which Mary referred in her farewell letter, saying that Mayerling reminded her of Schwarzau. She also travelled on her own, visiting brothers in Pardubitz, sisters Elizabeth and Marie-Virginie in England, and Charlotte in Hungary. But as far as is known, she never visited Albin at any of his posts.

Apart from bringing up her children, which with plenty of staff took up little of her time, Helen Vecsera was determined to establish herself as a hostess in the so-called First Society. In the second half of the 19th century there were three social strata in Austria. The First Society was just another name for the princely and old aristocratic families, whose sixty-four quarterings entitled them to be received at Court, and who looked down upon other mortals.

The Second Society consisted of high grade civil servants (some of whom wielded great power), top ranking soldiers, untitled nobility (some of these families were much older than those of the great nobles); heads of the big banks and big business concerns; and possibly some composers as the Viennese prided themselves on their love of music; and a very few intellectuals, like Professor Theodor Billroth. These people received Helen Vecsera with open arms as one of them; but she had no intention of remaining on their rung of the social ladder.

The Third Social Layer was made up of the wealthy Jewish families like the Rothschilds, joined by new multi-millionaires like Baron von Hirsch; Jewish intellectuals like Maurice Szeps, poets like the part Jewish Hugo von Hoffmansthal, some gentile businessmen in whose interest it was to keep on friendly terms with their Jewish competitors.

Helen set about her social campaign with great skill. First of all she got herself a superb chef, and her brothers built up her cellar. Then she began to entertain in perfect taste, which was soon the talk of Vienna. In 1886, Albin bought her a large house, Salesianergasse [which was pulled down in 1921]. Through her brothers she met a number of aristocrats[12] in the racing world, who accepted Helen's hospitality, even if they did not return it. Some of the wives came and could not help being impressed by the delightful manners and exquisite food of 'the Levantine woman'.

It is very likely that Marie Larisch also helped—for a consideration. She took money from little Mary Vecsera for introducing her to the Crown Prince; she is sure to have asked to be rewarded for introducing Helen Vecsera to aristocratic families. At any rate, Helen did make progress; she also cultivated diplomats, among whom she acquired friends. She was invited to the large parties of the German Ambassador, Prince Reuss, and—in view of her English connections—by the English Ambassador, Sir Augustus Paget.

In 1879, when the Crown Prince was twenty-one years old and she thirty-two, she tried to start a flirtation with him, and rented a villa for the summer in Gödöllö, contriving opportunities to be in his company. Countess Marie Festetics, who missed little in the life of the Court, recorded in her diary on December 3, 1879, that one day at luncheon the Emperor remarked digustedly: 'That woman's antics with Rudolf are outrageous—riding after him wherever he goes. Today she has even given him a present. She will stop at nothing.'[13] Imperial disfavour had little effect, but in fact Rudolf was not to speak to Helen Vecsera for ten years.

Her daughter Mary had no interest in anything besides clothes and racing; her whole nature was shallow and frivolous.[14] Her uncles taught her everything about racing from the age of ten. She met the Prince of Wales on a racecourse in Baden-Baden. At Freudenau, the Viennese racecourse, she was well-known and the jockeys nicknamed her the Turf Angel. She also visited her father in Cairo at least three times and acted as hostess for him when she was fifteen. Countess Marie Larisch says in her book, *My Past*, that Mary had a passionate love affair with an Englishman in Cairo, and that she became his mistress.[15] Walburga Lady Paget in her *Embassies of Other Days* openly writes about Mary's lovers; so does Victor Wolfson.[16]

Mary was much more developed than the average Austrian girl, with marvellous 'speaking eyes', which attracted men of all sorts. Stephanie says in her memoirs[17] that the Vecsera girl was described to her as 'bewilderingly lovely, tall, slender, beautifully made, with small hands and feet, she has masses of dark silky hair, and the complexion of a lily. The contrast between the black eyelashes and the periwinkle blue eyes is remarkable.' Helen planned a brilliant season for her favourite child during the winter of 1889. Mary's eighteenth birthday was on March 11. Helen knew that her daughter was infatuated with the Crown Prince, but she regarded this as a silly, childish phase, which she would duly outgrow.[18] The three-years-older Hanna knew her sister far better, and took a very different view of the hysterical, highly sexed Mary. She even suspected that Mary was pestering Marie Larisch to arrange a meeting with the Crown Prince. Helen would not even listen to Hanna's warnings—until it was too late.

She took her two daughters to London in 1887 and in 1888; she ignored Mary's efforts to stay at home in Vienna in 1888 so that she should not miss seeing Rudolf occasionally. In London, Helen Vecsera moved in distinguished circles (as I had occasion to find out[19]) but neither trip brought any desirable suitor.

Walburga Lady Paget described Mary Vecsera as a 'pretty but very fast girl. I never liked her on account of her flirtations with married men.'[20] With her mixed ancestry, brought up in self-indulgent circles as she was, it is no surprise that Mary Vecsera became the tragic victim of Mayerling. Circumstances conspired to form her so that she became ideal material for the romantic part and *grande passion* she had dreamt up for herself, centred around the glamorous personality of the Crown Prince. Longing for drama, and without any good sense or humour to counter-balance her silly romantic notions, on November 5, 1888, Mary Vecsera met the Crown Prince.[21]

20

Mary Vecsera provides Distraction

It is a commonplace that men and women are thrown into each other's arms not merely by mutual, or one-sided infatuation, but by the pressure of outside events. Infatuation is all the more irresistible when it provides a diversion and release from the burdens of reality. Such indeed was the case with Crown Prince Rudolf. When he and Mary Vecsera first met, and faced each other alone, on November 5, 1888, the Crown Prince was being driven to the verge of nervous collapse by four factors in his life.

In the first place, he found himself the victim of a vitriolic newspaper campaign which Szeps had predicted would be launched against him. It began on November 20, 1888, the day after Rudolf had a heavy fall from his horse, and suffered from excruciating headaches and from stomach upset. In the handwritten, stencilled Viennese news-sheet, *Dehnsche Korrespondenz*,[1] appeared an article entitled 'Austria's Hostility to Germany'. It referred unmistakably to the Crown Prince as the source of this policy. It based its case on articles in the Paris *Figaro*, the Viennese weekly *Schwarz-Gelb*, and the Budapest *Pester Lloyd*. All these articles were re-published in full in the *Dehnsche Korrespondenz* which called on the German public to take notice of the existence of political attitudes antagonistic to Germany and of the desire of certain circles to change Austria's political alliances. The implication was that Rudolf approved—if he had not actually initiated—this change in policy. The subject was promptly taken up in Germany by the *Deutsches Tageblatt* and the *Schlesische Zeitung*. Bismarck's directives were at the back of this campaign, and were specifically intended to distract Rudolf's shattered nerves.

These controversial articles were calculated to arouse the greatest agitation in the German Empire as well as in the Monarchy. Of course the Austrian and the Hungarian papers were not going to take these attacks on Rudolf lying down. The *Wiener Fremdenblatt*, the *Pester Lloyd*, and a number of other papers challenged their veracity. Whereupon the *Nord-Deutsche Allgemeine Zeitung* entered the lists, and the *Neue Preussische Kreuzzeitung*, the official paper of the Prussian Conservatives,[2] came out with an article expressly directed against the Crown Prince. There developed a regular newspaper war. It is revealing of the treatment Rudolf received from the Ballhausplatz that he was not provided with copies of these papers; he had to ask Szeps to send him, as soon as he could lay hands on it, at least a copy of the *Kreuzzeitung* which attacked him personally by name.

But a newspaper war in which the German Emperor—whose extravagantly hostile comments were common knowledge—and the heir to the Austrian throne were involved, could not be regarded lightly. It was the central subject of public debate in Germany and in the Monarchy; so much so that the *Deutsches Tageblatt* said on November 25: 'With the decease of Francis Joseph and the accession of Crown Prince Rudolf, the demand for a change of Viennese policy will be upon us.' What is more, and Rudolf of course knew it, the German Government was not at variance with the views expressed in the German Press; certainly not Bismarck who had masterminded it. When at last both Governments wanted to call a halt, the *Nord-Deutsche Allgemeine Zeitung* did not at once withdraw its attacks on Rudolf personally and its stance in this respect certainly had official encouragement.

First the Crown Prince expressed his suspicion to his great friend Ladislaus von Szögyény-Marich, Head of Department at the Foreign Ministry, that the whole affair had been instigated by his enemies of the conservative clerical and the anti-Semitic factions. Rudolf tried to defuse this danger by making fun of it. The leading article in the *Wiener Tagblatt* was certainly inspired, if not written, by him. He said that Germany's keen interest had contributed to the development of a state consciousness in Austria, where this had not existed before. Let the Germans be a little less aggressively patriotic, wrote the *Wiener Tagblatt*, and the Austrians would soon cool down. Later Rudolf changed his mind and told Szögyény-Marich that this campaign originated in Germany with the approval of Bismarck. In the spring of 1888 similar attacks had already appeared; in October in a much-discussed book, *La Fin D'Un Monde*, the author—Edouard Adolphe Drumont[3]—was extremely critical of Rudolf; in the introduction he re-printed the Pernestorfer speech in Parliament, implying that the Crown Prince was the guilty party who had jumped his horse over a funeral hearse; on November 11, *L'Epoca* in Italy reported: 'It is well known that Prince Rudolf leads a most dissolute life.' What was particularly sinister was that Szeps and his friends could not find out who was the author of the *Kreuzzeitung* article. All they knew was that the ideas came from someone in the reactionary Court circle.

The German Government was also in a difficult position. It had to determine whether Rudolf was directly or indirectly connected with the incriminating articles in the periodical *Schwarz-Gelb*. From these articles the Russian *Moskowskaya Wiedomosti* drew the conclusion that Austria was merely waiting for the accession of Rudolf to take firm steps against hated Prussia. The official assurance from the Ballhausplatz that the Crown Prince had nothing to do with *Schwarz-Gelb*, or with any of the articles published in connection with the anti-Prussian campaign, was received with relief in Berlin. This time Bismarck's minions had overshot the mark. Nevertheless, whoever examines today the propagandist essays of *Schwarz-Gelb*, must admit that they are in line with the Crown Prince's utterances about the Monarchy's mission in the Balkans, with his impatience over Prussian domination; with his conviction of the strength of the French Army and his interest in the Southern Slavs. But for once, it suited Bismarck to bring the revealing—the far too revealing—newspaper campaign to an end. Whoever had written the original article in *Schwarz-Gelb*, whether a professional journalist, a wild ultra-montaner, or a member of the *Golden International* (as the bankers and financiers were called), one thing is certain: the unknown author scored a signal and surprising success.

The Chief of the German General Staff at this time was Alfred Count Waldersee.[4] He had been appointed by the Kaiser and was an implacable foe of Bismarck, whom he hoped to succeed. It was his trusted agent in Vienna who reported: 'The last Press war has also made a very bad impression on the Austrian Army. The loyalty of our intentions has begun to be questioned. Such is always a favourable moment for our enemies to start agitating, and baiting us. The reprinting of the attack, as tactless as it is untrue, on the Austrian Crown Prince by our great conservative paper, is looked on with particular disfavour. Let us hope that the honourable efforts, made on both sides, will be successful in preventing the little superficial crack from becoming through machinations of our enemies a yawning chasm.'[5]

This report enabled General von Waldersee to lash out against the chancellor for his 'harmful attack' against Rudolf. Normally Waldersee, who was also an anti-Semite, was as opposed to the progressive Austrian Crown Prince as Bismarck, and would have fought him on political as well as ideological grounds.

While he was the centre of this embarrassing and enervating Press campaign, Rudolf suffered a deep humiliation in his plans for reform of the Army. He had been working extremely hard on a long and incisive report based on the deductions he had drawn from his strenuous inspection tours since his appointment as Inspector-General of the Infantry. He had incorporated them in a proposal for the modification of the drill programme of the infantry, which he intended to submit to the Emperor, with a covering letter which he had already drafted.[6] 'My inspections have brought me to the conclusion,' he wrote to his father, 'that it is high time to put an end to the abuses by revising the drill programme. I may add that the desire for such a revision, which I consider imperative, is very strong among the infantry.' Rudolf drew attention to the German Drill Book, a model of brevity and precise exposition, which contained a massive and most authoritative analysis of military problems, based on the experience of the latest campaigns. In fact, Rudolf had written new service rules, and hoped that they would form the basis for the reorganisation of the armed forces, especially the infantry.

Rudolf revised his report once more and sent it the next day to his father. On November 20, 1888, he received an answer not from the Emperor, but from Field Marshal Archduke Albert, who wrote in his own hand: 'With regard to the revision of the Drill Book of the Imperial Infantry proposed in this report, such has been under consideration for some time, and I have already expressed my opinion thereon to the Chief of the General Staff.[7] I cannot conceal, in conclusion, the fact that, as I have since his appointment endeavoured as far as possible to make up for the deficiencies of the General-Inspector of Infantry, I think I am justified in claiming the chairmanship of the proposed Commission.'

This slap in the face was the final blow for Rudolf. That his seventy-one-year-old Uncle Albert, whom he considered 'no longer equal to his work physically and perhaps even more, morally',[8] should have the effrontery to say that he had 'to make up for the deficiencies of the General-Inspector of Infantry', that is for the deficiencies of Rudolf, was the ultimate insult. His father, the Emperor, did not rebuke Archduke Albert: he did not even point out how conscientious Rudolf's work had been. Clearly, Rudolf had no future in the Army if Albert's views prevailed, and if Albert could again pose as the Emperor's closest and most influential adviser.

Rudolf also had financial problems which were pressing, if not catastrophic. Like Queen Victoria, Francis Joseph gave his son and heir a comparatively modest allowance. With his limited means, Rudolf could neither invest, nor participate in large-scale enterprises; he could not even give the kind of presents he wanted to give, especially to Mizzi Caspar, for whom he was anxious to provide. For instance, Mizzi's furniture had not been paid for.[9] As a result—like the Prince of Wales, he borrowed large sums first from Eduard Palmer,[10] a wealthy banker, then from the celebrated Maurice Baron von Hirsch.

Hirsch was born in 1831 in Munich, the eldest son of Baron Joseph von Hirsch and grandson of Baron Jakob von Hirsch, the first Jewish landowner in Bavaria, ennobled in 1818. From his father and grandfather Hirsch inherited considerable wealth, which was augmented by the large dowry of his Belgian wife, Clara Bischofsheim. Encouraged by her, he embarked in railway enterprises in Austria and in the Balkans, and took up the railway building concession Crown Prince Rudolf had obtained from Sultan Abdul Hamid in 1883. He formed a construction company, employed the best railway engineers in Europe and personally superintended the laying of the railway lines through the Balkans to Constantinople. Then he formed a company to run the soon famous Orient Express for him. That is when the Austrians with their wry sense of humour nicknamed him *der Türkenhirsch*.[11]

The enormous success that crowned Hirsch's work, contrary to the predictions of conservative bankers—the Rothschilds in particular—made him the leading captain of industry and finance in the world. In 1886 his fortune was estimated at 300 million *Gulden*—the equivalent of £30m. at the time, at 1976 valuation over £500m.[12]

This was a man after Rudolf's heart, and through Szeps he came to meet and befriend him. Hirsch and his wife had social ambitions, in which Rudolf was only too willing to help. According to Stephanie, who detested both Baron and Baroness von Hirsch, the baron loaned considerable sums to Rudolf who—in exchange—had to provide him with political information. This was most unlikely, as Rudolf did not possess any special information. Szeps could and did place at Hirsch's disposal all the latest news he had collected. But Rudolf helped Hirsch in a different manner; for instance in 1886 he introduced him to the Prince of Wales, whose financial adviser and creditor Hirsch became, and remained until his death in 1896.

Unfortunately Rudolf's correspondence with Hirsch has not come to light, but in view of the enormous donations Hirsch made for establishing schools in Galicia and the Bukovina, and Rudolf's sympathy for Jews in general, it can be assumed that he discussed these far-reaching schemes with Rudolf. There may be reports and comments on Rudolf's relations with Hirsch in the Rothschild archives, but they are not at present available to researchers.

Rudolf was far too intelligent not to realise that the treatment and medication he received did not improve his venereal disease; on the contrary, the pains in his loins and his joints grew worse; his eyes worried him very much; not only were they constantly inflamed, but he saw badly and towards the end of his life he felt as though he were going blind. For his eyes his physician prescribed the then standard remedy of yellow mercury precipitate, as well as eye drops containing *Zincum Sulfuricum* in 50 g. Ag. Dest.

Rudolf also suffered from severe ear-ache; and for all these ailments he had only one answer: more and more morphine. He could obtain a certain amount on his physician's prescription, but with the increasing quantities he used, this did not begin to suffice. Therefore he had to obtain the rest by other means. No wonder Rudolf spent his time with cab-drivers and prostitutes—he was gradually sinking into despair and had no one, apart from Szeps, with whom he cared even to discuss his plight.

He realised what his life would be like if this deterioration continued. The physicians either talked unintelligible medicalese, or gave tactful non-committal answers to his questions; his parents noticed nothing. His immediate entourage were at last becoming concerned and discussed the prince's condition among themselves, but they would not have dared to suggest anything to Rudolf. The servants were very worried about the changed appearance of their master; the devoted Rudolf Püchel was overheard to tell a valet: 'What is the matter with Rudolf?[13] He is quite unlike his usual self—he looks terrible, he shouts, bangs the doors. . . . *Du lieber Gott*, I hope he is not really ill. . . .'

The one person who was aware of Rudolf's deteriorating condition, and who wanted to do something about it, was Stephanie. In her memoirs she wrote: 'On my return from Greece in October . . . I was horrified as soon as I set eyes on the Crown Prince. His decay was so greatly advanced as to have become conspicuous. He was frightfully changed; his skin was flaccid, his eyes were restless, his expression was completely changed. It seemed as if his lineaments had lost the inner substantiality, which can only come from strength of will, as if a process of internal dissolution were going on. I was profoundly sorry for him, and wondered how the devastation would end.'

Stephanie then decided to take the one action that might have saved the situation. 'In my intense anxiety I determined to go to the Emperor and speak to him unreservedly in such a way as could not fail to open his eyes about everything, without reserve and ruthlessly. I clung to the thought that his intervention would save us both from disaster. I was only twenty-four . . . I had not yet completely lost confidence in my elders.

'Although it was contrary to all rules of etiquette to approach the Emperor uninvited, I took my courage in both hands and asked the chamberlain to announce me. The Emperor received me kindly. I began by telling him that Rudolf was extremely ill, and that my husband's appearance and behaviour caused me great anxiety. I earnestly begged the Emperor to send his son on a journey round the world which might remove him from a life which was wearing him down. Emperor Francis Joseph interrupted me by saying: "You are giving way to fancies, my dear. There is nothing the matter with Rudolf. I know he is rather pale, gets about too much, expects too much of himself. He ought to stay at home with you more than he does. Don't be anxious!" The Emperor embraced me; I kissed his hand. I had been dismissed, and had not been allowed to pour out my heart in the way I expected.' Francis Joseph intimated to her that in future she was to approach him only through his equerry. 'Tottering and trembling, I made my way into the ante-room, where I had to sit down for a time. Was nothing more to come of this last hope? It seemed to me that the Crown Prince's fate was sealed. I feared the worst—a wasting away which would be more horrible than death.'[14]

Why Stephanie did not take her grave problem to the Empress who, according to Frau Schratt and her ladies in waiting, was also deeply concerned over Rudolf, is inexplicable. She was the one person who, had she so wished, could have talked to her son and influenced the Emperor. But Stephanie (perhaps because she knew that Elizabeth did not like her) never thought of confiding in her mother-in-law. Admittedly in October 1888 Elizabeth was in Greece,[15] but Stephanie could at least have written to her.

Burdened as he was to the point of desperation, it is not surprising that Rudolf was the willing recipient of consolation from the love-sick girl who threw herself at him on November 5, 1888. At about eleven o'clock of that morning, Marie Larisch drove in her un-numbered *Fiakker* to 11 Salesianergasse in Vienna. She had arranged with Baroness Helen Vecsera to take her daughter Mary out shopping. Yet their way led not to Vienna's smart shops, but to the Augustiner entrance approach of the Hofburg, one of the few parts of the medieval fortifications to survive the city's extension in 1887. Marie Larisch ordered the cab-driver to stop by a small black iron door, which gave access to an oval staircase leading up to the flat roof, which formed a kind of terrace with a railing, extending as far as the *Schweitzerhof*, where the Crown Prince's bachelor apartments were.

'An old servant was waiting for us,' Marie Larisch has written in her book, *My Past*. 'He led us up several stairs and through several rooms until we reached one in which he left us. At our entrance a black bird—some kind of raven—flew at my head.' According to a well-known tradition, a black raven appeared whenever a member of the Habsburg family was to die. This was a tame raven which lived in Rudolf's gunroom, hung with quantities of antlers and trophies. Mary Vecsera was startled by the bird, but as she had not heard of the legend, it made no great impression on her.

The Crown Prince received them with great courtesy. Using all his charm, he apologised to Mary for leaving her on her own for a few minutes as he had something important to discuss with his cousin. As usual, Marie Larisch was heavily in debt, and she tried to get some money from Rudolf. This time he refused. As Marie Larisch had to meet a debt of 25,000 Gulden, a few days later she got Mary Vecsera to write a letter to Rudolf to the effect that she and her sister Hanna had given the Countess this money out of their own pockets.[16] Mary, feeling indebted to her friend Marie, asked the Crown Prince for 25,000 Gulden, and a Court footman brought it the same day. At a later date Marie again asked, this time for 10,000 Gulden, but presumably Rudolf got the truth out of Mary, and refused to provide a single *Pfennig*. Baroness Nancy (Ferdinanda) Vecsera, Mary Vecsera's niece,[17] possesses a copy of Hanna Vecsera's memorandum whose postscript describes Marie's extortions in detail.

In Rudolf's apartment it took Mary Vecsera a little time to collect herself; later in the day she wrote to her confidante, Hermine,[18] an almost incoherent letter: 'The greatest wish of my life has been consummated—I have made his acquaintance—I have met HIM.' He had spoken to her, and he was even more charming than she had expected. 'I examined everything that was lying on the writing table. A revolver, a skull[19] . . . I picked up the latter and looked at it from all sides. All at once he came in, and quite startled took it out of my hands.' The visit lasted only half an hour. As they were leaving, Rudolf told Marie Larisch: 'Bring her to me soon again, please!'

Marie Larisch ushered Mary out of the apartment and, guided by a servant called Hloček,[20] they reached the Augustiner entrance by the same complicated way as they had come.

Mary was in a state of ecstasy. Her happiness was greater than she had dared to hope—her dream had at last come true.

Rudolf was flattered by the unbounded adoration of the young girl who did not try to hide her feelings for him. In his profound depression, this cheered him somewhat, and he talked about it to his cousin, Otto, and his brother-in-law, Philip Coburg. Their ragging about his irresistible charm even to a young beauty like Mary Vecsera did some good to Rudolf's pitifully low morale.

21

Death Planned by his own Hand

In November 1888 Rudolf reached the point at which he felt that he had nothing to look forward to in the Army; as long as his father lived, he could have no influence on general policy-making; the only chance he had had of attaining power legitimately—the Junior Kingship offered him by Tisza—he had thrown away. His marriage was a wreck, and it was his fault that Stephanie could not produce an heir. His health was not only deteriorating but he had the impression that he was going to pieces.

The anonymous author of the *Berliner Börzen Courier* article, whose identity has never been revealed, put it this way: 'Crown Prince Rudolf's mental life showed signs of serious disturbance for two years; he seemed to have been noticeably unbalanced since the autumn of 1888. If people had been as well acquainted then as they are today with the mode of life and certain typical utterances which escaped him, he would have been carefully watched and placed under medical care.' This is what Stephanie wanted so badly, but she found no support from anyone.

Dr Anthony Stevens, the English psychiatrist who has read the accounts of Rudolf's mental condition, has commented: 'Rudolf had not only to suffer what you have mentioned; he also foresaw political disasters which his father refused to allow him to attempt to prevent. It was enough to make anyone depressed and attracted to suicide. But in Rudolf's case there were the additional factors of gonorrhoea, syphilis and morphia addiction, to say nothing of an excessive dependency on alcohol. These factors would account for his restlessness, irritability, moodiness, tension and outbursts of rage.'[1] To this must be added indications of one more calamity: Anton, Count Monts, reports in his memoirs: 'In 1886 young Austrian aristocrats told me, according to authentic confidences of certain beauties, that the Crown Prince was like Abelard after his operation.'[2] If Rudolf had become impotent, no wonder he considered his physical condition hopeless and decided to make an end of it. If Mary temporarily restored his virility, obviously she had an influence on him.

In the 1880's the condition from which Rudolf suffered was not recognised, as it is today, as a mental illness. Oscar von Mitis gives the following description of it: 'A typical case of this disease often presents striking contrasts; the sunshine of a perfect joy of living, great mental ability and a highly principled temperament gradually or suddenly dissolve into the shadows of deranged mental processes, pleasure in the commonplace, uncontrolled eroticism, rejection of the moral laws, restlessness, repellent outbreaks of anguish and despair cast on the life of the afflicted person. Such people stand on the borderline between health and indubitable mental disorder, and a study of their character consequently means a study of the disease.'[3]

It is Dr Anthony Stevens' opinion that Ruldolf suffered from what would nowadays be recognised as a form of depression.[4]

Rudolf had been talking of shooting himself ever since the summer of 1888. He said that he had to make an end of it because his honour demanded it.[5] Why his honour demanded it, he did not explain either to Mizzi Caspar or to Stephanie.

At this advanced stage of his illness Rudolf proposed to Victor von Fritsche, that they should commit suicide together.[6] When the amazed Fritsche refused in some agitation, the Crown Prince made the same proposal to Colonel Baron Arthur von Giesel,[7] one of his staff officers, with the same result. As both these men categorically refused to die with him, in December 1888 Rudolf asked Mizzi Caspar whether she would commit suicide with him in the *Husaren Templ* in Mödling?[8] With his theatrical inclination, Rudolf wanted to take his life in this sham Greek temple in the company of Mizzi, because he was afraid that he might not have the courage if he tried to do it on his own. But Mizzi had no intention of dying; on the contrary, she wanted to save Rudolf and went to see the Police President, Baron von Kraus. He listened to her, but tried to make light of her story; when Mizzi explained persuasively that the Crown Prince was determined to die, Kraus threatened her if she dared to say one word to anyone about this.[9]

Krauss must have discussed Mizzi's revelations with the Prime Minister; what advice he received from Taaffe is not known; but he certainly was not told to report to the one person who could and would have done something: the Empress. It was common talk subsequently in Vienna that Taaffe did not want to stop Rudolf from committing suicide, because he disliked him and feared for the future if Rudolf ever had a chance of introducing his liberal principles. Krauss could not have acted on his own, especially as the year before he had failed to prevent Queen Natalie of Serbia being cheered by her fellow nationals, and the Emperor demanded his dismissal. Krauss, with the help of Taaffe, cleared himself. He could not risk any move that might annoy the Emperor, or his protector, Taaffe.

For Christmas, 1888, the Imperial Family foregathered as usual at the Hofburg. It was a happy occasion, for Rudolf's sister, Marie Valerie, announced her engagement to Archduke Franz Salvator. At first Rudolf had disapproved of the prospective groom, but then, probably under Elizabeth's influence, he changed his mind. During the Christmas festivities Rudolf warmly embraced Valerie and wished her much happiness; Elizabeth then asked him to give her a solemn promise that he would always aid and support his little sister. Rudolf solemnly promised, but with such a sad expression that Valerie felt almost frightened—she had an uncanny premonition that something would happen to Rudolf. He had presented the Empress with some handwritten copies of Heine's poems, which Szeps had managed to buy for him, because she was extremely fond of Heine. There were three Christmas trees; one for the Emperor and the Empress; another for Valerie and her groom; a third for Rudolf, Stephanie and little Erzsi, who was by then five and a half years old.

Rudolf and Stephanie then went together to Abbazia, where Rudolf left his wife to her own devices and returned to Vienna. On December 31, 1888, he wrote to her the following letter:

Dear Stephanie!

I send you every good wish for the New Year, health and pleasant days, cheerful times, the fulfilment of all your desires. It is not cold here but far from being as warm as Abbazia, and it is very damp with perpetual fog. The little one has a cold but, thanks be, no sore throat. She is very cheerful and rompish. Uncle Louis thought he was dying yesterday. The Hofburg chaplain was in attendance; the next of kin, the Emperor at the head of them, were assembled round the bed of the dying man. I was conspicuous by my absence for apparently no one knew whether I was back in Vienna, and where I was to be found. Widerhofer[10] says Uncle Louis is now out of danger, can get up tomorrow, and dine the day after with his usual excellent appetite. Now I must drive off to Adler with Pausinger. With renewed good wishes and fondest love,

Your most affectionate
Coco'[11]

Typical of a person suffering from a depressive condition, Rudolf wrote this humorous letter to Stephanie while trying to find a partner with whom to make a suicide pact. On the one hand Stephanie saw very clearly what was happening to Rudolf; on the other, her non-comprehension of Rudolf's state of mind was astonishing. Compare these two passages of Stephanie's memoirs: 'During the last two years of his life, there occurred a change in the Crown Prince's whole nature. He suffered more and more from nervous unrest and from violent temper, culminating in what was tantamount to complete mental decay, added to the ill-effects of his transitory *amours*, which became more and more frequent, and more and more entangling was the fact that he drank heavily. By the immoderate consumption of alcoholic liquors, he tried to whip up his nervous system for the efforts demanded by unceasing activities, by military duties which he took very seriously, and by his eager participation in political affairs, and by the irregularities of his personal life.'[12]

Stephanie continued: 'The Crown Prince, in fact, was of a strangely two-fold nature, mingling contrasts in a single personality. He had a great respect for the Emperor; but was ready to fling this respect to the wind as soon as anyone reminded him that he himself would one day mount the throne. His conviction was that he was pre-destined to inaugurate a new era, and he was ready to hazard everything on a single cast of the dice.'[13] And then she gave her own explanation of Rudolf's unstable mind in the following terms: 'The roots of all the Crown Prince's later troubles lay in his education. It was exemplary as far as it was concerned with drilling him for the occupation of a ruler, much as one drills a recruit for soldiering. Nothing was omitted that would serve his knowledge or studies. Only one thing was overlooked: that the most important thing for a young man is the education of his soul. Although reverence and obedience to the Church and its usages were impressed on him, he was never permeated by the spirit of Christianity. The training of his heart was neglected; he had no true fear of God; he lacked a sense of duty and responsibility—so that later, when life came to make its claim on him, he lacked the power of religious faith and moral restraint.'[14] In view of his farewell letters, it is clear that he had a good deal more religious faith than Stephanie gave Rudolf credit for.

To quote once more the anonymous *Berliner Börzen Courier* article: 'In addition, Rudolf had the gnawing restlessness of the Wittelsbach character inherited from his mother, which was apparent even to comparative strangers, and might be thought responsible for the transformations of his appearance, such as repeated changes in his fashion of growing his beard. Towards the end . . . people were surprised by the lightning changes in his opinions, and this is a warning to us to exercise great care in the valuation of changes in his political outlook.'

One such was Rudolf's attitude *vis-à-vis* Russia. For years he had insisted on the necessity of having a well prepared war against the tsarist empire in order to ensure the Monarchy's civilising mission in the Balkans, and he put up with the German alliance because Austria needed German support for this war. Suddenly, after Christmas, 1888, Rudolf begged the Emperor to send him to St Petersburg to clear up the interests of the two states in the Balkans. It could be explained by Rudolf having learnt of the so-called Re-Insurance Treaty, in which Bismarck had agreed that the Russians should have the whole of the Balkans as their sphere of influence; if there could be no war to evict Russia from the Balkans, Rudolf thought that a division of their respective spheres of influence would be best, and urgent, for as soon as Russia negotiated an alliance with France, which Rudolf foresaw, Russia's price would go up. After prolonged reflection, the Emperor gave his approval to Rudolf's journey, on condition that he first accompanied him on a State visit to Berlin.

After the Mayerling tragedy László Szögyény-Marich told the Russian Chargé d'Affairs, Kantakuzene, that the Emperor's decision had given no end of pleasure to Rudolf, and had been the only ray of light after months' of disappointments and humiliations.[15] Szögyény, who for years had seen a good deal of Rudolf, had no idea, in fact would not believe when subsequently told, of the mental derangement of the Crown Prince. Rudolf had never shown Szögyény the suicidal side of his personality.

Whether Rudolf gained the impression that the Emperor had in theory agreed to his Russian plan, but in fact would go on postponing the visit indefinitely, or whether he just was driven to suicide by his depression, it is impossible to tell. It may have been a combination of both reasons.

By January, 1889, he had decided to make an end of it all.

22

The Last Hours of Rudolf with Mary

The little Vecsera girl, who was so wildly in love with the Crown Prince, was just the person he needed for the desperate plan to do away with himself. Mary had been to see Rudolf five times at the Hofburg; they had met a few times either in the Prater or on short drives with Bratfisch. On January 13 she had become his mistress; on January 18 she had given him a golden cigarette case, in which was engraved: 'With gratitude to a kind fate. January 13, 1889.' Rudolf, who showed this to his brother-in-law, Philip of Coburg, was convinced that Mary Vecsera was willing to die with him. Stephanie wrote in her memoirs: 'Since he could find no male friend willing to join him in this sacrifice, he traded upon Mary Vecsera's passion to ask her to join him. She agreed unhesitatingly and blindly. Mary Vecsera was a typical species of her race, the kind of woman frequently to be encountered in the East. There were plenty of far more beautiful women in Vienna, and the Crown Prince was used to finding that no woman could resist him. He was not in love with Mary Vecsera, she was to him only one woman among many. But she was passionately attached to him; and in view of the fact that her love for him brought her in a position from which there was no sane issue, she gladly accompanied him to death. This acknowledgement that Mary Vecsera had a profound and sincere love for the Crown Prince can be the flower which I, the deceived wife, place in forgiveness upon the resting-place of the poor misguided girl.'[1]

Rudolf felt that he had to die because his honour demanded it, and because his life had no more meaning. Yet had there been any real change in his father's attitude, he would have been glad to live, for he told his sister Valerie:[2] 'If only I could live to be a hundred, it is awful to think that in the end one has to die.' But there was no change in the Emperor's attitude; moreover the psychiatric authorities of Vienna were to state after Rudolf's death: 'Even rigorous interference in September or October 1888 could not have prevented the calamity; the Prince indeed might not have killed himself, but he would have pined away slowly. Fate would have left him but two alternatives—either to share the destiny of King Ludwig of Bavaria [suicide after he was to be declared insane], or that of Prince Otho of Bavaria [natural death in a state of complete mental derangement]. Both were cousins of the Crown Prince. The hopes entertained of his future career would never have been realised.' This much of the pychiatrists' report was published in the *Berliner Börzen Courier*.

On January 13, 1889, Mary Vecsera wrote to Hermine:[3] 'Dear Hermine! Today I must make a confession to you which will make you very angry. I was with him yesterday from seven to nine. We both lost our heads. Now we belong to each other with body and soul.' She added that now she had to do whatever he asked her. And what he asked her we can infer from the fact that on January 19, 1889, Mary Vecsera made her will. Her sister Hanna suspected that her many excuses for not going to the opera or to parties had an ulterior motive; unfortunately she did not know that Mary corresponded with the Crown Prince through her maid, and Rudolf's faithful old Nehammer.

When Mary could get away, which was surprisingly often, the Crown Prince waited for her in Bratfisch's unnumbered cab in the Marokkanergasse, just round the corner from the Salesianerstrasse. She also begged her chaperone not to reveal to her mother that she had bought a golden cigarette case, nor that she had gone to a fortune-teller who, most unusually, told her that she would die in the near future.

On January 26 Mary's chaperone reported to Baroness Vecsera that on January 15 Mary had bought a golden cigarette case and had something engraved on it. She begged her not to tell her mother; thinking it was a surprise for the Baroness, the chaperone agreed. But on January 25 Mary forced her to accompany her to a fortune-teller, with whom she had a secret discussion. This visit was so unpleasant that the chaperone decided to make a clean breast of it all.

Mary had several hysterical attacks; once she fainted in Marie

Larisch's sitting-room at the Grand Hotel; when Marie brought her home she fainted once more in her bedroom to the great distress of her sister Hanna, who insisted that her mother should at last question her. This time Helen was firm with her favourite child and, ignoring Mary's sobbing, made her open her iron deedbox, in which she found her will and a steel cigarette case with Rudolf's initials and coronet on it. Amidst more sobs Mary swore she had received the cigarette case from Marie Larisch—a lie—who had given it to her because she knew how much she admired the Crown Prince. Marie Larisch, when asked by Helen Vecsera confirmed Mary's lie and said that she had indeed given her the steel cigarette case. Mary owned up to her mother that she had sent, anonymously through a serviceman, a golden cigarette case to Rudolf. In fact she had given it to him personally. Marie Larisch promised Helen Vecsera that she would get it back from Rudolf. 'I know he will do it,' she said, 'he is very gracious to me these days.' What Marie Larisch did not tell her friend was that Rudolf was furious with her because of the money she tried to extort from him to pay her debts.

On January 27 (some historians think it may have been on January 26) the Emperor summoned Rudolf and took him severely to task about his relations with Mary Vecsera. According to General Albert Margutti[4] of the Adjutants' Office, the interview was a stormy one, yet at the end agreement was reached between father and son; Rudolf promised to give up Mary Vecsera, but asked his father for permission to see her once more, to which Francis Joseph agreed. The Emperor told Elizabeth of this, and she was extremely worried. As she told Kati Schratt, she knew her son and was certain that Rudolf would do something quite different from what the Emperor expected. But astonishingly Elizabeth still did not send for Rudolf to have a frank talk with him.

When Stephanie came back from Abbazia on January 12, she wrote 'When I returned from the south, I was once again struck by the change in the Crown Prince, and this time more strongly than ever. He was rarely sober, he did not get home to the Hofburg until dawn; and as for the company he kept, the less said the better. His restlessness and nervous irritability had become intensified. He spoke menacingly of horrible things, and, in my very presence would cruelly toy with the revolver he always carried about. I was so worried (and frightened) that I tried not to see him without a third person being present.'[5]

On January 27 Rudolf appeared for the last time in public at the ball given by the German Ambassador, Prince Reuss, in honour of Kaiser William II's first birthday as ruler. Francis Joseph also made an appearance at the party. There has been a lot of gossip about this ball: some guests related that Mary Vecsara had refused to curtsey to Crown Princess Stephanie; others that she was impertinent to her; yet others that the Emperor Francis Joseph cut his son dead. None of this is true, but it is a fact that Rudolf never took his eyes off Mary Vecsera, who was remarkably beautiful that night; Count Josef Hoyos said in his memorandum written three days after the Mayerling tragedy: 'The young lady of about twenty attracted my attention by her great beauty. Her eyes seemed much larger than they actually were and glittered almost mysteriously. Her whole person seemed on fire.'[6]

The impression Rudolf made on one very reliable witness, Walburga Lady Paget, wife of the British Ambassador, is on record. She left two days after the tragedy for Paris, where on February 3, 1889, at a luncheon at the German Embassy she told Count Alexander Hubner: 'I had a long talk with Crown Prince Rudolf at the Reuss reception. Like everyone else, I found him strikingly changed. He seemed dejected, sad and just fought back his tears.'[7] In her memoirs, *Embassies Of Other Days*, Walburga Paget also wrote that on January 24, at a dinner at the British Embassy, 'Crown Prince Rudolf seemed somehow different, less sarcastic, less down on people, and for the first time, he looked me in the eyes when speaking. . . . The only person he mentioned with bitterness was the Emperor of Germany, once his devoted friend, and he said: "How horrible is this constant fight with the ghost of his father . . ." '[8]

There is evidence that Rudolf appeared deeply perturbed by his decision, and by no means enthusiastic either about Mary Vecsera or about dying. In his book *Kaiser Karl*[9] Polzer-Hoditz, relates that he had occasion to read the telegrams that had passed between the Crown Prince and Mary Vecsera which, like all telegrams of the Imperial Family, were preserved at the Ministry of Communications. These showed quite plainly that 'the Baroness's love had become an inconvenience to the Crown Prince. This was obvious in spite of the careful language in which his refusals were couched.'

From the German Embassy Rudolf and Stephanie were back at the Hofburg about half-past eleven. Towards midnight the Crown Prince received Szeps in his bachelor apartment. Szeps recorded that 'the Crown Prince was indescribably upset, again and again he repeated: "The Emperor has openly affronted and degraded me. From now on all ties between us are broken. From now on I am free." ' Bertha Szeps connected this with the allegation that the Pope had returned Rudolf's letter requesting permission to divorce Stephanie, but Dr Fritz Judtmann has proved that this was untrue.[10] Then Rudolf went to see Mizzi. Dr Florian Meissner, the police informer, next day reported to Baron von Krauss: 'Archduke Rudolf was with Mizzi until three in the morning; drank a great deal of champagne, and gave the *concierge* 10 Gulden for letting him out. On taking leave from Mizzi, totally counter to his custom, he made the sign of the cross on her forehead.'[11]

It has been said many times—and Crown Princess Stephanie certainly believed it—that Rudolf's end was precipitated because he was involved in a conspiracy against his father: that, in fact, he had committed high treason. In her memoirs she wrote: 'When his secret plans had led him into a blind alley, he had no stamina to face the situation and could not back out. True, the real scope of his political plans will always remain wrapped in obscurity for written documents bearing on the matter have been destroyed. The Crown Prince never initiated me into the true nature of his designs. He had perhaps good reason for lacking confidence in me as far as these matters were concerned. What I gleaned of his intentions was wholly repugnant to me.

'I had an instinctive detestation of his favourite associates, and of those who involved him within the orbit of their liberal ideas. As regards the so-called "Hungarian schemes", of which, since his death, there has been much talk, the matter will for ever be veiled in darkness.

'When Count Szögyény in accordance with the terms of the

Prince's will opened the drawers of his writing table in my presence, the last documentary evidence about these matters was destroyed.'[12]

On this point Stephanie lied: in his final instructions to Szögyény Rudolf willed that he should open the drawers alone; hence Stephanie was not present. On April 8, 1889, Szögyény told the German Ambassador that he had finished sorting Rudolf's papers and had destroyed nothing.

The Hungarian writer, Emil Szittya, has made a case of the accusation of treason. He says in his book *Self-murderers* that in 1883, at Sáromberke, Teleki's country-house, in a state of heavy inebriation, Rudolf had signed a document promising the Hungarians to work for an independent Hungarian Army and an independent Hungary. Szittya knew of course that Teleki had gone to Africa in 1886, but he believed that the conspiracy of the other Hungarian aristocrats, headed by István Károlyi, had continued, and that they were planning to defeat the Government of Kálmán Tisza over the Army estimates which were to be debated in Parliament towards the end of January. At first Károlyi attacked the Government, but he did not say that he had received encouragement from 'high quarters' that an independent Hungarian Army would soon come into being. Károlyi's innocuous speeches were not published, and the general public was left to believe the untrue gossip about his having referred to the support of a very highly placed personage whom, in view of his friendship with the Crown Prince, everyone took to be Rudolf.

What cannot be stated with any certainty is in what activity Archduke Johann Salvator was involved. Many historians believe that he did carry on negotiations with Rudolf's Hungarian friends, and that they seriously discussed their plan to dethrone Francis Joseph, and make Rudolf King of Hungary, and to entrust Johann Salvator with the administration of the Austrian part of the Monarchy. In view of the tremendous respect Hungarians of all classes had for an anointed king, crowned with the Crown of St Stephen, it is highly improbable that these negotiations were very serious. How much Rudolf knew about them, or how much he cared when he had already decided to commit suicide, it is impossible to establish.

Marie Larisch tells a wild story about Rudolf having brought an iron deed-box to her at the Grand Hotel, to hold and to hide, and only hand over to the person who would use the pass-word: R.I.O.U. Marie relates that a few days after Rudolf's death she received a note requesting her to meet the anonymous writer at the dead of night in the Schwarzenberg Platz. She was approached by a man who gave the pass-word: R.I.O.U., and then revealed himself to be the Archduke Johann Salvator, who told her that the deed-box contained the documents which the Prime Minister, Taaffe, was desperately anxious to obtain as the basis on which he could have arraigned both Rudolf and himself before a military tribunal. Johann Salvator added: 'Rudolf has betrayed me—Rudolf was a weakling . . .'

In view of the many lies told by Marie Larisch, this episode is probably invention. To this day there is no firm evidence that Rudolf's death at Mayerling was attributable to his involvement in any treasonable plan against his father. The only serious indication that Rudolf had been involved in some Hungarian intrigue is a statement by Karl von Werkmann, Emperor Charles IV's Personal Secretary, quoted by Werner Richter in his biography of Rudolf, p. 241: 'We believe that Crown Prince Rudolf . . . had involved himself in a Hungarian adventure; later on he wanted to withdraw from it, but he could not find the way back. The personality who transmitted to us this as his conviction, knew from the Emperor Francis Joseph all the details, and therefore he really did know.' But even von Werkmann does not imply that Rudolf committed high treason.

And now the sands were running out. The story of how Marie Larisch took Mary Vecsera on January 28, 1889, at 10.30 a.m. to the Hofburg, where the cab-driver Josef Bratfisch waited for her, how he drove her to the *Roten Stadl*, a summer excursion place, where she met Rudolf, how they drove together to Mayerling; how on January 29 Rudolf breakfasted with his brother-in-law, Prince Philip of Coburg, and his old friend, Count Josef Hoyos; how he excused himself from going out with them to shoot because of a heavy cold, are well-known.

Equally well-known is the fact that he sent the following telegram to Stephanie:[13] 'Alland, January 29. Please write to Papa that I ask his pardon most obediently for not appearing at dinner, but because of a heavy cold I wish to avoid the journey this afternoon and stay here with Josl Hoyos. Embracing you all most warmly. Rudolf.'[14]

Stephanie was considerably embarrassed when she arrived alone at the dinner and had to hand the Emperor the telegram which she had just received. Agitated and frightened though she was, she did not have the courage to suggest to the Emperor that a doctor should be sent immediately to Mayerling. Anyone who wishes to read the details will find them in a number of books, the most up-to-date and extremely well-researched is that by Dr Fritz Judtmann, *The Facts Behind the Legend.*

From this and other accounts of Mayerling, it is clear that Crown Prince Rudolf intended to take his life because of his despair, enormously magnified by his mental illness. Everything that mattered to him in his personal life seemed to have gone.

Rudolf knew that his venereal disease was incurable; what he did not know was that he had also infected Mary Vecsera. In his original *post mortem* findings, Dr Auchenthaler stated that Mary as well as Rudolf suffered from gonorrhoea. These *post mortem* findings were communicated to the Emperor by the first Lord Chamberlain, then sealed and deposited at the Lord Chamberlain's Office. The findings were never published, except an excerpt. The original document has vanished.[15] General Baron Artur von Giesel made a statement about the original *post mortems* to *Lónyay*, who published it.[16]

Rudolf was convinced that the Monarchy was doomed because of Taaffe's reactionary policy, and the Hungarian ill-treatment of the nationalities. As he was not allowed to go to St Petersburg to reach an accommodation with the Tsar, he was certain that the Russians would ally themselves with the French, and be backed by the English. (And this is what happened—1914.)

At this time Rudolf began to toy with ideas about the soul, and about life after death, which he had hitherto rejected as contrary to biological law, and sheer nonsense. Yet that he intended to commit suicide is confirmed beyond any doubt by his farewell letters. The following were found in Mayerling and attested by witnesses:

1. A telegram to the Prior of Heiligenkreutz, its text partially known, asking him to come and pray by Rudolf's and Mary's side.

2. A note to his valet, Loschek, text known: 'Dear Loschek, Fetch a priest and have us interred in a common grave at Heiligenkreutz. My dear Mary's valuables and letters please hand over to Mary's mother. I thank you for your invariably loyal and devoted services throughout the many years which you served me.

   'See that the letter to my wife reaches her by the shortest route. Rudolf.'

To the Loschek instructions, Rudolf added a postscript: 'My greetings to Count Hoyos. The Baroness sends him the message that he is to remember what he told her about Mayerling on the evening of the reception of the German Ambassador, Prince Reuss. Hoyos is not to telegraph Vienna, only send to Heiligenkreutz for a priest that he should pray by my side.'

Owing to this mysterious message, Hoyos was questioned by members of the Imperial Chancellery, and by the Emperor himself, who wanted to know whether Hoyos had had an inkling of the relationship between Rudolf and Mary Vecsera. To prove that he had known nothing, and was barely acquainted with the Baroness who—to his surprise—had spoken to him twice at the Reuss reception, Hoyos wrote a long memorandum in two parts, on February 2 and 4, 1889. This is invaluable evidence for reconstructing what happened, and as Hoyos had been a devoted friend of the Crown Prince for ten years, it provides some indications as to why Rudolf wanted to die. The head of the Hoyos family made the Memorandum available to historians in 1923, after Josef Hoyos's death. It is kept at the Austrian State Archives in Vienna.

3. An undated letter to Szögyény which read:

   'Dear Szögyény, I must die—that is the only way at least to leave this world like a gentleman.

   Be so good as to open my desk here in Vienna, in the Turkish room where we so often sat together in happier days, and deal with my papers as set out in my last will, herewith enclosed.[17] With warmest regards and with all good wishes for yourself and our adored Hungarian Fatherland. I am yours ever. Rudolf'
4. A codicil to Szögyény's letter in German: 'Departmental Head

von Szögyény-Marich will be good enough to open my writing desk in the Turkish room in Vienna at once and alone. The following letters will be delivered: 1. To Valerie; 2. To my wife; 3. To Baron Hirsch; 4. To Mizzi Caspar. Any money that is found, please hand it all over to Mizzi Caspar. My valet Loschek knows her precise address.[18] (The Secretary to the Court of Enquiry reported that 30,000 florins were found and handed to Mizzi.) All letters from Countess Marie Larisch Wallersee and the little Vecsera to me are to be destroyed at once. As for the remaining papers, Szögyény can deal with according to his own judgement. As for military papers, he should first get in touch with Lt. Col. Mayer. Rudolf'

5. The letter to Valerie is only partially known. Corti read it, but quoted only a few sentences: 'I do not like dying. . . . After the Emperor's death, emigrate with your fiancé, since it is unforeseeable what may then happen in Austria.'
6. The letter to Stephanie was published by her in her memoirs: 'Dear Stephanie! You are freed henceforth from the torment of my presence. Be happy in your own way. Be good to the poor little girl who is the only thing I leave behind. Give my last greetings to all my acquaintances, esp. to Bombelles, Spindler, Latour, Wowo, Gisela, Leopold, etc., etc. I face death calmly—death alone can save my good name. With warmest love from Your affectionate Rudolf.'[19]

The letter to Hirsch has vanished; that to Mizzi, which according to Szögyény and Hoyos 'was brimming over with love' Mizzi must have destroyed, for not one word of it has ever been read by anyone except Szögyény and Hoyos, who were as silent as the tomb.

Mizzi's behaviour was quite remarkable: she too remained silent until her death in 1907. No one could get a word out of her. Yet she could have told a lot; Orsini-Rosenberg, in his evidence, and Hoyos in his Memorandum stated that Rudolf took Mizzi with him on his journeys and inspections, and that she was seen in his living quarters at night.[20] This figured in the secret police reports on Rudolf, and also in the routine reports of the Controller of the Imperial Household. Mizzi, Loschek, Bratfisch, the three simple people closest to Rudolf, who in their different ways knew everything about him.

The Empress Elizabeth showed Rudolf's letter to her devoted Ida Ferenczy, who either let Corti read it, or read it out to him. In accordance with Elizabeth's wishes, Ida destroyed it after the Empress's death. Corti quoted from it: 'I have no right to go on living, I have committed murder . . . I have broken my word as an officer and a gentleman. I am not worthy to be his son and to wear an officer's sword-knot." Then Rudolf wrote about the afterlife of his soul, and said that she who died with him was a touchingly pure angel. He requested the Empress to have him buried by the side of the girl.[21] Hardly the letter of an atheist.

It was the view of several contemporaries, such as Anton Monts; Rudolf's A.D.C.'s, especially Colonel Giesel; a number of aristocrats, mainly in Court circles; etc. and it is the view of the psycho-graphologist, Mrs Klára Ács, that when it came to the crunch, it was Mary Vecsera who insisted that Rudolf should carry out their plan and first shoot her. Once she had found out that he had to break with her, that he had given his word to the Emperor (see the half-finished letter to her sister Hanna) she did not want to live and be regarded as a paid-off 'ex-mistress of the Crown Prince'. The fact that Rudolf kept Bratfisch waiting all night to take Mary back to Vienna, also indicates that in spite of farewell letters and all, Rudolf was not quite decided to commit suicide.[22] In other words, in the end, it was Mary Vecsera who forced Rudolf's hand.

Two more letters were found at Mayerling. One Police President Baron Ferdinand von Gorup found in a desk drawer at Mayerling and copied it:

Mayerling, January 30, 1889

Parting!

Time is running short. I conclude: The Emperor will not abdicate in the foreseeable future.

He is heading for decline. Eternal waiting with deeply injurious slights and repeated serious conflicts unbearable! Aspirations with regard to Hungary magnifique [sic], but dangerous. Be watchful! No understanding anywhere for crushing matrimonial relations! Young Baroness chooses the same way because of hopelessness of her love for me. Expiation!

Rudolf[23]

This letter has no addressee, whether Baron Gorup forgot to copy the name or decided to withhold it so that it should not become known, it is impossible to establish. Rudolf was a true Habsburg: even in the state of despair in which he was, he tidied up his affairs and left precise instructions regarding his effects.

Mary Vecsera wrote six farewell letters. That to her mother read:

Dear Mother!

Forgive me for what I have done; I could not resist love. In agreement with him I wish to be buried by his side at Alland churchyard. I am happier in death than in life.

Your Mary

P.S. Bratfisch whistled quite beautifully.

Then she wrote to her sister Hanna: 'To Hanna! We are both going blissfully into the uncertain beyond. Think of me now and again, be happy and marry only for love. I could not do so, and as I could not resist love, I am going with him. Your Mary.'

'Do not cry for me, I am crossing over peacefully. It is wonderful out here. It reminds me of Schwarzau. Think of the line of life in my hand. Once again—farewell.'

Mary also asked her sister to send a gardenia to be put on her grave, or to put it there herself, on January 13 each year, and concluded with the words: 'As a last dying wish I ask Mama to continue to provide for the family of Agnes Ungar [her maid] so she does not suffer through my fault.'[24]

To her brother Franz, Mary wrote: 'Farewell, I shall watch over you from the other world because I love you very much. Your faithful sister Mary.'

The second letter, half-finished, found at Mayerling in Mary's clothes was written to her sister Hanna: 'Today he finally confessed to me openly that I could never become his; he has given his father his word of honour that he will break with me. So everything is over! I go to my death serenely.'[25]

As regards Mary's fifth letter, written to Don Miguel Braganza,[26] Hoyos in his Memorandum had this to say: 'Among the letters left, which did not include any for His Majesty, there was one addressed to His Royal Highness Don Miguel of Braganza. The young Baroness (who knew the Duke from the country since he was stationed near their rented castle at Schwarzau) wrote to him a cheerful letter dealing briefly with a boa (a feather wrap) which she bequeathed to him and which he was to hang over his bed. A postscript by the Crown Prince merely said: "Servus, waterboy!" and signature. Waterboy was a nickname given to the Duke on the occasion of a hunt in Görgény because of the red neckerchief he wore.'[27]

Three weeks after the tragedy, Marie Larisch had the following letter delivered to her: 'Dear Marie! Forgive me all the sorrow I have brought upon you. I thank you most warmly for all you did for me. If life should become difficult for you, and I fear it might after what we have done, follow us. It is the best you can do. Your Mary.'[28]

As far as they go these agonizing letters spell out truthfully enough the appalling tragedy of that January morning in Mayerling. The question remains: did they spell out the whole truth?

23

'The Truth is Far Worse . . .'

There is ample evidence that the whole truth about Mayerling has never been disclosed.

The Emperor Francis Joseph said at the opening of the Mayerling Covent which was installed at the scene of the tragedy: 'The truth is far worse than any of the versions.'

The Emperor also wrote in 1889 to King Leopold of the Belgians: 'Anything is better than the truth.'

Archduke Karl Ludwig in a letter to Duchess Ludovika of Bavaria, the mother of Empress Elizabeth: 'The truth is so frightful that no one can speak about it.'

Archduke Victor to his brother: 'The whole truth is so frightful that one can never confess it.'

Prince Philip of Coburg to his wife: 'It is terrible! But I cannot, I must not, say anything except that they are both dead.'[1]

Josef Hoyos to Archduke Johann Salvator: 'His Highness is dead. That is all I can say. Do not ask for details. It is too frightful. I have given the Emperor my word that I shall not say a word about what I have seen.'[2]

On March 7, 1965, Edward Taaffe, grandson of the Prime Minister who was opposed to Rudolf, wrote to Dr Fritz Judtmann: 'It is entirely correct that I said what my father publicly stated before me—that the circumstances of the Mayerling affair were far more frightful than was imagined.'

It is undisputed that Rudolf intended suicide; but it is likewise undisputed that the official announcement that he had committed suicide made no pretence of telling the whole truth. If the fate of the Crown Prince was, in fact, even more appalling than the accepted verdict of suicide, three questions may be legitimately asked.

Did Rudolf have the courage to carry out the deed for which

at Mayerling and also on three previous occasions he sought a partner because he feared that at the last moment his will power would desert him?

Did he somehow bungle the job?

If this was the truth of the matter, who then killed the Crown Prince?

The dilemma confronting historians who have tried to solve the mystery of Mayerling arises from the total secrecy which the Emperor Francis Joseph imposed on the tragedy.

Officially the following facts were admitted. On January 29, 1889, at 6.15 a.m. Rudolf called Loschek, his valet, and told him to instruct the beaters where to go, see to the breakfast, and call him at 7.30. When Loschek, having carried out Rudolf's orders, knocked on his door at 7.30, there was no answer and the door was locked. So was the other door leading to the dressing-room. As Loschek could not wake Rudolf, he went to fetch Count Hoyos, who also banged on the door. As there was still no response, they waited for Prince Philip of Coburg, who was due back at 8 a.m. from Vienna. Together Coburg and Hoyos decided that Loschek was to break in a square panel of the door. Loschek looked in first, then Coburg, then Hoyos. Only Loschek—who having put his hand through the hole, unlocked the door from inside—went into the room and came out convinced that Rudolf had been poisoned with strychnine. Hoyos drove off to Baden to catch the express train to Vienna.

Officially the following facts were not admitted: Mary Vecsera was in Mayerling and lay dead in Rudolf's bed. Loschek admitted that at 6.20 he heard two shots in quick succession. Why he did not call Count Hoyos he did not explain. If Bratfisch—who sat in his cab outside Rudolf's window—heard the shots, he did not tell anyone about it. Finally the express Hoyos wanted to catch stopped at Baden, a town near Mayerling, but was not allowed to take passengers. To induce the stationmaster to make an exception Hoyos told him that the Crown Prince was dead, and he had to convey the terrible news to Their Majesties. The stationmaster reported the news to the Rothschilds, the majority shareholders of the railways,[3] so that they knew an hour and a half before the Empress and the Emperor of the Mayerling tragedy.

At the Hofburg[4] Hoyos went to the Emperor's Adjutant

General, Count Paar, who refused to break the terrible news to Francis Joseph. He said the Empress was the only person who could do this; therefore he sent for Baron Ferenc Nopcsa, Controller of the Empress's Household. Nopcsa ran to Ida Ferenczy and asked her to tell the Empress. Elizabeth was having a Greek lesson when Ida appeared, white to the lips, and announced that Baron Nopcsa had something urgent to tell. The Empress, who was irritated by this interruption of her Greek lesson, said he must wait and come back later. Only when Ida at last added softly, 'He has bad news, grave news, from His Imperial Highness the Crown Prince,' did Elizabeth dismiss the Greek teacher, and Ida pushed Nopcsa into the room. He carried out his duty with utmost delicacy. When Ida re-entered the room, Elizabeth was in floods of tears, sobbing. At this moment a light step was heard—Francis Joseph. 'Not yet! Do not come in!' cried Elizabeth. Ida rushed to the door: 'I implore Your Majesty most earnestly to wait a moment longer.'

Francis Joseph stood outside with Nopcsa, who was controlling himself with a great effort. Having dried her tears, Elizabeth asked Ida: 'Is anything noticeable? No? Very well, then, show him in and may God help me.'

Ten minutes later, Francis Joseph left the room with drooping head, a broken man.

'Come with me, Baron Nopcsa,' he said.

Elizabeth went downstairs to Ida's room as it was time for Fräulein Schratt's visit, and she usually went straight there. Elizabeth felt that the Emperor was in need of consolation from an outside person which a grievously stricken mother could hardly give. She accompanied Fräulein Schratt to the Emperor and then went to Valerie, but she was not in her apartments. Elizabeth sent for her to be fetched.

Valerie found her mother sobbing. 'Rudolf is very, very ill,' she stammered, 'There is no hope.'

Valerie threw her arms around her mother's neck and sat on her knee. 'It will blanch your cheeks with horror—the worst has happened.'

'Has he killed himself?'

Elizabeth started. 'Why do you think that? No, no. It seems probable, even certain, that the girl poisoned him.'

Steps were heard. 'There is Papa,' said Elizabeth. 'I entreat you be as calm as I am.' When Francis Joseph came in, both Elizabeth and Valerie threw their arms round his neck, and the three stood together in a close embrace. Then they sent for Stephanie—Elizabeth met her kindly, lovingly. Then Valerie's fiancé hurried in.

Meanwhile Ida returned to her apartment, and found Baroness Vecsera sitting in her ante-room. 'What do you want here, Baroness?' Ida said sharply. 'I cannot see you now. Kindly go away.'

But the Baroness repeated persistently: 'I must speak to Her Majesty the Empress.'

'But, Baroness, that is impossible.'

'I must, I must. I have lost my child, and she alone can restore her to me.' Helen Vecsera had been advised by Taaffe: 'Go to Her Majesty, she alone can do anything.'

Ida returned to Elizabeth.

'Does she know all yet?' asked the Empress.

'No.'

'Poor woman! Very well, I will go to her.'

Ida suggested that Nopcsa should talk to Helen Vecsera first and prepare her. He did not tell her all. When Elizabeth entered, Nopcsa withdrew, but Ida stayed in the next room with the door open. She heard the Baroness demanding her child, and saying that the Crown Prince must have taken her away with him. In a gentle voice the Empress said, 'Collect all your courage, Baroness; your daughter is dead.'

The Baroness cried out in wildest grief, 'My child, my dear, beautiful child . . .'

'But do you know,' continued Elizabeth in a firmer voice, 'that my Rudolf is dead, too?'

The Baroness fell to the ground before the Empress and clung to her knees. 'My unhappy child!' she cried. 'What has she done? Can this be her doing?'

After a silence Elizabeth left the Baroness, saying as she went: 'Now mind! Rudolf died of a heart attack!'

Two official enquiries were set up. One Commission of which the secretary was Dr Heinrich Slatin,[5] was sent to Mayerling with the specific task of searching for Rudolf's will. Another Commission (which did not include a forensic expert either) was sent with general terms of reference to establish the circumstances of Rudolf's death. A third unofficial Commission was sent by the Prime Minister to make general enquiries. The report of the first official Commission was published but later disappeared. The findings of the second were laid down in a protocol which was never published; the results of Taaffe's enquiries never saw the light of day.

Another incident is worth recording. In Baden rumours spread that the Crown Prince had been shot by an unknown third party. Therefore the Judge of the Baden District Court sent an official, Dr Siebenrock, to enquire whether the intervention of the District Court was required. Bombelles, who was a member of the Lord Marshal's Commission, came out of the billiard-room, where the Commission was assembled, white as a sheet and very excitedly said: 'Out of the question, quite out of the question! There is no occasion for intervention by a criminal court!'

At Dr Siebenrock's request, Bombelles confirmed this in writing on the back of a visiting card, which was filed with a protocol of the Prosecutor's office in Wiener Neustadt, which on the following day ordered the suspension of all criminal enquiries.[6]

No one therefore knows for certain what the secret Mayerling papers consist of. The best attempt to identify them has been the research of Dr Fritz Judtmann who drew up the following probable list:

1. The Protocol of the official Commission of the Lord Marshal's Office which searched for Rudolf's will. This Commission entered the room in which Rudolf had died on the afternoon of January 30. The Protocol is mentioned in the list of papers used in the probate proceedings but is, in fact, missing from the file. It may have contained references to the body of Mary Vecsera.

2. The Protocol of the official Commission to establish the circumstances of the incident, which was drawn up on February 4, the last sentence of which ran: 'Evidently the Crown Prince used a looking glass at the last moment,'[7] has disappeared. The dispatch of this Commission is also recorded in the Protocol of Ceremonies[8] which is thought to have been deposited under seal at the Lord Chamberlain's office, but has also disappeared.

It is to be noted that by the time this Commission to establish the circumstances of the death had arrived, the bodies were no longer at Mayerling.

3. Possible statements by Bratfisch, Mizzi Caspar, Loschek, and the servants at Mayerling.

However, Hoyos states in his memorandum that the questioning of witnesses by the Commission to establish the circumstances of the death arranged for 5 p.m. on January 31 was cancelled, and never reconvened.

4. The originals of the autopsy findings, which, according to the Protocol of Ceremonies were communicated to the Emperor personally by the first Chamberlain, then sealed and deposited in the archives of the Lord Chamberlain's Office.[9]

These documents have disappeared but an excerpt was published on February 2, 1889, under the heading: *Medical Opinion*, which read:

> In connection with the dissection of the body of His Imperial and Royal Highness, Crown Prince Rudolf, on the 31st of January, 1889, in the imperial palace at Vienna, undertaken in observance of legal ordinance by the legally appointed medical specialists, a verdict of the findings of the stipulated *post mortem* certified and signed by the operating doctors, was submitted, which verdict reads as follows:

Verdict

a. His Imperial and Royal Highness the Crown Prince died from a fracture of the skull and destruction of the front portions of the brain.
b. This fracture was caused by a shot fired against the right anterior temporal area at close range at the right temple.
c. A bullet fired from a revolver of medium calibre would be likely to produce the injuries in question.
d. The projectile was not found, as it made its way out through a bullet hole discovered above the left ear.
e. There can be no doubt that His Imperial and Royal Highness fired the shot himself and that death was instantaneous.
f. The premature cohesion of the sagittal and coronal suttures, the remarkable depth of the skull cavity and the so-called 'finger-like' impression on the inner surface of the skull

bones, the evident subsidence of the brain passages and the enlargement of the brain-chamber (vestricles) are pathological circumstances which experience shows are usually accompanied by abnormal mental conditions, and which therefore justify the assumption that the deed was committed in a state of mental derangement.[10]

Privy Councillor E. Hofman, m.p. Professor of Forensic Medicine	Professor Doctor: Hans Kundrat, m.p. Director of the Institute of Pathological Post Mortem Operator:

Post Mortem Operator:
Prof. Dr Hermann Widerhofer, m.p.
Imperial and Royal Physician-in-Waiting

Given by His Imperial and Apostolic Majesty's Chief Controller of the Household. February 2, 1889.

5. Documents regarding the journey of Count István Károlyi, leader of the Hungarian Opposition, to the Crown Prince.

These disappeared from the Political Archives of the Ministry of the Imperial Household and Foreign Affairs. This may have happened in 1899, when these archives were reorganised. They were in a box labelled Secret XXV.

6. Information about Rudolf's financial business with Baron Hirsch. Any papers regarding this matter have disappeared from the Archives of the Directorate of Imperial Private and Family Property. There is merely a notification from the Privy Purse that 150,000 *Gulden* were paid back to Baron Hirsch. These documents presumably also included Rudolf's letter to Hirsch found after his death, or at least a copy of it.

7. Numerous papers concerning the removal of the female corpse from Mayerling, which Taaffe, in his capacity of Minister of the Interior and Supreme Chief of the Police, must have received from Krauss, the Police President, and from the District Governor of Baden.

8. Reports from confidential informers and newspaper cuttings about the tragedy.

The reason why the Mayerling papers as listed by Dr Judtmann —and any others—have disappeared and their contents remained secret is easily explained. The Emperor Francis Joseph in his anxiety to maintain total secrecy about the Mayerling affair made his Prime Minister, personally responsible for safeguarding all the papers relevant to the incident, since he feared that they would sooner or later become public property if deposited at the *Haus, Hof und Staatsarchiv* at 1 Minoriten Platz, Vienna.

It may well be asked why did the Emperor not burn the Mayerling papers. That would have been the surest way to keep them secret for ever. The answer lies in the nature of the Emperor. Not merely did he have the meticulous mind of a bureaucrat (in a census form he wrote under the occupation heading: 'Self-employed civil servant'), but with his deep feeling that the history of the House of Habsburg belonged to posterity, it would have been unfitting to destroy documents which were an essential part of that history, even though they were kept secret for an extremely long period.

The subsequent history of the Mayerling papers shows without doubt that officially only three persons knew of their contents, the Prime Minister, Count Eduard Taaffe, his son Heinrich, and his grandson Edward. The Prime Minister, obedient to the Emperor's command, entrusted the papers to his son, Heinrich, who died in 1928. Heinrich passed the papers on to his son, Edward, whom he required to give his most solemn word of honour that he would not show them or reveal their contents to a single person.

It is thus beyond dispute that Edward Taaffe knew the whole truth about Mayerling and could have given a complete answer to the question whether, contrary to the official verdict of suicide, the Crown Prince did not in fact die by his own hand. It is indeed through Edward Taaffe that it is at long last possible legitimately to question the proposition that Crown Prince Rudolf took his own life. How, despite the undertaking of secrecy which he had given to his father, Edward Taaffe is the source from which the whole truth about Mayerling has finally come to light must now be related.

On November 11, 1931, Edward Taaffe married Mabel Grace MacLaughlin at Dunboyne, near Dublin. In 1939 he returned to Ireland where he lived in Dublin until his death in 1967 and was survived by a cousin, Group Captain Rudolph Taaffe, who has greatly assisted me with the material appearing in this chapter.

And it was Edward Taaffe who was approached by Dr Fritz Judtmann with the request to show him the Mayerling papers, to which request he replied: 'that his family archives were not at the moment accessible. He would like to help, but could see no possibility of doing so for the present'.[10] Thereupon Dr Judtmann drew up a report on what he had achieved by way of untiring researches, and in August 1964 he wrote to Edward Taaffe again, asking also a few questions to clarify the fate of the Rudolf documents.

On August 12, 1964, Edward Taaffe replied: 'My letter will disappoint you—it begins with the word—unfortunately! Unfortunately I had to give a solemn promise to leave unanswered any question concerning the Crown Prince or anything to do with the affair, and to decline to answer anything in this respect. I have considered the matter carefully—hence the six days which have elapsed since the arrival of your letter. Although you have taken so much trouble with this business and have done such intensive research, yet I may not help you.

'As long ago as 1929 (William) Randolph Hearst, the American newspaper king offered me 200,000 dollars for any information and papers concerning the Crown Prince Rudolf; I refused all information or help by pointing out that these were not my secrets which I was keeping merely in the capacity of (inherited) trustee. Since then hundreds of questions, either from curiosity or in order to make capital, have begged me to reveal the facts known to me. You *Herr Professor*, are the first to try to solve the mystery purely for scholarly purposes, and that is why I am sorry to have to refuse you.'[11]

In July 1965 Dr Judtmann appealed to Edward Taaffe to assign the Crown Prince Rudolf papers and archives of his grandfather to the Austrian State Archives. Edward turned down the suggestion.[12] He did not say that they no longer existed, he merely wrote to Dr Judtmann that he would not hand over the Mayerling papers to the Austrian Government.

In 1967 Edward Taaffe died quite unexpectedly, an unhappy man. His wife, Grace, had left him by mutual agreement; although in 1939 he had returned to Ireland, from where the family originated, he was still in a way a stranger. He spent some of his time with his cousin, Rudolph Taaffe.

The following is the text of the letter which Rudolph Taaffe wrote to me, dated September 6, 1975.

'Edward, Yaxi to the family, was born in 1898 and died at 17 Lower Baggot street, Dublin, on July 4, 1967. He left no will. He had no relatives left in Austria, thus it fell on me to clear up his effects. And I have most of the papers he had at my home, Inch House.

'My opinion of the whereabouts of what we call "the Mayerling Papers" is summed up in the late Professor Judtmann's book, *Mayerling, the Facts Behind the Legend*, in the postscript at p. 355 in the English translation. I am the relation of the Count referred to in this Postscript.'

Professor Judtmann's postscript reads as follows:

'In the course of an extensive correspondence the Count's heir obligingly provided me with the following important information: "the file with the documents which the Emperor handed over to Count Eduard Taaffe, and which were known in the family as the Mayerling papers, these papers are definitely not in my possession and I do not know where they are." He possessed no papers which could throw any further light on the Mayerling affair. The documents in his possession were Taaffe letters of a much earlier date.

'In reply to further questions the heir informed me that he had indeed talked about the papers with the Count, who had died quite suddenly, but he had never seen them himself. He believed that only the Emperor[13] and the three Counts Taaffe had ever seen the papers. He also knew that the Count's divorced wife, Countess Mabel Grace, née MacLaughlin of Dunboyne, in Ireland, knew nothing about the papers and had never seen them. The Count had never discussed them with her. When I asked his own personal opinion of what had become of the documents, he replied, on April 23, 1968: "In my opinion the papers still exist." '[14]

In his letter to me Taaffe continued: 'Yaxi left Ellischau[15] in Bohemia in the summer of 1939; the property was confiscated by the Czechs. The papers were never in the library in Ellischau, but bricked up in the cellars.[16] There was, indeed, a fire in that room (meaning the library) but the Mayerling papers were not burnt there. I do not think Yaxi brought them to Ireland. From about 1952 to his death in 1967 I frequently talked to Yaxi about them; but he would never tell me where they were. He could have burnt them when he left Ellischau, but I doubt it and I have an idea they are still in existence—but where? I repeat that I do not think anyone ever read them except the Emperor, Eduard the Minister-President, his son Henry, and Yaxi, Henry's son.[17] I knew Henry and stayed at Ellischau while he was alive and it was most unlikely that he would have allowed anyone to see them. And I know Yaxi had a similar outlook.'

Taaffe may be mistaken in thinking that Heinrich Taaffe showed the Mayerling papers to no one, for he commissioned Professor Arthur Skedl of Prague University to publish his father's political writings under the title: *The Political Papers Of The Late Count Edward Taaffe*. In the Preface to this book, published in 1922, Professor Skedl says: 'There are only a few documents relating to the most deplorable misfortune in the Imperial House which occurred during Taaffe's Ministry in 1889; the others I have not published in accordance with Count Taaffe's wish that these should not be made available to the public. Strictly speaking, the documents concerning the Crown Prince's death should have been deposited with the Ministry of the Imperial Household. At the Emperor's express wish, however, these documents were handed over to Count Taaffe, as the Emperor's trusted friend, to make sure that they should not as a result of some unforeseen event, come to the knowledge of the public. Hence Count Taaffe's wish is understandable and entirely justified.'

Skedl published only: (1) the report of Police Commissioner Habrda about the transfer of Baroness Mary Vecsera's body from Mayerling to Heilingenkreutz. The original of this report was discovered in 1953 in the secret file of Police President von Krauss. (2) The police report about Baroness Helen Vecsera, dated April 22, 1889, and (3) the report about the exhumation of Mary Vecsera's body dated May 16, 1889. Skedl adds: 'As for the other papers left by Count Taaffe and concerning the so-deplorable death of the Crown Prince, I cannot publish these, since Count Taaffe has requested that these should never be made public.'

Group Captain Taaffe is convinced that Professor Skedl may have seen some Mayerling papers, but not the secret dossier.

Among Edward Taaffe's papers he has found the following letter, which he sent me on October 16, 1977.

Count Taaffe
11 Raglan Road
Dublin
January 27, 1938

Dear Sir,

Your paper published an article on January 22, 'The Taaffes and European Events" . . . etc.

Para 3.

The Mayerling Dossier has 'disappeared' is nonsense. The Dossier was entrusted in 1889 after the tragedy to my grandfather, Count Eduard Taaffe, who was then Prime Minister of Austria, and has been since in the personal guardianship of the Head of the Family and its contents and hiding place known only to him. As I am the Head of the Family now, I was not likely to discuss the matter with stray acquaintances or waste my time looking for something which I knew to be in perfect security in a very different place. [This refers to a search made in Ellischau Castle, Bohemia, for the Dossier.] The wording 'The Dossier has disappeared' has no sense, as the Dossier has always been well hidden from the public and certainly no secretary or Professor Skedl have ever had it in their hands. And it will stay well hidden away.

. . .

Yours truly,
(Signed) Edward Count Taaffe

Certified True Copy.
(Signed) Rudolph Taaffe

The following is the transcript of my long conversation with Rudolph Taaffe:

Conversation Between Group Captain Rudolph P. H. Taaffe and Judith Listowel on November 15, 1974

R.T.: I do not believe that Crown Prince Rudolf committed suicide. I believe he was murdered.

J.L.: By whom?

R.T.: By personnel of the Austrian Army.

J.L.: Why should they have killed him?

R.T.: Because of the conspiracy in which he was involved—with Hungarians—which amounted to high treason.[19]

J.L.: Do you think the Austrian Army did it on their own, or were they ordered to do it?

R.T.: They acted under orders.

J.L.: Whose orders? The Army High Command—the General Staff—or Archduke Albert?

R.T.: They would have known about it—connived at it. Mark you, I have no proof of any kind that this happened, but I have formed this opinion. I also believe that Taaffe (the Prime Minister) was aware of the plot and that it was he who informed the Emperor.

J.L.: But surely not before the deed was perpetrated? The Empress broke the terrible news to Francis Joseph, and he left her room ashen white, slumped, walking with difficulty.

R.T.: Taaffe told the Emperor after the funeral—of course that is just my opinion.

J.L.: What led you to form this opinion?

R.T.: I formed my opinion from certain letters I have read and from my conversation with my cousin Edward. He talked about Mayerling, but he never showed me the papers, for he had given his word to his father that he would not show them to anyone.

J.L.: Are you sure he did not destroy the papers?

R.P.: I am certain, although I do not know where they are. They may be in the Vatican.

Following up this suggestion I approached the Vatican authorities and the discreet reticence of their reply is not without interest. On June 8, 1975, I applied through the good offices of H.E. the Apostolic Delegate to Britain, Archbishop Bruno B. Heim, to the Vatican for permission to see the letters the Holy Father sent to the Emperor Francis Joseph on February 2, February 8 and February 25, 1889, which have never been made available to students of history. I also requested permission to read the autopsy report of the Crown Prince which has disappeared in Austria. To this the answer, through the Apostolic Delegate, was first that the letters would be read in Rome, and even if they could not be made available, I might be informed of their content. On November 6, 1975, I wrote to the Apostolic Delegate once more, pleading with him to induce the Vatican to allow access to the secret Mayerling papers. To this the reply was that regretfully the Vatican could not make the papers available 'at this period as they are not being free yet.'[20]

This is how my conversation with Rudolf Taaffe continued:

J.L.: When did Edward smuggle the papers out of Ellischau Castle?

R.T.: He got them out in 1939. There was a fire in the library at Ellischau (some papers from this room are in my possession and they are scorched) and the Czech authorities thought that they had been destroyed. The Mayerling papers had never been in the library; they had been bricked up in the wall of the basement, and no one except Edward knew about it. He showed me the spot where they were. When the Czech authorities thought that they had been burnt, it was easier to get them out. . . . I was one of the heirs, but he did not leave these papers to me, nor did he tell me where he had deposited them.

Group Captain Taaffe signed the transcript of our conversation when he gave me permission to publish it as follows:

Rudolph Taaffe (m.p.)
November 24, 1974.

Such then is the solution to the mystery of Mayerling propounded on the basis of information from Edward Taaffe, the last man to see the secret Mayerling papers—Rudolf did not kill himself but was murdered by members of the Austrian Army.

24

Solution to the Mystery

And now for the evidence.

There are two reasons for concluding that Edward Taaffe's proposition is indeed credible and correct. Although he put it in general terms, he was the only man who knew the truth, and his proposition is wholly consistent with a detailed statement, never published before, by a direct descendant of the Crown Prince. But first it is necessary to recite the facts of the Mayerling tragedy as they are known from recognised sources.

Crown Prince Rudolf killed Mary Vecsera: this he admitted in his letter to his mother which I publish in part on p. 221.

According to the doctors' statement, Mary died between midnight and 2 a.m. The Crown Prince sat with the dead girl until 6.15 in the morning, when he sent Loschek to the other side of the Mayerling Hunting Lodge.[1] Rudolf walked away from the door whistling—Loschek heard it distinctly.

In this context it is legitimate to comment that it is strange in the extreme in the case of a purported suicide pact that Rudolf was indisputably alive some five or six hours after Mary Vecsera had died.

At about seven o'clock the Court Huntsman-in-Ordinary, Franz Vodička,[2] walked towards the part of the Lodge where Rudolf's apartment was. Bratfisch was sitting on his cab waiting, his instructions were to drive Baroness Mary Vecsera back to Vienna. He called out to Vodička: 'No good rallying the beaters, there will be no shoot!'

'And what makes you say that?' Vodička answered somewhat peeved.

'Because the Crown Prince is dead,' Bratfisch said this so emphatically that Vodička turned on his heels and went back to the kitchen quarters to find out what was happening. An hour later, he learnt that Bratfisch had been right. What Bratfisch had seen or heard is not known, for the transcript of his interrogation by the police has never been published. But it may be among the Mayerling papers entrusted to Prime Minister Taaffe.[3]

It is at this point that the general proposition of murder which emanates from his grandson becomes vital in its revelation of the whole stark truth about how the Crown Prince died. It provides convincing confirmation of a detailed account of the tragedy which might otherwise be dismissed as mere sensationalism. This account was given to me by a descendant of the Crown Prince. For obvious family reasons this descendant must remain anonymous, but this version of the tragedy is unequivocal and confirms in explicit detail the general proposition of murder.

This is what I was told. Ten soldiers of Archduke Albert's Roll Commando were despatched to Mayerling. The Roll Commando were specially trained troops of the Austrian Army kept ready to carry out special orders at any time and in any place. The detachment, two of whom were experienced sharpshooters, were hidden in the garden of the Hunting Lodge. They were given explicit orders that if the Crown Prince had not taken his own life by 6.30 a.m. they were to shoot him. Rudolf was unable to carry out his desperate intention and accordingly at about 7 a.m. the two Roll Commando sharpshooters entered his room through the window and shot him.

Startling though murder may be as the truth about Mayerling, it nonetheless rings true not merely because Edward Taaffe, who propounded this solution as a broad proposition, was uniquely placed to know the contents of the Mayerling papers but because it offers a logical explanation of the exceptional secrecy which, on the express orders of Emperor Francis Joseph, descended on the whole affair. Furthermore, Edward Taaffe's account and the detailed account of Rudolf's descendant, both give credence to and are themselves confirmed by other contemporary accounts. These other accounts—which could not be checked because of the disappearance of the Mayerling papers but which strongly hinted that Rudolf did not die by his own hand—are now given added importance. Thus the broad proposition now derived, through Rudolph Taaffe, from his cousin Edward Taaffe, and substantiated by Rudolf's descendant, confirms the contemporary theories of what happened at Mayerling put about by the Papal Nuncio, Mgr. Luigi Galimberti, and the German Ambassador, Prince Heinrich VII Reuss-Schleitz-Koestritz.[4]

Reuss sent three despatches to Bismarck, all three based on information provided by the Nuncio.[5] In the first, of February 5, he reported the Nuncio as accepting the official verdict of suicide while of unsound mind: 'The Papal Nuncio told me of the great embarrassment in which the Pope found himself concerning his consent to the Church burial of the Crown Prince. Had this consent not been forthcoming and had it been necessary to bury the suicide without the blessings of the Church, the population of Vienna would undoubtedly have let itself be swept away in the worst possible excesses. His Majesty the Emperor was therefore supremely worried until the autopsy was completed and the physicians and legal officials assembled declared the probability of insanity.

'The Emperor immediately despatched Kálnoky to the Nuncio to submit to him the officially authorised findings. Monsignor Galimberti reported it to Rome by telegram and dispelled all the scruples of the Church. In this country, too, the Nuncio has received many inquiries from bishops as to what attitude they should adopt. He pointed out that insanity excuses suicide also in the eyes of the Church.

' "My official conscience is clear," the Nuncio added to me. "I only have to believe what the Minister of Foreign Affairs tells me. Nevertheless this is probably the first time in history that the Papal Nuncio in *Pontificalibus* will attend the funeral of a murderer and a suicide."

'As for the rumour that the late Crown Prince had been working on his divorce and had written to the Pope in this connection, a rumour much spread about in recent weeks, Monsignor Galimberti denied all knowledge. Certainly nothing concerning this matter had passed through his hands. He gave it as his opinion that it would not be impossible for the Pope, provided such a letter existed, to have sent it to Brussels and for it to have become known to the Emperor from there. I have no ground for attaching any credence to this rumour, even though the Crown Prince was most unhappy in his marriage.'

On February 7 Reuss sent another despatch to Prince Bismarck, to the effect that Rudolf's suicide had had a most unfortunate effect on the deeply religious population of the Alpine Provinces. The clergy was strongly antagonistic; in several places the priests refused to read requiem masses. In some the churches remained closed, not even the bells were rung. In Laibach, however, the liberal and free-thinking German population forced the Bishop, Mgr Missim, to celebrate mass—there were considerable demonstrations against him. The Nuncio, Mgr Galimberti, had complained to Reuss about his difficult position between Vienna and Rome. He had been especially bitter about the deceitful attitude of Archbishop Franz Count Schönborn. Galimberti held to the principle that if the scientists had established mental derangement, the Church had no cause to question this. He had told Schönborn to provide proof to the contrary if he was so full of doubts.

On February 9, 1889, Reuss sent Bismarck two further despatches, which show that during the four days that elapsed since February 5 very important new evidence had reached him. It came mostly from Monsignor Galimberti who, in the intervening four days, clearly had found reasons for revising his first opinion. Additional details may have been provided by Anton Count Monts, Counsellor of the German Embassy.

In his first despatch of February 9, Prince Reuss reported his long conversation with the Foreign Minister, Kálnoky, who neither admitted nor denied that Mary Vecsera had also died in Mayerling. Kálnoky told Reuss that a love affair could not have been the real cause of the catastrophe 'as the Vecsera family does not belong to those with whom one could not have reached agreement, hence this would not be a credible reason for the Crown Prince committing suicide'. Kálnoky was far from believing that the Crown Prince had been insane, but he said that Rudolf had a monomania for suicide, which had come to the fore already earlier on. Reuss reported that during his last talks with Rudolf, Kálnoky had gained the impression that the Crown Prince was looking forward to his trip to Berlin, and his other plans, although he was extremely restless. Kálnoky expressed the opinion that Rudolf's attitude was that of someone who had no future, of an old man, and that had been borne out by his autopsy which showed that he had the skull of an old man. This is how Reuss reported the end of Kálnoky's statement: 'Unhappiness in his marriage? No heir? Yes, one could not have pretended that he was happy in his marriage, but he was not the man to shoot himself for that. Marriages which go badly can be put right over the years and an heir to the throne may yet have appeared. Both were still young. There was no question of divorce, the Minister assured me this most emphatically. The fixed idea of suicide existed; it disappeared at times, to surface again. While the Crown Prince talked about it before, he was silent with everyone when the fixed idea ripened and was about to be carried out. In none of his letters was there even an indication of the cause of his suicide.'

Reuss's second despatch of February 9, 1889, is so important that it is here published in full:

> SECRET
>
> By Royal Courier Vienna, February 9, 1889
>
> As I have had the honour to report in a different context today, the version that the Crown Prince Rudolf shot himself is still being officially maintained, while the accompanying circumstances, though more or less public property by now, are being hushed up.
>
> I must once more return to the subject because some very serious people doubt this version, and increasing support is given to the rumour that the Crown Prince as well as the young lady found on his bed were murdered.
>
> This would seem to be supported by the following circumstances: Once the heart-failure story proved no longer tenable, the suicide version was launched in order to conceal the fact that a female corpse was present—and not only from consideration for the Crown Princess or with an eye on public morals, but also because it was feared lest the Church should make difficulties in connection with the burial. The evidence that the murder victim was found in concubinage would have made ecclesiastical honours equally difficult, if not impossible.

How intent the Court were on keeping secret Mary Vecsera's presence at Mayerling may be gauged from the well-known macabre account, reported by innumerable historians, of how Alexander Baltazzi and Georg Count Stockau, Mary's two uncles, drove in a *Fiakker* the dressed-up corpse of the wretched girl propped up between them to give the impression that she was alive. In Heiligenkreutz the police certified that she had committed suicide, yet the Abbot Heinrich Grünbock agreed to a church funeral. A coffin was hurriedly knocked together at the Abbey's workshop, a grave dug with difficulty in the frozen ground, and next morning (February 1, 1889) Mary Vecsera was quickly buried in it.

When Rudolf's death was announced, some Viennese newspapers, Reuss, Monts and other diplomats reported that Mary Vecsera was in Venice with her mother. Her death at Mayerling only gradually leaked out to the general public.

Reuss's despatch continued as follows: 'If murder had been conceded, then public opinion would have demanded the establishment of the culprit and his punishment; but this in turn would have required detailed judicial investigation of the circumstances, and the entire not very moral circumstances would have come out. In order to avoid this the Emperor is said to have decided to make the possibly much worse and more damaging admission of suicide, which could then be exonerated by insanity.

'Herr Galimberti, who no doubt commands good sources of information, shares these views.[6] Nevertheless he immediately accepted the official version in order to save the Pope and also the Court here great embarassment. He also sticks to this version *vis-à-vis* everybody.

'However, he has told me the following in strict secrecy. The bullet did not pass from right to left, as is officially stated, but from back left behind the ear upwards, where it had left the head again. Moreover, other wounds were found on the body. The shattering of the top of the skull is being explained by the fact that the revolver had been held quite close to the head and the escaping powder caused this devastation—however, such an effect is thought to be doubtful. The revolver found by the bed did not belong to the Crown Prince, and all six bullets had been fired.'

It is a fact that no ballistic expert was called in to pronounce about the revolver found in the Crown Prince's bedroom.

Reuss continued: 'The bullet wound of the young girl, it is further said, is not at the temple, as has been maintained, but at the centre top of the head. She too is said to have had other wounds. These details had been given to the Nuncio by the Grand Duke of Tuscany and from other quarters.'

Here is one point on which there is irrefutable evidence from modern times. In 1959, a wealthy lady from Trieste, who wishes to remain anonymous,[7] was informed that Mary's grave had been broken open and that something should be done about it. Dr Judtmann subsequently approached the Baden undertakers who had carried out the work. From them he learnt that the persons who had broken open the coffin had severed Mary's head from her body with the hoe found in the grave. It had been carefully examined. 'Nowhere on the skull was a bullet hole to be seen, unless it had been at the very spot where the top of the skull was missing,' the director of the undertakers has written in his report which he made available to Dr Judtmann.[8] This suggests the possibility that Mary Vecsera was shot from above and that the bullet in consequence did not leave her body. This confirms the information Monsignor Galimberti gave the German Ambassador. It is interesting to recall that Dr von Auchenthaler, the Court physician who did the *post-mortem*, stated that the entry-wound of the bullet was on the left temporal bone and a small jagged exit opened two centimetres above the right outer ear. The Baden undertakers could find no sign of this shot.[9]

In his despatch to Bismarck, Reuss continued: 'The above information, however, does not fit in with the fact that a great many circumstances point to suicide having been premeditated, that the Crown Prince announced his death in letters which can be proved to have been written by him while still in Vienna, and in particular it does not seem likely that, had death been preceded by a struggle, he would have found enough time to write to Herr von Szögyény[10] and send him his keys, which the latter in fact showed me on the morning of February 1. Admittedly I did not see the letter.

'I may add that I now know for certain that Count Hoyos and the Prince of Coburg saw the two bodies immediately after the door had been broken down,[11] that the Count really believed this to be a case of strychnine poisoning, which is said to produce haemorrhage also, and that, without satisfying himself more accurately, he hastened to Vienna to make his report. Both of Their Majesties learnt this version and believed it until the following morning. For that reason the attempt was made to ascribe death to heart-failure.

'At the sight of the scene before them, Hoyos says he did not even enter the room but left for Vienna at once. Josel Hoyos says the Vecsera woman was dead hours before Rudolf himself.

'The mother of the young girl is now in Venice, where, in a way, she is parading her daughter's disaster without making any secret of the romance. This throws a clear light upon this person, who claims to have received a promise that, provided she disappeared and kept quiet before the burial, everything would be published later. Blackmail cannot be quite excluded here. Heinrich Reuss.'

The last paragraph is inaccurate. Baronness Vecsera did not go to Venice; she got out of the train at Klein-Reifling, in the Gesäuse mountains, and turned back to Vienna. But it was true that the Baroness 'paraded' her daughter's tragedy and allowed her friends to read the farewell letters. See Monts' memoirs, p. 107.

That, as now revealed by Yaxi Taaffe and the Crown Prince's descendant, Rudolf was murdered by the Roll Commando sharpshooters, fits in with the two accounts written by Szeps in two separate editions of the *Wiener Tagblatt*, not to be confused with the *Neues Wiener Tagblatt*, on February 1, 1889. In the first Szeps wrote that no one believed suicide to be a possibility since suicide was hardly compatible with a Prince of the Imperial House. He regretted that something was hushed up and he was afraid that rumours would arise which would be far worse than the true facts. Szeps' second report differed in one significant respect from the official medical opinion. 'The Crown Prince,' Szeps wrote, 'had placed the revolver to his throat below the right ear, the barrel aimed obliquely upwards. The bullet entered the brain and shattered the top of the skull and the upper part of the forehead. This is also the reason why yesterday only the face of the corpse was visible, and the head covered with a cloth.' The censor did not stop publication of this account which did not glaringly contradict the official verdict of suicide; but Szeps' account differed from the official *Medical Opinion* published on February 2 which stated, at Point B, that Rudolf shot himself through the right temple and not from below the right ear. Given his position as an extremely well-informed journalist and a close friend of the Crown Prince,

Szeps must have had a pretty shrewd idea of what actually happened at Mayerling, but he would have known that the account which eliminated suicide altogether would never have passed the censor. At least, however, this account drew attention to the shot having been fired below the ear and not through the temple, and thus contained a hint that the official verdict was not to be believed. That the official verdict was indeed untrue was shown by the Papal Nuncio who informed Reuss on February 9 that the fatal shot was fired from behind the left ear—that Rudolf's death was not suicide, but murder from behind.

That the tragedy of Mayerling was something much worse than Rudolf's suicide, explains why the official Commission investigating how the death happened was dismissed before such informed witnesses as Bratfisch, Loschek and Mali—who had cooked during the two days the Crown Prince was at Mayerling—could be questioned. Likewise it is now explicable why although Bratfisch was questioned for several hours by the police, his statement has disappeared, as has that of Mizzi Caspar. The version of Edward Taaffe, the Prime Minister's grandson, makes it all too clear why only an excerpt of the *post mortem* ever saw the light of day. Neither the full autopsy, nor any report on the condition of the furniture at Mayerling, etc., was ever published. And no forensic or ballistic experts were ever called in to make a report. Small wonder that the Emperor ordered all traces of what happened at Mayerling to be obliterated. For instance Latour, who was called in to participate at the secret State Council meeting immediately after the catastrophe, in his will instructed his stepson, Wilhelm Wagner-Latour, to burn immediately after his death a thick envelope in a secret compartment of his writing desk. Another piece of vital evidence went up in smoke. It is also significant that on February 25, 1889, the Hungarian Minister of Justice stopped the Public Prosecutor from taking action against the *Neue Temesvarer Zeitung* because of an article on Rudolf's death it had published on February 16, 1889, on the grounds that (a) he regarded the subject as unsuitable for public discussion; (b) because the defence 'might provoke the members of the jury to acquit the accused'. When Bombelles died in July, 1889, *rigor mortis* had not yet set in when representatives of the Emperor came to remove all his papers.

Two simple people were close to Crown Prince Rudolf—Bratfisch, the coachman of the *Fiakker* who waited all night at Mayerling, and his valet, Loschek, who knew every detail of his private life. Bratfisch took his secret to the grave; Loschek kept his silence for thirty-nine years.

Taaffe, the Prime Minister, certainly had the motive for wishing Rudolf dead. For years he regarded the Crown Prince's liberal ideas as a menace to the Monarchy. He was also, of course, fully aware of the political conversations Rudolf had not only with reliable and serious people like Szeps, but with wild and irresponsible individuals, chiefly Hungarian, some French. After the Mürzsteg incident the Emperor had Rudolf watched; this is how the authorities found out about Rudolf's frequent talks with Archduke Johann Salvator, and Johann Salvator's Hungarian intrigues.

With access to all police reports and all information submitted to the Emperor about the Crown Prince, Taaffe was fully aware of Rudolf's constantly deteriorating health and his desperate frame of mind. He knew from Mizzi Caspar's statement to Police President Krauss that Rudolf was planning to kill himself. Had he wished to do so, he could have taken action to prevent any suicide. Since Monday, January 28, 1889, Taaffe and Krauss realised that something terrible was in the making, yet on the excuse that the police had no legal powers in the Crown Prince's premises, did nothing. Had they informed the Empress, Rudolf would not have died at Mayerling. The Prime Minister however took no precautionary action and the only possible inference is that Rudolf's death suited Taaffe's book both from a political and a personal point of view. From deciding deliberately to refrain from preventing a planned suicide, it is but a short step to deciding to give the *coup de grace* if the victim failed in his own purpose. In any event, had Rudolf survived the death of Mary Vecsera, he would have been guilty of murder. In view of Rudolf's incurable illness, and his general distressing physical and mental condition, as the Vienna psychiatrists have pronounced,[12] he could not have been a successful ruler—if a ruler at all. In the extremely difficult situation in which the Monarchy found itself, this too must have weighed with Eduard Taaffe.

One thing is certain. Eduard Taaffe, the Prime Minister of the

Austrian half of the Monarchy, knew how Rudolf had met his end. Though he drew back from revealing the truth, another Prime Minister of the day had no such inhibitions. In his letter of February 12, 1889, the Prince of Wales wrote to Queen Victoria: 'You tell me that Lord Salisbury is positive that poor Rudolf and that unfortunate young lady were murdered . . .'[13]

And so the truth will out. The Crown Prince Rudolf, a most talented if wayward scion of the House of Habsburg, the man who might have dragged the Monarchy into the 20th century, and saved it in a democratised, federated form, died from a bullet at the time he wanted to die, but the trigger was pulled by agents of his arch-enemies, the man whom he considered 'the gravedigger of the Monarchy'[14] and his uncle, the Archduke Albert, Colonel-in-Chief of the Roll Commando Execution Squad.

Epilogue

Everyone connected with the tragedy of Mayerling is long since dead. The buildings where the ill-starred Crown Prince played out his life still stand, but they stand only as monuments to the age which, for the modern reader, must seem infinitely remote.

Rudolf's shooting lodge was transformed, within a year from his death, into a convent for the Carmelite Order of nuns, whose duty is to pray for the soul of the Crown Prince—and, one hopes, to say a few prayers for Mary Vecsera.

The Hofburg, Schönbrunn and the Belvedere are all museums. Rudolf's bachelor quarters house the Federal Office of Monuments; Archduke Albert's palace, now known as the Albertina, is a picture gallery. He died on February 18, 1895, and he had the humiliating experience of having to preside when a military commission, set up by Francis Joseph, re-examined Rudolf's drill book and found it so good that it was promptly introduced in the Austrian Army and was in use until 1916.

Laxenburg Castle, the birthplace of the Crown Prince, has suffered many vicissitudes. That it has survived since its foundation in 1273, when the Habsburg Dynasty began its career, is thanks to the devoted efforts, since 1966, of a well-known Austrian actor, Bernard Hall (born Bernard Koller).

During World War I the last Habsburg Emperor, Charles IV, spent his summers in Laxenburg with his Empress, Zita. From 1919 the castle stood empty until 1938, when the Germans—after Hitler had occupied Austria—set up offices there. From 1945 to 1955 the Russians were in possession and left the place in ruins. Emperor Franz's Biedermeyer furniture, Napoleon's Empire furniture, and the Empress Elizabeth's furniture all disappeared; the parquet floors, made of precious Caucasian wood, had been used as firewood; the superb plasterwork of the ceilings was badly damaged; the rare wooden frames of the twenty-one window niches had to be scrubbed and scraped ten times to restore the original glowing patina of the timber. The

Rococco stoves had gone—not a single piece could be found; irreplaceable crystal chandeliers had been picked off, bit by bit, by revolver shots. In 1966, however, Bernard Hall, the actor, leased part of the derelict castle for an annual rent of one Schilling per square yard: for an area of 480 square metres, his annual rent is Sch. 5,860. The estimates Hall obtained for restoring Laxenburg ranged from Sch. 1.6m to Sch. 2.5m. So he decided to do the work himself. He began with a hammer and a spade—by now he owns equipment worth Sch. 25,000, though this is woefully inadequate for a proper restoration. After ten years' work, Hall has achieved the incredible: he has made the room of Emperor Franz, Napoleon's bedroom and the room in which Rudolf was born, not only habitable, but modern and lovely in a new way. The Empress Elizabeth would surely approve of what Bernard Hall is doing, and of the simple happiness the actor has found in her apartments . . .

The people close to Rudolf when he met his end were with few exceptions themselves, beset by tragedy. The Emperor Francis Joseph lived until November 21, 1916; and had to endure two more terrible blows: the murder of his beloved wife, Elizabeth, by the anarchist Luigi Lucchini on September 10, 1898; and that of his nephew, Crown Prince Francis Ferdinand by a Serb nationalist, on June 28, 1914, in Sarajevo. In his old age—he was eighty four years old—Francis Joseph agreed to the sending of an ultimatum that was bound to lead to war with Serbia, knowing that Russia would back her. Rudolf had wanted a showdown with Russia, but before she had made her alliance with France, and before she was sure of English support. Fortunately Francis Joseph did not live to see the outcome of World War I, and the dissolution of the Monarchy, the catastrophe he had dreaded all his life.

The former Crown Princess Stephanie refused to marry Archduke Francis Ferdinand for reasons of state, but married for love the Hungarian Count Elemér Lónyay; Francis Joseph stripped her of her title of ex-Crown Princess, even of Archduchess and her father refused to allow her to call herself Princess of the Belgians. In 1904, when Stephanie came to the assistance of her sister Louise who caused a world scandal by divorcing her husband—Rudolf's friend Prince Philip of Coburg—and running away with a Croat Uhlan lieutenant, Geza von Matasits, the Emperor wrote to Stephanie that he never wished to see her again. In Hungary out of courtesy Stephanie was usually addressed as Royal Highness, but even when on February 9, 1917, the young Emperor Charles IV elevated Elemér Lónyay at Stephanie's urgent request to the rank of prince, she still could not call herself royal highness, which she minded very much.

As she could not have any more children, and as she quarrelled with her only daughter, Archduchess Elizabeth, she was very embittered. After Archduchess Erzsi's marriage to Prince Otto Windisch-Graetz[1] had broken up in 1924 and they were divorced, Rudolf's daughter married Leopold Petznek, a schoolteacher of working-class background. Mother and daughter never met again. Petznek was a man of parts. In 1921 he was elected member of the Lower Austrian *Bundestag* (Parliament), and in 1927 became its President. In 1934 he was detained for five months on account of his extreme Leftist views. He lived in retirement until early 1945, when Austria's Nazi rulers sent him to a concentration camp. After World War II, Petznek became President of the Court of Audits, finally President of the Highest Court of Audits. He died in 1956; Archduchess Erzsi survived him by nine years.

When at the end of World War II military operations engulfed Hungary, Princess Stephanie fled to the Benedictine Abbey of Pannonhalma, as Oroszvár,—her husband's lovely country house —was first looted by German and then by Russian soldiers; finally the area in which the house stands had to be ceded by Hungary to Czechoslovakia. Prince Elemér Lónyay also took refuge in Pannonhalma; Stephanie died there on August 23, 1945; Elemér on July 20, 1946. At present Oroszvár—called Rusice—houses the Klement Gottwald School for Communist Pioneers.

Rudolf's sisters, Archduchess Gisela and Archduchess Marie Valerie were the two members of his immediate family who did find happiness. Gisela lived until 1932, Marie Valerie until 1924, and both were surrounded by loving families. In 1975 Marie Valerie's son, the seventy-five-year-old Archduke Theodor of Habsburg-Lothringen, invited all the grandchildren and great grandchildren of Emperor Francis Josef for a family reunion at

Castle Wallsee on the Danube. Over one hundred and thirty members of the Habsburg family turned up; the event had taken over a year to organise. Relatives came from Austria, Belgium, Australia—and Russia. But the long shadow of the *Mayerling* tragedy stretched out even over this happy family party in that the highlight of the celebrations was when Archduke Theodor read from Archduchess Valerie's diaries her description of what had happened at the Hofburg at the time of Rudolf's death at the time of her mother's murder and at the outbreak of World War I.

Gossip had it that Archduke Johann Salvator was somehow connected with Rudolf's death. This cannot be so, as he was in Trieste at the time, and his telegram of condolences is extant at the Vienna archives. Whatever the Austrian secret police discovered of Johann Salvator's negotiations (or merely irresponsible talk) with Hungarians, is not known, and will not be known until the *Mayerling* papers become available. The fact remains that on October 8, 1889, Johann Salvator had to renounce officially his rank, position, income, even his nationality according to the formidable Spanish Etiquette rules of the House of Habsburg. He would have liked to retain his rank as captain beginning his new life, but the Emperor refused his request. Johann Orth left Austria a few days later with Miltschi Stubl, the little ballet dancer whom he adored, and married her in London.

Later he set sail from Chatham on his boat, the *Santa Margherita*, for La Plata. Allegedly the *Santa Margherita* sank in a storm near Cape Horn. But from the first there were doubts. Count Wilczek, who was greatly interested in maritime matters and well informed in all things nautical on account of his Arctic travels, was convinced that the *Santa Margherita* did not go down; Johann Orth carried several sets of ship's papers so that no one would suspect his craft of being the *Santa Margherita*. He had dismissed his Austrian crew at the first port he reached, and in his disguised vessel no one recognised him.

Count Wilczek told Marie Larisch that the Court knew perfectly well that Johann Salvator was alive, they had had information from South American police authorities. When Julia von Stockhausen worked for Princess Stephanie, she found a letter from Archduchess Antoinette, Countess of Cazerta, Johann Salvator's niece, who had met him in Cannes when he was on his way to

Japan. One final witness: Arthur Count Polzer-Hoditz, the Chief of Emperor Charles' Cabinet. In the autumn of 1907 he accompanied the young Archduke Charles on a ride across Lobau to Orth. He spoke of Johann Orth, remarking that recently newspapers had revived the story that he was still alive. 'The Archduke looked at me in surprise and asked laughingly whether I really believed that he lost his life off Cape Horn.' 'He is as much alive as you or I. Papa[2] corresponded with him to the last.' The Archduke Charles added that Johann Orth lived a contented life as a farmer in South America.'[3]

Wilczek firmly believed that the Emperor had authorised Johann Orth to return to Austria and to live in his castle near lake Gmunden without his old titles and prerogatives, provided he testified to the identity of the little boy in America who was alleged to be Rudolf's illegitimate son. It is not known why Johan Orth refused to do this. In 1911 the Hofburg Chancellery announced that the former Archduke Johann Salvator had died.

After Rudolf's death, the police sent their informer, Dr Florian Meissner, to sound out Mizzi Caspar. Completely heartbroken, she kept on repeating that Rudolf had told her that his honour demanded that he should die—but would never explain why. In his report Meissner said that for this reason an American duel[4] could not be excluded. In this Meissner was entirely mistaken. Then the police also questioned Mizzi; this is confirmed in the *Mayerling Original*, although it did not contain the protocol of her statements. Some historians believe it was kept at the Justizpalast and destroyed in the fire of 1927; others say it was kept under lock and key at the Vienna *Rathaus* (town hall) until 1932, when it vanished. It may be among the Mayerling papers. E. C. Corti says in his biography of the Empress that a letter exists relating to the planned suicide pact of Rudolf with Mizzi, but he did not reveal where it is.[5]

Mizzi died on January 28, 1907, as a result of a very painful spinal disease. She wished to be buried in the cemetry of Mödling, near the place where Rudolf had wanted to commit suicide with her. I went to Mödling to photograph her grave. As I was unable to find it, and the Mödling cemetery is not a large one, I went to the manager in charge. Thus I learnt that on 'higher orders' Mizzi's grave had to disappear; she was buried in another one, the plinth carrying the name: Familie Fischer; later her remains were once more transferred, and now she lies in a grave carrying the name of Familie Kubischta.

Thanks to the good offices of Professor Walter Hummelberger, I learnt that the 'higher orders' did not emanate from the Hofburg but from the Austrian Cemetery Authorities, whose ordinances lay down that every so often graves must be renewed' (*erneuert werden*)' and graves of persons without descendants must be 'dissolved' and the remains they contain 'rebedded' in another grave. The President of the Austrian heraldic and genealogical *Verein Adler*, Dr Hans Jäger von Sunstenau, stated categorically on August 16, 1977, that Mizzi's remains were twice moved for the above-mentioned reasons.

Johann Loschek, Rudolf's devoted valet, was born in 1845 in Wiener Neustadt, and died in 1932 in Kleinwolgersdorf. Officially he was keeper of the Outer Door, in fact he waited on Rudolf. How devoted he was to the Crown Prince is borne out by the letter the Prince of Wales wrote to Queen Victoria on February 12, 1889: 'Nobody knew that the young lady was with him but his valet. The latter seems to have had orders from the Emperor not to leave him alone—but regardless of the poor man's wishes, Rudolf peremptorily ordered him to leave before the deed was committed.'[6]

Loschek was not popular with the Hofburg, possibly because he would not report on his master. He received a pension of 1,300 *Gulden* a year; due to the post-World War I inflation, this became worthless. On April 19, 1928, aged eighty-three, Loschek dictated to his son, Johann Loschek Jr., a memorandum of what he remembered about that night in Mayerling. But he still would not say one word about Rudolf's private affairs.[7] He did, however, describe his visit to the Hofburg on February 2, 1889, where he had been summoned to the office of the Lord Chamberlain, Prince Konstantin Hohenlohe, to take the oath of secrecy. Unexpectedly Taaffe walked in—gay,debonair, his hat at the back of his head and a cigar in his mouth. He called out cheerfully: 'Hallo, Konstantin, here I am.' Even so many years later, Loschek was still shocked by the evident pleasure of the Prime Minister over Rudolf's death. 'He behaved as though organising a reception and not the interment of the Crown Prince.'[8]

Loschek added the following postscript to his memorandum:

It has been claimed again and again that I received a large sum of money, etc. This is a complete fabrication as so much else about Crown Prince Rudolf. Rudolf remembered all his employees in his will. In this way I received 2,600 florins as well as guns, clothes, etc., and I possess a receipt for every single item. It is a fairy tale to claim that Loschek now became a rich man. What little capital I have, I have earned honestly and fairly. Besides, on our many journeys I was able to put aside my travel expenses entirely. To be honest, I am proud to die a poor man.

Johann Loschek
Valet to the late Crown Prince Rudolf, retired.
Kleinwolgersdorf, 19. I.1928

The fat *Fiakker* coachman, Josef Bratfisch, who drove Mary Vecsera to Mayerling, and spent the night of January 29–30 outside Rudolf's bedroom, must have known what happened. He wrote no memorandum, and never spoke to anyone about his memories, unless it was to Mizzi Caspar, whom he frequently visited.

Josef Bratfisch, nicknamed *Das Nockerl* (the dumpling)[9] was born in Vienna on August 26, 1847, the son of Franz Bratfisch, a master-saddler. They lived in Loudongasse 52; later he was employed as *Fiakker* coachman by Leopold Wallner, Breitenfeldergasse 13, VIIIth *Bezirk*, Josefstadt. Rudolf twice visited Bratfisch at his home. Before going there, he sent word to Frau Bratfisch, who was an excellent cook, to prepare for him roast beef, Pariser sausages, and dressed *Liptauer* cheese. On his second visit, when he was accompanied by Mizzi, *Das Nockerl* and his wife sang Viennese songs, and Rudolf was so pleased with their performance that he rewarded Bratfisch with two Bosnian pistols. After Bratfisch's death, his collection of presents from Rudolf was sold at auction.

Bratfisch was questioned several times by the police, on one occasion by Krauss himself: he was then offered by the Court Chancellery a considerable pension and a large lump sum of money if he left Austria. He refused to go; instead two months after Mayerling he bought No 8 Annagasse (now Lacknergasse) in

Hernals, the 17th District of Vienna, and there ran his own cab business. *Kommerzialrat* Egon Wallner, son of Bratfisch's employer, on January 7, 1966, wrote to Dr Judtmann: 'I am firmly convinced that Bratfisch received a major sum from the Court Chancellery and according to my father's accounts, he started a business of his own after the Mayerling tragedy.'[10]

Bratfisch died at his home on December 16, 1892, from cancer of the larynx. He is buried at the Hernals cemetery; on his tombstone he is proudly described as: The *Leibfiakker* of Crown Prince Rudolf. He took his secret with him to the grave. The police report on his statements has disappeared—as has that of the cook at Mayerling, Mali and her kitchenmaid, Kati. Bratfisch revealed nothing of what he knew about the night at Mayerling; he only said that he thought he had taken the Baroness to meetings with H.I.H. about twenty times.

The death of Rudolf had a shattering effect on his three great journalist friends. Maurices Szeps, Dr Berchtold Frischauer and Julius Futtaky carried on, but their chief moral and financial support had disappeared. Szeps died in 1908, Frischauer in 1924 and Futtaky in 1895, aged only forty-five. It is a great loss that his diaries, which contained very important information about Crown Prince Rudolf, were 'inadvertently destroyed'. He never talked about Rudolf, nor did Szeps, who must have known all the facts, nor Frischauer. They took their secrets to the grave. All of them had handed over their letters from Rudolf to the Emperor's Cabinet Chief, and some were returned to them later on. What happened to the rest is not known; presumably they form part of the Mayerling papers.

Rudolf's devoted Hungarian history teacher, J. J. Rónay, also had an unexpectedly unhappy end. He had gained the complete confidence of Empress Elizabeth, who on March 31, 1872, put him in charge of the education of her youngest and favourite child, Archduchess Valerie. This kept J.J. for nine years in closest contact with the imperial family and enabled him to see Rudolf often, especially in Hungary, at Gödöllö. In 1874 he had become titular Bishop of Szkodar, which made him a member of the Hungarian Upper House, where his speeches were noted for the many English examples on which he drew.

In 1888, Valerie's education completed, J.J. retired on his full salary for life. Two of his sisters came to live with him, he was surrounded by friends and was looking forward to contented old age. Then Rudolf died at Mayerling. Apart from his personal distress, all of a sudden ugly attacks rained down on him: he was accused of having implanted destructive ideas into Rudolf's mind and taught him without giving him any religious grounding. In Budapest the *Egyházi Közlöny* (Ecclesiastical Gazette) published an article with the title: 'Freemason'—stating that he had introduced Rudolf to Freemasonry. Several papers bluntly said that Bishop Rónay was responsible for Rudolf's death and printed scandalous, completely fictitious reports.

J.J. was too unhappy and too stunned even to try to answer the infamous lies spread about him. He died on April 17, 1889, at 5.30 in the morning, having become in less than three months a withered old man—with a broken heart. He was buried on April 19, 1889, with the rosary that Rudolf had brought him from Jerusalem wound round his hands.

The mother of Mary Vecsera, Baroness Helen Vecsera, lived until February 1, 1925. Her life was no longer an easy one, as the inflation wiped out her personal fortune, and the Czechoslovak Government refused to pay her her husband's pension because he had been absent from Slovakia during all his adult life. Her eldest son, Ladislaus, lost his life in the Ringtheater fire in Vienna in 1881; her second son, Franz, was killed in World War I. Her daughter Hanna married on June 26, 1897, a distinguished Dutchman, Hendrik Graf Bylandt, with whom she was very happy, but she died in childbirth on February 20, 1901, aged thirty-three. By the end of World War I Helen's four dashing brothers were dead, and she lived under very straitened circumstances.

If in the context of Mayerling anyone can be dubbed villain of the piece, it is the Prime Minister, Taaffe, and Marie Larisch. Whatever may be said against Taaffe, he was at least motivated by legitimate interests of State as he saw them. With Marie Larisch, who conspired to bring Rudolf and Mary Vecsera together for money, there was no redeeming feature.

Count Eduard Taaffe remained Prime Minister until July, 1893, and died on November 29, 1895, aged 62. His son Heinrich died in 1928 and his grandson Edward in 1967. As related earlier, in

1939 Edward Taaffe returned to Ireland, smuggled the Mayerling papers out of Czechoslovakia, but would not reveal where he had placed them even to Group Captain Taaffe, a close friend as well as one of his heirs.

When Edward Taaffe left for Ireland, he had no more relations in Austria, and with him not only did the line of the Counts Taaffe die out, but all connections with Austria ceased. After 230 years, the Taaffes are practically forgotten in Austria, except by historians who still want to see the Mayerling papers to find out for certain how Rudolf died.

Vienna is still there, outwardly full of memories, inwardly happy under a social democratic regime of which Eduard Taaffe would certainly not have approved, but which has undoubtedly brought general well-being to the population, and a neutrality which has given Austrian politicians great opportunities to make their views heard. Dr Kurt Waldheim was re-elected for another five-year term as Secretary-General of the United Nations. The Austrian aristocracy has lost its titles, no one is interested in quarterings, but Rudolf and Elizabeth—if they were on this earth—would be pleased for small, neutral Austria has realised many of the ideals they had dreamed about.

The ultimate fate of Marie Larisch was one which befitted a woman whose consistent aim in life had been squalid self-seeking. In 1896 she divorced Georg Larisch, and on May 15, 1897, she married the Bavarian *Kammersänger* Otto Brucks. That marriage also broke up, and in 1924, aged sixty six, she married for a third time in the USA a farmer called W. A. Mayers; him she also divorced and allegedly married a fourth time a man called Fleming who had helped her with her memoirs.

Marie Larisch was an irresponsible, wildly extravagent woman, who squeezed money not only out of Rudolf, but even out of young Mary Vecsera. And yet she would have got away with her nefarious role had it not been for Tadeusz Ajdukiewicz, the Polish painter, who was engaged on painting a portrait of Rudolf in his uniform of General of the Infantry. Ajdukiewicz asked to be allowed to keep Rudolf's uniform as a souvenir after his death, and this wish was granted. Ajdukiewicz went through the pockets of the tunic and found a compromising letter from Marie Larisch to Rudolf. He saw to it that this letter reached the

Emperor; the secret police soon pieced together Marie Larisch's role in the Mayerling tragedy and the amount of money she had extracted from Rudolf. She was banned from Court for ever, her letters were returned unopened. It was the end of her life in Austria: no one would speak to her. Her second son, Georg Larisch, born in 1886, committed suicide in 1909 when he discovered the part played by his mother in the Mayerling drama.

Marie Larisch avenged herself for her humiliation by viciously libelling the Empress Elizabeth in her books. For instance, she related in detail in her book, *Secrets of a Royal House*, how Elizabeth bore an illegitimate child in Sassetôt, France; had she taken the trouble to consult the Empress's travel dates, she would have found that she had not been to France ever after 1875, while Countess Zanardi-Landi, her alleged illegitimate child, was born in 1882. And yet, having practically lived at the Hofburg for thirteen years, Marie Larisch did know a great deal of what went on during this period; though the utmost caution is advisable, some of her impressions and reports relating to Rudolf and others are worth using. She died in America in 1931. It is not known where she is buried; she lies rejected to the bitter end.[11]

Let this book end on an extraordinary prophecy relating to Crown Prince Rudolf by Sister Catherine Filljung, a Dominican nun who founded an orphanage at Biding, Alsace, and travelled to Vienna in June, 1886. Sister Catherine was to collect donations for her foundation, and had a letter of introduction from the Bishop of Alsace to Archduchess Maria Theresa, the second wife of Archduke Karl Ludwig. The Archduchess invited Sister Cathérine to watch the Corpus Christi procession. As Sister Cathérine caught sight of the Crown Prince, she had a vision which she immediately told the Archduchess: 'I saw the Crown Prince sleeping, entangled in a thin net, and hanging dangerously over the edge of a precipice. Then my vision changed in a different direction. I saw the Prince in a pavilion with many windows right in the middle of a thick wood. He was lying lifeless on a bed, his whole body covered in blood.'

Sister Cathérine explained to the alarmed Archduchess: 'If the Crown Prince persists in his foolish passion, he will die a violent death.'

The Archduchess Maria Theresa knew that Sister Cathérine had on previous occasions had visions of events which subsequently came to pass. Deeply moved by the prophecy, she told it to Bishop Dr Marschall, who reported it to the Emperor. On May 27, 1886, Francis Joseph invited Sister Cathérine to his presence, and asked her to tell him everything she knew about his son.

The nun closed her eyes as if seeking inspiration from higher powers. Then she gave the Emperor the following interpretation of her vision: 'If the Crown Prince continues to persist in his vain excesses, the father will lose what he holds dearest on earth. In an explosion of insanity the idol of a powerful empire will pass away like a dream. He will die like the hero of a gloomy saga . . .'

After a few minutes of thoughtful silence, the Emperor dismissed her. Nineteen months later, to the day, Rudolf died at Mayerling.

Shortly after the event, the Emperor and the Empress decided to invite Sister Cathérine to Vienna in order to discover from her whether she could get in touch with their deceased son.

The Emperor dispatched Bishop Dr Marschall to request Sister Cathérine to come to Vienna for an interview; at the same time the Archduchess Maria Theresa wrote her a letter with the request to let the imperial family know everything she could see of the dead Crown Prince's fate in the other world.

Sister Cathérine had had another vision of the dead Crown Prince, but declined to come to Vienna. She told Bishop Dr Marschall: 'I saw it all. There is no need for me to come to Vienna. There would only be many confusing questions which I have no desire to answer.

'But tell the Emperor he may rest at peace in his grief. There is no need to deprive the Crown Prince's unfortunate soul of Christian charity. Requiem masses may continue to be said for the peace of his soul. Tell the Emperor that his son did not commit suicide. He was murdered. It would have been easy enough for the Imperial Court to find the guilty person if it had wanted to do so.'[12]

Notes

The Birth of a Crown Prince, pp. 7–15

1 From a letter in the possession of Széchen family.
2 Joan Haslip. *The Lonely Empress*, p. 120.
3 The last Rudolf of Habsburg was the antithesis of the first. He was ahead of his time; conscious of and sympathetic to the wishes of the people, he wanted to transform the Habsburg Empire into a liberal commonwealth, within which all nationalities would meet on equal footing and remain united of their own accord. He foresaw the break-up of the Empire founded by the first Rudolf of Habsburg but, for reasons this book will tell, he failed to prevent it.
4 Actually Rudolf was a very delicate nervous baby.
5 Somewhere in the Tirol a bewildered Austrian sentry was accused of having overstepped an invisible borderline. A shot was fired, and returned, and over this incident the war began. Lord Palmerston wrote: 'The conflict was contrived after some exertion by the meddlesome mediocrity, Napoleon III, in whose foolish mind ideas multiply like rabbits.'
6 Grünne was Adjutant General in charge of higher military appointments.
7 Harry Holmes was forty-nine years old at this time. He had an exceptional knowledge of horses. He trained the Empress's mounts and prepared them for the hunting field. Later he was put in charge of the Empress's stables in Gödöllö which in 1872 contained 26 horses, I pony and 1 donkey.
8 John Welcome; *The Sporting Empress*, p. 24. The only member of the imperial family who was a passionate horseman was the Emperor's younger brother, Archduke Ferdinand Maximillian—Maxl to his mother. Maxl tore about at a mad gallop, but the Empress was more than his match. Francis Joseph had drilled himself into perfect mastery over his mounts, yet he did not ride for pleasure. Elizabeth was instinctively aware of this and preferred to ride with Maxl, which Francis Joseph realised and resented.
9 See Chapter III of *Gold and Iron, Bismarck and Bleichröder*, by Fritz Stern.
10 Carl Count Lónyay; *Crown Prince Rudolf: the tradegy of Mayerling*, p. XV, said of Grünne: '. . . he had the ruthlessness of the autocrat and the harshness of the bureaucrat.'
11 This brought to the fore Francis Joseph's latent jealousy of his brother. In 1860 the English Foreign Secretary, Lord John Russell, added fuel to the fire by strongly advising Francis Joseph to place Archduke Ferdinand Maximilian at the head of an independent Hungarian State. This proved to the Emperor what he had already heard—that Maxl had made an excellent impression in England, and that Queen Victoria and Prince Albert wished him well. It was probably owing to his jealousy of Maxl that Francis Joseph allowed him to embark on the Mexican adventure—because this would take him away from Austria. Francis Joseph had a very good idea that Maximilian could not succeed in Mexico without considerable European help, and he was determined that his impoverished Austria should not get involved.
12 See Chapter IV, p. 63.

13 Joan Haslip believes that she consulted a doctor in Vienna.
14 Joan Haslip, op. cit., p. 400.
15 By a strange coincidence, in 1921 the last Habsburg ruler, Emperor Charles IV, and his family were exiled to Madeira by the Conference of Ambassadors.
16 She returned to Madeira once more, a few months before her death, and stood near the place where Emperor Charles IV was to be buried in 1924.
17 Archduchess Sophie's Mistress of the Household.

Crisis over Rudolf's Education, pp. 16–21

1 Extant in the Vienna State Archives.
2 Common knowledge, quoted by E. C. Corti, *Elisabeth die seltsame Frau*; Dr Oskar Freiherr von Mitis, *Das Leben des Kronprinzen Rudolf*; Viktor Bibl, *Die Tragödie Eines Sinkenden Reiches*; and many other historians.
3 V. Bibl. op. cit., p. 120.
4 Richard Barkeley; *The Road To Mayerling*, p. 11.
5 Understandably the Viennese medical profession was offended that the Empress had called in a Bavarian doctor to give a 'final verdict'. Dr von Fischer was a passionate shot who longed to add the antlers of a stag of the Danube marshes to his hunting trophies. On his way to the marshes he drove through the Prater. No one had told him that in the Prater there were tame stags, fed and petted by visitors—some even had names given to them. Dr von Fischer shot the first stag that approached his carriage. Of course the story spread like wild fire, and the unfortunate Dr von Fischer became the butt of endless malicious jokes. His jealous colleagues organised a regular campaign against him. John Welcome, *The Sporting Empress, p.* 26, and other sources.
6 Joan Haslip, *The Lonely Empress*, p. 16.
7 Dr P. Mellisch, *Fürst Auersperg*, Vol. 51, p. 203.
8 Under the pseudonym Anastasius Grün Prince Auersperg wrote lyrical and political poems. The latter created a sensation by their originality, bold liberalism and fine ironic humour. Some were translated into English. Francis Joseph appointed Prince Auersperg life member of the *Herrenhaus*, the Austrian Upper House.
9 *Kriegsarchiv*, Vienna, *Gerichtsakten*, 1866.
10 *Kriegsarchiv*, Vienna, Gondrecourt's *Erziehungsplan*, 1886.
11 E. C. Corti, op. cit., p. 110.
12 E. C. Corti, op. cit., p. 32.
13 Gondrecourt got another appointment and in 1867 was retired as a Lieutenant-General.
14 E. C. Corti, op. cit., p. 111.

The Right Man in Charge, pp. 22–33

1 Actually it was in his nineteenth year,
2 Edmund von Glaise Horstenau, *Franz Josephs Weggefährte, pp.* 230–31 F.
3 See *Latour's Gesammelte Schriften* (Latour's Collected Writings), Cartons 3 and 4, at the Vienna State Archives.
4 Vienna State Archives, in one of the Rudolf Cartons.

5 Aged eight, Rudolf told Latour: 'I simply follow the religion forced on me at Court because I have no means of resisting it.' C. Count Lónyay, *Crown Prince Rudolf: the Tragedy of Mayerling*, p. 43.
6 Vienna State Archives.
7 Letter extant at Vienna State Archives. In August, 1871, Rudolf wrote about Germany; 'Maintained and drilled by military police and a wooden bureaucracy, the spirit of empire and unity floats on the wings of a patriotism enforced and cultivated at the point of the bayonet.'
8 Rudolf's diary is preserved at the Vienna State Archives.
9 Rudolf had picked up Hungarian from one of his former wet nurses. Rimely's main problem was to cure him of the strong provincial accent he had caught from her.
10 In Austria and in the whole of Europe it was believed that Austria would easily defeat Prussia. But the Prussian envoy to France, von der Goltz, reported to King (later Emperor) William I: 'It is said that the House of Rothschild is determined to use all its influence to prevent Prussia from causing a war to break out.' The Rothschilds knew which side would win. E. C. Corti; *The Rothschilds*, p. 273.
11 Letter extant at the Vienna State Archives.
12 The first owner of Gödöllö, Antal Count Grassalkovich, erected a monument to his favourite grey horse, which Elizabeth found very *sympatisch* (congenial).
13 As Ida had no title—she belonged to the untitled landed gentry—according to Spanish Etiquette she could not be a Lady-in-Waiting in the Austrian Court. In Hungary, where Spanish Etiquette was unknown, there was no such difficulty. Elizabeth invented the position of Reader for Ida Ferenczy. She became devoted to her, addressing her in the familiar second person singular, and Ida remained her closest friend until Elizabeth's last day, when she was murdered. Ida was one of the executors of Elizabeth's will.

Rudolf's Hungarian History Teacher, pp. 34–37

1 Hyacinth John in English. In this text I am using the Hungarian initials, J.J.
2 Györ is at the centre of four rivers, three of which pour into the Danube, and to this day the area suffers from flooding, the last time being in 1974.
3 The water was frozen solid in the trenches Father Rónay had helped to dig.
4 The role played by Hungarian Jewry in the War of Independence was outstanding; in recognition of their heroism Kossuth granted them full citizenship rights, cancelling all previous restraints on them.
5 Arthur Görgei, born in 1818 in Toporcz, Upper Hungary, died in Budapest in 1916. He was the most successful general of the uprising, who won a series of brilliant victories against the Austrians. Thanks to him Kossuth's Republic would have prevailed had not Tsar Nicholas I come to Francis Joseph's rescue. Görgei was the only insurgent general not executed due to the personal intervention of the Tsar. He was imprisoned until 1867, when he was pardoned. The son of a saxon family, he did not like the Hungarians, and several of them have accused him of treason because Francis Joseph spared his life. After 1867 Görgei worked as an engineer, at which profession he was as talented as at soldiering.
6 In this century no paper of Communist Hungary could have published such letters as the *Pesti Napló* (Gazette of Pest) did last century. It is also questionable

whether a similarly dispassionate and well informed source of information as Father Rónay was, would have been available.

7 J. J. Rónay's *Diary Fragments* consist of eight red-leather-bound volumes, published by himself. One of the 150 series is in the British Library, British Museum. This quotation is from Volume II, p. 281.

8 Daughter of the second Earl Grey; died in 1859.

9 Széchényi's harsh criticism was so telling, and his wit so pungent that the Austrian secret police restarted their harassment of the voluntary inmate of the Döbling Lunatic Asylum. They drove Széchényi to the point that he committed suicide on April 7, 1860. The indignation and grief this caused in Hungary can be imagined.

10 Kossuth had been interned in Turkey for two years. On October 23, 1851, he landed in England, where he was the object of extraordinary enthusiasm. In the USA his reception was equally rapturous. Other Hungarian exiles protested against Kossuth's claim to have been the only hero of the Revolution, accusing him of arrogance, cowardice, and duplicity. Kossuth had, against the advice of Széchenyi, forced the pace to war with the Habsburg dynasty to gain Hungary full independence. Széchényi for his part wanted reforms and concessions, but he realised that a Hungary ruling over a large number of national minorities —Slovaks, Rumanians, Saxons, Croats, Serbs—was not viable, especially as Kossuth would not grant the minorities equal status with the Hungarians. From America Kossuth soon returned to England, and with his wife and sons lived here for eight years. In 1859 he went to Italy where he tried unsuccessfully to organise a Hungarian Legion to participate in the Crimean War. He remained in Italy, refusing to reconcile himself to the new regime in Hungary, or to avail himself of the amnesty of 1867. Though elected to the Diet that year, he never took his seat. He died in Turin on March 20, 1894, and was buried in Budapest.

11 Father Rónay contributed more and more articles to Hungarian publications; his Sketches of *The English Theatrical World*, published in Pest in 1865, proved a great success. *Budapesti Szemle* (Review of Budapest) asked him for a review of T. H. Huxley's *Evidence of Man's Place in Nature*, but when in print the author's name was —Ágost Greguss! Fear of the censor was the explanation of this alias, which greatly upset J.J. In 1864 his book, *The Formation of Races, Man's Place in Nature and Age*, containing his collected essays and the Huxley review, appeared anonymously. When the original publishers went bankrupt, Mór Ráth, a brave Jewish publisher, bought up the remaining copies and put J.J.'s name on them. Paul Hunfalvy's *Reguly—Traditions*, which J.J. translated for Prince Lucien Bonaparte, dealt with ancient religions and the Hungarian–Vogul language groups.

Historic Truth instilled into Rudolf, pp. 38–46

1 At present the Embassy of the Hungarian People's Republic is housed in this building, Bankgasse 6, Vienna.

2 Francis Joseph's memorandum is extant at the Austrian State Archives; Latour's statement is taken from Father Rónay's *Diary Fragments*, Vol. V., p. 7.

3 Ibid., Vol. V, pp. 7 and 8.

4 It is now known that not all the Hungarian tribes came by this route; some came from the south, having followed the Danube.

5 Ibid., Vol. V, p. 13.
6 According to the five-volume *Magyar Történet* (Hungarian History) by Bálint Hóman and Gyula Szekfü, Vol. I, p. 56, some of them were mercenaries, others criminals.
7 Hóman–Szekfü, op. cit., Vol. I. p. 370. Men from the Netherlands and from Saxony joined the Emperor's crusading force. Later the French King, Louis VII, also passed through Hungary with his approximately 60,000 crusaders, and there was no trouble.
8 Rónay, op. cit. Vol. V, p. 59.
9 Ibid., Vol. V, p. 62.
10 Miklós Jankovich, a distinguished Hungarian historian has found documentary proof that Gábor Bethlen was murdered by Habsburg agents.
11 C. Lónyay. *Crown Prince Rudolf: the Tragedy of Mayerling* p. 16.
12 op. cit., Vol. V. p. 276.
13 About £10,000.
14 One of the best sources for this and the following passages is the five-volume Hóman-Szekfü Hungarian history.
15 Rónay, op., cit Vol. V, p. 305.
16 This quotation and the following paragraphs are from Rónay, Vol. V, pp. 312–13.
17 Some years later the General came to London and visited the Guinness breweries, where with the cry: 'General Hyena!' the workers gave him a good beating.
18 Count Andor Semsey, great-grandson of Carolina Károlyi, remembers seeing her as a small child. In a letter to Miklós Jankovich, who showed it to me in Budapest in 1975, Semsey wrote that his mother told him the story of the curse. The Hungarian writer and historian, László Passuth, also related this story to me. Princess Stephanie included it in her memoirs, p. 52. Michael Károlyi, in his memoirs published in Budapest in 1977, added that his grandmother would not allow one word of German to be spoken in her presence, nor could any relative appear before her in a 'uniform of Francis Joseph'.
19 The text of Francis Joseph's speech is extant in the Austrian State Archives, and in Father Rónay's *Diary Fragments*, Vol. V, p. 324.

Rudolf comes of Age—his Foreign Travels, pp. 47–61

1 According to spanish Etiquette, Rudolf should have completed his studies at eighteen. Although I have been unable to find direct proof (many documents have been lost from the Austrian State Archives during World War II) it seems probable that Latour induced the Emperor to allow Rudlof to complete his studies according to plan. This happened about July 20, 1877; Rudolf was declared of age four days later.
2 *Eine Orientreise* is the original title: first published in 1879, it was well received and there were three more editions, the last in 1884, with one hundred illustrations.
3 Lajos Benedek was a Hungarian of modest parentage and a Protestant. An outstanding soldier, he had proved his ability in many battles, particularly in Italy. In 1866, when he was offered the command of the Austrian forces, at first he refused on the grounds that he was not the right person to handle such large numbers, and moreover he did not know the terrain. Then he objected

to the deployment of the Austrian Forces, but was overruled by the Army High Command. Forced to serve, after the debacle the Emperor accepted his sacrifice and the ruin of a distinguished military career. When he died, General Benedek left instructions that he should be buried in civilian clothes.

4 C. Lónyay. *General Benedek*, p. 435.

5 O. von Mitis *Das Leben des Kronprinzen Rudolf*, p. 73.

6 Original in the Austrian State Archives.

7 For the text, see Vienna Archives.

8 Original in the Austrian State Archives.

9 Mrs Klára Ács has done some interesting graphological work for the Hungarian Academy of Sciences, and as a result of her analyses several historical mysteries have been solved. But graphology is still not an exact science, and it is possible that Rudolf caught gonorrhea somewhat later. He certainly had it; it figured in the autopsy report. For the text of Mrs Ács's report, see Appendix.

10 Original in the Austrian State Archives.

11 O. von Mitis, op. cit., p. 52.

12 C. Lónyay, *General Benedek* p. 31.

13 The Rev. Kantor, *Reminiscences*,

14 O. von Mitis, op. cit., p. 52.

15 Diaries of Archduchess Marie Valerie, extant in the archives of her grandson, Archduke Theodore, in his castle Wallsee-on-the-Danube; and from E. C. Corti's books on members of the Habsburg family.

16 O. von Mitis, op. cit., pp. 53–54.

17 A report at the Austrian State Archives. Also Mitis, op. cit., pp. 56–57.

18 O. von Mitis, op. cit., p. 224.

19 The present Austrian Embassy is in the same building, almost the sole embassy that has preserved its 19th century premises.

20 O. von Mitis, op cit., pp. 24–25.

21 The text of this important passage is in the Appendix.

22 Princess Margaret of Connaught married King Gustav V of Sweden.

23 Beust had been Prime Minister and Chancellor from 1866 to 1871; then Ambassador to London and to Paris.

24 Rudolf was accompanied by the Grand Duke Ferdinand of Toscana and the painter Franz von Pausinger.

25 Count Gustav Kálnoky, from November 20, 1881, until May 16, 1895, Foreign Minister of the Austro-Hungarian Monarchy.

26 Berta Szeps, *My Life and History* p. 37.

27 Leopold Wölfling, *My Life Story*, p. 34.

The Army and Marriage, pp. 62–73

1 In the words of Anton Bettelheim: 'With the publication of *Fifteen Days on the Danube*, all of a sudden a completely formed, original personality revealed itself in a loveable and self-confident manner. A spirit which looked deeper into thé inner essence of nature. He gives of his best in the description of the Lower Austrian Danube marshes, a masterpiece of lyrical mood, finely felt observation of nature and fine example of German prose writing.' O. von Mitis, *Das Leben des Kranprinzen Rudolf*, p. 161.

2 Imperial and Royal = *Kaiserlich und Königlich* = K. und K. was the usual abbreviation, used in speech and writing.

3 Ladislas Freiherr von Rieger was a popular Czech politician, and the son-in-law of František Palacky, the well known Czech historian, who wrote in German. He coined the famous phrase: 'If Austria did not exist, it would have to bé invented.'

4 I remember at a very early age hearing such views from my parents' relations serving in joint Austro-Hungarian regiments, and counter arguments from relations serving in Hungarian regiments.

5 Letter, dated 2, August 1879, by the Commanding Officer, Major Friedrich Hotze, of the 36th Infantry Regiment.

6 In a letter to Latour, Rudolf said that he even considered the possibility of an unauthorised issue of bank notes to cover the cost of the occupation as Parliament would not vote the money.

7 Letter extant at the Austrian State Archives.

8 See Appendix for the anonymous article which also appeared in the *Neues Wiener Tagblatt* on March 18, 1883.

9 Strictly translated, the Cabbala means the traditions handed down from Moses to the Rabbis of the Misnah and Talmud. Later the sense of the Cabbala was expanded to mean the tradition of the mystical interpretation of the Old Testament; it had become an occult science.

10 Two years later, when Cardinal Schwarzenberg died, Rudolf wrote a very critical article about him, which appeared anonymously on August 15, 1883, in the *Neues Wiener Tagblatt* heavily edited by Szeps. Its title was: 'The Jubilee Celebrant of the Hradžin'. Rudolf designated Cardinal Rauscher as a *Josephiner* (meaning enlightened liberal), beside whom Cardinal Schwarzenberg had played a none to gratifying role. Szeps rejected the adjective *Josephiner* and prudently termed Schwarzenberg's role 'an essentially different one'. He also supressed the part of the MS in which Rudolf said that Schwarzenberg was never able to appreciate really broad ideas of Government, and that he always retained a feudal–federal outlook.

The following passage was also blue-pencilled: 'The ridiculous conceit, the assumption that one is something apart and superior, the "innate and inherited aristocracy of the Bohemian nobility", are in the marrow of the Cardinal's bones. . . . He has collected the Bohemian aristocracy around him and he will be largely responsible for the outlook entirely unsuited to the 19th century, of the "blue blooded youth", and for the catastrophe which must result of it . . .'

11 Bertha Szeps, *My Life and History*, pp. 25–26.

12 It was the same Cardinal Archbishop with whom Rudolf had had so many differences of opinion in Prague.

13 At this moment the Empress burst into floods of tears, and for about two minutes could not regain control of herself.

14 Bertha Szeps, op. cit., p. 112.

15 Ibid., 46. At the request of Archduchess Elizabeth, daughter of Crown Prince Rudolf, the Austrian Government banned Princess Stephanie's memoirs when published in 1937. In Hungary they were not banned,

Strain between Emperor and Crown Prince, pp. 74–82

1 See 'Shackles of Spanish Etiquette' in the Appendix.

2 Raoul, Ritter von Dombrowski (published anonymously), *Kronprinz Rudolf von Österreich Ungarn als Forscher und Weidmann*, p. 37.

3 Ibid., pp. 120 and 137.
4 Ibid., p. 123
5 October 27, 1881.
6 The nearest English equivalent is hobbledehoy or hoyden, but *Trampeltier* has a perjorative meaning absent from hobbledehoy or hoyden.
7 Árpád Kendeffy died in 1882; his son Gábor successfully petitioned the title of count which an extinct branch of the Kendeffy family had been granted in the 17th century.
8 Görgényszentimre is now a school for training forest guards; it is beautifully restored: in the park the rare trees and shrubs are protected. It is also a tourist attraction, and the Rumanian guides point to a gazeboo on a small island in the lake of the park as the place where Rudolf and Mary Vecsera held their trysts. Needless to add that Mary Vecsera had never been to Transylvania, let alone Görgényszentimre.
9 Count Eduard Taaffe, 1833–95: was Prime Minister of Austria from 1879 to 1893.
10 Taaffe's concessions had been to the Czechs.
11 Prime Minister.
12 Chief of the Emperor's Cabinet Office.
13 Head of the Armed Forces.
14 Friedrich Baron von Beck-Rzikowsky was Chief of the Imperial and Royal General Staff. On his retirement he was created a count.

Rudolf Misses his Greatest Opportunity, pp. 83–92

1 Born in 1830, he died in 1902; he was Hungarian Prime Minister from March 1875 to March 1890.
2 In 1945, peasants, instigated by the Russian occupying soldiery, carried into the courtyard all the books of the library and all the documents of the archives of Geszt, the ancestral home of the Tisza family. The books were burnt in a vast bonfire; the precious documents collected by some fourteen generations, were put into sacks, and handed out to the villagers to light their fires with. The late Count Kálmán Tisza, rescued a few sacks and deposited their contents in Debreczen at the Museum and in the care of the Protestant Church—for the Tisza's are staunch Calvinists. So far, these documents have not been sorted out, and it is not known whether the grandson of Kálmán Tisza rescued important documents, with possible relevance to the strange offer of Junior Kingship to Crown Prince Rudolf.
3 See at the bottom of page 89.
4 Hungarian historians believe that the two Ministers who accompanied Tisza on his mission to Rudolf were most likely to have been Baron Béla Orczy, the Hungarian Minister in charge of the Emperor-King's personal affairs; and Count Gyula Szapáry, the Hungarian Minister of Finance. The distinguished public figure 'at that time not in an official position' they believe to have been Károly Kerkápolyi, who had served in Tisza's Cabinet for years, and was one of his closest friends. With these three men Kálmán Tisza would have talked openly and he would have sought their advice and support.
5 Tisza's conception of Rudolf's role would have been similar to that of the Queen of England in relation to England, Scotland and Wales, when the Scots and the Welsh achieve the independence they are now declaiming about.

6 Count Steven Tisza played an important part in Hungarian politics since his young days, and was Prime Minister of Hungary from 1913 to 1917.
7 Austrian State Archives.
8 O. von Mitis, *Das Leben des Kronprinzen Rudolf*, p. 118.
9 Bertha Szeps, *My Life and History*, p. 71.
10 There was also nationalist agitation in Bosnia and Herzegovina, which the Croats wanted to attract to their side and form with them and Dalmatia the Greater Croatia of their dreams; while the Serbians courted them so as to include them in a southern Slav—Yugoslav—state, as came to pass after World War I.
11 Subsequently it came to light that Dávid had had instruction from Budapest gradually to magyarise the common institutions: anything connected with defence, finance, and foreign affairs. With a wide stretch of the imagination, the post office and schools could be classified under headings of communications and finance (as they cost money!) but the Croat nationalists would have none of this Hungarian interpretation. At the request of Baron Pejacevic, who correctly foresaw the trouble in Zagreb, Dávid had postponed the coat of arms change for two years.
12 For Rudolf's article see the Appendix. Szeps not only edited it, but altered several passages so as to avoid having the *Tagblatt* issue confiscated.
13 A strong-handed Lord Lieutenant of County Zólyom. Béla Grünwald, tried to counter Slovak nationalism by founding a Slovak Cultural Association— —*Felvidéki Magyar Közmüvelödési Egyesület*— in October, 1882. But the leading young Slovaks boycotted it. Grünwald eventually committed suicide in his distress over what seemed to him not only unwarranted Slovak demands, but outright Slovak ingratitude.
14 Erzsi is the Hungarian pet name for Elizabeth.

Rudolf at the Apex of his Career, pp. 93–105

1 Ibid., pp. 147–48
2 January 9, 1884, letter to Maurice Szeps.
3 Ibid., pp. 53–55.
4 Rudolf applied on December 12, and the appointment was published on December 26, 1883
5 Ibid., pp. 151–53.
6 With the exception of Serbia, whose king, Milan Obrenoritch, was relying strongly on Austria.
7 Ibid., p. 160.
8 Abdul Aziz was deposed on May 30, 1876, and murdered on June 4 of the same year; Murad V was deposed on August 31, 1876: he was only banished from Constantinople.
9 Hirsch, born 1831, died 1896 at Szeszélyes, County Komárom, in Hungary, while organizing a shoot for the Prince of Wales. He was believed to be the richest man in the world. See p. 101 and pp. 199–200.
10 O. von Mitis, *Das Leben des Kronprinzen Rudolf*, pp. 254–56.
11 Ibid., p. 170.
12 When sailing around the Peloponnesus, *Miramar* was once more followed by dolphins. Rudolf shot some of these charming animals—to the horror of the sailors, who firmly believed that this doomed him to an early violent death.

13 This memorandum has disappeared; fortunately Bertha Szeps copied the most important passages from it and published them in her memoirs, *My Life and History*, p. 100. A rough draft of the memorandum has been found in the Austrian State Archives.

Crown Prince and Iron Chancellor, pp. 106–116

1 June 15, 1882.
2 Ibid., 139–49.
3 The Dual Alliance, *der Zwei-Kaiserbund*, signed in the Hotel Imperial in Vienna on October 7, 1879.
4 For Rudolf's report on it see Appendix.
5 The Prince of Wales, Rudolf and their intimate friends referred to Prince William of Prussia as 'Little Willie'.
6 March 2, 1883. Emperor William I's views were somewhat changeable. For instance, after Sadowa he had set his heart on marching into Vienna, and holding his victory parade in the Austrian capital. It was Bismarck, foreseeing that Germany would need Austria as an ally, who prevented this, and negotiated an acceptable peace treaty at Nikolsburg, so as to spare Francis Joseph's feelings.
7 Ibid., p. 55.
8 P. 229.
9 Béla Wodianer von Maglód, 1831–96, obtained untitled nobility in 1867. Member of the Hungarian Parliament, great businessman with international connections.
10 Rudolf fought anti-Semitism whenever and wherever he could. It pained him particularly when it spread to Hungary, where in the Counties of Zala and Somogy there was Jew-baiting and Jew-plundering. In Austria his rage was concentrated against Georg Ritter von Schönerer, who founded a conservative anti-Semitic party, of which later a very young Adolf Hitler became a member. See the Appendix for Rudolf's article castigating anti-Semitism in Hungary: *Wachsmaske—Wechselschein.*
11 On the application to the Emperor there is no exact date.
12 Maurice Jókai, 1825–1904, a brilliant and prolific Hungarian novelist. Many of his novels were translated into English.
13 Stearin is the general name for three glycerids (monostearin, distearin and tristearin) formed by a combination of stearic acid and glycerin; chiefly applied to tristearin which is the chief constituent of tallow or suet. Our white candles are stearin candles, invented in Austria in 1817.
14 On August 16, 1883, an article entitled 'A Thousand and One Days' appeared anonymously in the *Neues Wiener Tagblatt*. Its theme was that electricity and other miraculous inventions belong not to the inventors but to all mankind. 'They become communal property for the use and enjoyment of all humanity. The fairy tale is an aristocratic dream; its realisation through research and invention connected with it is the democratic reality.' The 19th century had created the marvellous things to be seen in the *Rotunda* and 'A Thousand and one Days' are its thoughtful motto. Rudolf was the anonymous author.
15 J. Szeps, *Politische Briefe an einen Freund*, p. 73, December 31, 1883.

Rudolf and Women, pp. 117–131

1 According to C. Lónyay this happened when Rudolf was twenty years old; according to Klára Ács when he was seventeen.

2 On February 18, 1853, a Hungarian tailor called János Libényi made an attempt on Francis Joseph's life. The young Emperor was walking with his A.D.C., Captain Karl Karnauer, along the Schottenbastei when Libenyi tried to stab him in the neck with a sharp, thin knife. But it slipped on the heavy golden embroidery of the collar and Karnauer threw himself on Libényi, and pulled him down to the pavement. It is on record that this incident contributed to turning Francis Joseph into a suspicious and withdrawn person. Libényi was hanged on February 9, 1856.

3 Copyright Ferenczy Verlag A.G. Zürich.

4 In addition to ordinary cabs there were the un-numbered cabs, a kind of superior carriage without number plates, as a rule a closed coupé with blinds. These could be hired for longer periods. Un-numbered carriages were substitutes for private carriages. But even persons who owned their own carriage would frequently make use of an un-numbered cab, especially for 'discreet' journeys. Discretion was the first duty of any 'personal cabby' (*Leibfiakker*). Cabbies had a fee: one florin for the first half-hour, and half-a-florin for every further half-hour.

5 Ibid., p. 119.

6 Windsor Royal Archives, Z 498.52.

7 Ibid., p. 55.

8 Ibid., p. 54–55.

9 See text in the Appendix.

10 Carl Count Lónyay was the nephew and heir of Princess Stephanie's second husband, who looked after their affairs when they were abroad, and who saved their archives. His book, *Crown Prince Rudolf the Tragedy of Mayerling*, (1949) is spoilt by many malicious comments.

11 Ibid., p. 115, based on the recollections of Victor Major von Fritsche, Crown Prince Rudolf's A.D.C. for six years, allegedly the illegimate son of the King of Würtemberg.

12 Lónyay, op. cit., p. 118.

13 Mizzi, unlike the rest of her family, spelt her name with a C—Caspar.

14 Ibid., 105.

15 *Grosse Österreichische Illustrierte*, dritter Jahrgang, Wien, Mai 5, 1951, No. 18; Titelkopf: *Der 4-te Bericht über die Tragödie von Mayerling behandelt die Rolle von Mitzi Kaspar*. But the photograph in the article is not one of Mizzi.

16 In a letter dated October 25, 1975, Professor Walter Hummelberger informed me that he could not establish whether or not Mizzi Kaspar went to secondary school. If she did, she did not finish it, for had she done so, she would have received a certificate, and there would be some indication of this.

17 Baron Maurice von Hirsch, see footnote on p. 200.

18 Archduke Otto testified that Mizzi had bought a house for 60,000 Gulden, See Lónyay, op. cit., p. 47.

19 Marie Larisch, *My Royal Relatives*, p. 116.

20 Ibid., p. 89.

21 Ibid., p. 106.

22 Ibid., p. 94.

23 Ibid., p. 153.

24 Ibid., p. 124.

25 Leopold of Bavaria, husband of Rudolf's sister Gisela; Ferdinand IV, Grand Duke of Tuscany.

26 Lieutenant of the Guard (later General) Heinrich Ritter von Spindler, first A.D.C. to Rudolf, later Head of the Crown Prince's Secretariat.

27 These are the inhabitants of an area in Moravia called Hana, whose capital is Kremzier, now called Kromeruz. They love and maintain their traditions, and still wear the costumes in which Rudolf saw them. They are exceptionally friendly and hospitable people.

28 October 7, 1883.

29 Marie Larisch, op cit., 153–154.

30 Ibid., p. 119.

First Signs of Decline, pp. 132–143

1 Extant at the Austrian State Archives.

2 The aristoctatic men's club of Hungary modelled on the London St James Club of the day.

3 Rudolf was wrong on this point; he did not know that agreement had been reached with the Tsar that the Germans should be present.

4 Reproduced in full in the Appendix.

5 Letter dated September 5, 1885.

6 Joachim von Küremberg; *Katherina Schratt*, pp. 99–100. In his introduction to her biography, Küremberg said that he had written the book on the basis of long conversations with Katherina Schratt, who honoured him with her confidence, and related conversations to him on the basis of her letters, especially those written to her friend, Pauline Lucca, in Berlin.

7 Ibid., p. 113.

8 In the archives of the former Cabinet Sectetariat of Vienna a whole bundle of documents covering the years 1867–70 has been found. From them it transpires that the Office of the Household Controller knew through secret sources of every step taken by the Empress Elizabeth. It is equally a fact that she never opened her heart about this to Rudolf—and they never exchanged their humiliating experiences; yet together they could have stood up to the Emperor.

9 W. Mayer-Gross in *Clinical Psychiatry*, writing about morphine addicts, says on pp. 372–73 that 'addiction does not lead to pronounced mental changes. There is no loss of intelligence, no dementia. . . . The great danger is ethical depravity . . . an all-embracing insincerity to family friends, colleagues . . . dishonest manœuvres of all kinds and flagrant breaches of the law.'

10 Many years later a young Adolf Hitler joined this party and imbibed Schönerer's ideas.

11 Rudolf's letter, extant in Vienna State Archives.

12 Bertha Szeps, ibid., pp. 95–96.

13 C. A. Macartney, ibid., footnote on p. 655.

14 Minister of Finance from 1880 until 1891.

15 Franz von Pausinger drew and painted in the style of Sir Edwin H. Landseer.

The Crown Prince's Illness, pp. 144–150

1 Ibid., p. 196.
2 Ibid., p. 197
3 Ibid., p. 197.
4 M.U. Dr Hofrat Max Braun, Royal Bavarian *Leibartzt* (personal physician) and hospital doctor in Munich. Born in 1831; died April 18, 1906—both in Munich.
5 Oroszvár was Prince Lónyay's country house, where he and Stephanie spent most of their time.
6 Julia von Stockhausen married Count Ferdinand von Gattenburg, who ghosted Princess Stephanie's memoirs.
7 From private conversations.
8 How common gonorrhoea was in the 19th century, is illustrated by a letter, dated July 31, 1811, written by Lord Byron to Charles Skinner Matthews from Newstead Abbey: 'The rest of my time has been spent on business and acquiring Gonorrhoea, which I regret as I was only just cured of a severe one contracted in Greece of all places.'
9 Ambrose King, 'These Dieing Diseases—Venereology in Decline' *The Lancet*, pp. 651–57, March 9, 1958.
10 Dr R. D. Catterall, F.R.C.P.E., Director of James Pringle House at the Middlesex Hospital in London.
11 W. Mayer-Gross, op. cit., p. 449: 'The condition which has been called syphilitic neurasthenia sometimes occurs in the primary stage. The patient complains of headache and difficulty in concentration, tires very easily, shows marked irritability. There is a general malaise with vague bodily discomfort, possibly pains in the limbs. . . . A similar picture may be observed in the secondary stage. . . . Associated with these mental changes there are physical signs. . . . The pupils may be abnormal, usually showing a failure to react to light, and they are generally unequal."
12 Eventually he found it and called it Lake Rudolf, which recently was re-named Lake Turkhana, after the tribe living around it.
13 Ibid., p. 208–9.

Rudolf's Assessment of the Future, pp. 151–157

1 Bismarck insisted after the defeat of Sadowa that Austria should formally resign from the German *Bund*. This formed a paragraph of the Treaty of Nikolsburg, 1866.
2 This is proved brilliantly by Fritz Stern in *Gold and Iron, Bismarck and Bleichröder*.
3 After World War II the Federal Republic of Germany, created by the victorious Allies, became in many respects what Rudolf had predicted; if East Germany were not under Russian domination, Rudolf's prediction probably would have come true.
4 See footnote on p. 39.
5 On September 25, 1886, the German Ambassador, Prince Reuss, reported to Bismarck that Emperor Francis Joseph had said: 'Rudolf is again holding forth.'
6 Princess Stephanie, *I Was to be Empress*, p. 206,
7 Professor T. Sollmann, *Pharmacology*, 7th ed, p. 371.
8 Paul Christophe has written a series of articles in the *Neue Illustrierte Wochenschau*

about Crown Prince Rudolf. In the issue of September 18, 1953, he pointed out that the prescription book of the Court pharmacy appears to have undergone various manipulations. Thus a sheet of thinner paper, containing prescriptions for the Crown Princess Widow Stephanie dated November, 1888, had been pasted in. But Stephanie did not bear this title until February 1889, after the Mayerling tragedy. It is possible that a new sheet was pasted in to conceal other prescriptions for Stephanie. In this article Paul Christophe confined himself to discussing the morphia prescriptions, without investigating those made for the Crown Prince for other ailments. in 1888.

9 Princess Stephanie, op. cit., p. 198.

10 Ferdinand of Saxe-Coburg-Gotha's visit was connected with the likelihood of his being elected Prince of Bulgaria. Archduke Johann Salvator having twice refused, the Bulgarians did eventually accept Prince Ferdinand. Emperor Joseph and Rudolf were neither in favour nor opposed to this. The general opinion was: 'What, another Coburg sovereign!' Stephanie says that she suffered from the attitude to her family.

11 Josef, Ritter von Weilen, editor of the German addition of *The Austro Hungarian Monarchy In Word And Picture*. See also footnote on p. 114.

12 Ibid., p. 211.

Mounting Tensions, pp. 158–169

1 Paul Clemenceau was Georges Clemenceau's much younger brother.

2 Letter to Szeps dated May 29, 1886.

3 Bismarck was generally referred to as the Iron Chancellor.

4 On June 16, 1886, Rudolf was the chief foreign mourner of his friend and cousin, King Ludwig II of Bavaria, who had committed suicide. As Desmond Chapman-Hoston says in his biography of Ludwig: 'Mourner and mourned understood and loved one another, subconsciously recognizing, even as did Rudolf's mother Elizabeth, that they were doomed to share a latent originality, a thwarted genius, a common fate.' *Bavarian Fantasy*, p. 292.

5 Rudolf's secret account of his conversation with Bismarck is printed in full in the Appendix.

6 Members of the Territorial Army or Force—the Army of Home Defence.

7 Ibid., p. 208.

8 The date roughly corresponds to the lack of response to his *Political Sketches*.

9 Ibid., p. 209.

10 Queen Victoria forbade the Prince of Wales to go to Rudolf's wedding in 1881 because of his reputation of leading a dissolute life.

11 In 1974, in Budapest, I talked to Imre Török, who is well over ninety years old. He was brought up in Vienna and spent his time not at school but with jockeys and *Fiakker* coachmen. He had seen the famous Bratfisch. Mr Török had heard about the Crown Prince's nightlife from humble, ordinary people. *Weinstube* is the equivalent of a pub in which mainly wine is being served.

12 Princess Stephanie was ill-informed on this point as Mary's sister was not yet married. However, she had two aunts, the sisters of her mother, Lady Nugent and Countess Stockau, who did live in England.

13 J. von Küremberg, *Schratt Katalin, a Császárváros Regénye*, pp. 128–30.

14 Waddington continued: 'In Vienna social circles Miss Vecsera was nicknamed '*La pic-nic*' because five or six men were regarded as her potential father. I can

guarantee you these details.' *Archives du Ministère des Affaires Etrangères*, Paris. Unprinted part of the confidential telegram no. IV, in *Documents diplomatiques français* VII, 5, 337, no. 321.

15 Original at the Benedictine Abbey of Pannonhalma, Hungary.

16 Count Charles Kinsky won the Grand National in 1883 on his mare *Zoedone.* In 1904 he became Prince Kinsky and died in 1907.

17 Stephanie, *I was to be Empress*, p. 44: 'When staying in London at Brown's Hotel, Rudolf was afraid to go out of the building after dark.'

18 Ibid., p. 36.

19 *Stenografisches Protokoll des Abgeordneten Hauses*, X Session, vol. 6, p. 6991.

20 Princess Stephanie, op cit., p. 220.

21 Ibid., p. 220.

22 Letter to Stephanie, March, 1888.

23 Princess Stephanie, op. cit., pp. 335–36; O. von Mitis, *Das Leben des Kronprinzen Rudolf*, p. 65.

24 E. C. Corti told me in 1933 in Budapest: 'The talented, clever, elegant, witty and so well-intentioned Rudolf had become in reality a mere shadow of his former self. His 1886 illness had never been fully cured: it impaired him physically, though externally this was not yet noticeable. He had bouts of fear, he was filled with fear, he took medicines to soothe his nerves and to choke his growing fear of the future. He drank a great deal, as though he wanted to enjoy to the full the years that were still before him. He gulped down greedily and immeasurably the sources of life. Women of all types, some belonging to a very low social strata, some society girls, filled his nights. One was bound to wonder at times whether this behaviour was compatible with his honour as son of the Emperor and an officer of the Austrian Army.'

Rudolf's Nerves at Breaking Point, pp. 170–178

1 Ibid., p. 227

2 Ibid., p. 230.

3 Austrian State Archives, letter dated March 21, 1888.

4 von Stronstorff memoirs, p. 52.

5 Letter dated February 21, 1888.

6 The dashing Otto.

7 Ibid., pp. 232–233.

8 Julius Szeps, *Politische Briefe an einen Freund*, pp. 163–64.

9 Lónyay, *Crown Prince Rudolf, the Tragedy of Mayerling*, p. 54

10 Ibid., p. 239.

11 For the story of Rudolf's secret romance in Switzerland and the fate of his illegitimate son by Princess K., see the Appendix.

The Kaiser Humiliates Rudolf, pp. 181–187

1 Bertie was his nickname in his family and among intimate friends.

2 Sir Philip Magnus, *Edward the Seventh*, p. 208.

3 In 1938 and 1939 Prince George Festetics, son of Prince Tassilo Festetics, told me this.

4 Original at Benedictine Abbey of Pannonhalma, Hungary.
5 O. von Mitis, *Das Leben des Kronprinzen Rudolf*
6 Ibid., p. 100.
7 V. Bibl, *Kronprinz Rudolf—die Tragödie eines sinkenden Reiches* p. 282; R. Barkeley, *The Road to Mayerling*, p. 212; etc.
8 Diaries of Count Lamsdorff, published by the State Publishing House, Moscow, 1926; report by Prince Gregor Kantakuzene.
9 See Appendix.
10 Sir Philip Magnus, *Edward VII*, p. 214.
11 Ibid., p. 239.
12 The *Heurigens* were and are unique Austrian entertainments. Twice a year people who grow their own grapes and make their own wine, fasten wreaths made of pine branches to the end of long poles, which they then stick over their doors. These are signs that they are making use of their ancient privilege permitting them twice a year to retail for a fortnight by the glass without a licence the new wine made of their own grapes. This custom has not changed since the visit of the Prince of Wales in 1888. Nor has the saying: 'A man should have an hour of happiness everyday. If he cannot get it, he can go to a *Heurigen* for a night of happiness.'
13 O. von Mitis, op. cit., p. 226.
14 Ibid., p. 224.
15 The Rev. Kantor, *Reminiscences*, p. 93.
16 Steven Kegl of Csala, in County Fehér in Hungary, shot himself because of card debts he could not meet.
17 Walburga Lady Paget, *The Linings of Life*, p. 468.
18 Ibid., p. 468.

Who was Mary Vecsera? pp. 188–197

1 For the data regarding Albin Vecsera's ancestors. I am indebted to the research of Herbert Fuhst, *Mary Vecsera im Lichte ihrer Abstammung und Verwandschaft*, Selbstverlag Herbert Fuhst, 1931.
2 Pozsony was from 1541 to 1784 the capital and the coronation town of Hungary.
3 The nearest equivalent of Town Captain in some Scottish towns was the sheriff (shire reeve), who had similar functions to that of the Town Captain in some Hungarian towns, among them Pozsony.
4 This house is still in existence in Bratislava, but the address is: Hviesdaslovo 4.
5 See H. Fuhst, op. cit., p. 27.
6 On March 24, 1867, Albin received the Austrian Leopold Order, and thus was raised to the *Ritterstand* (knighthood), becoming Albin Ritter von Vecsera, which title was hereditary; on October 2, 1869, Francis Joseph conferred upon him the lesser cross of the Hungarian St Stephen's Order with diploma, and on January 30, 1870, he created him a hereditary baron, obtaining the title his father had refused
7 In Austria, and later in Austria-Hungary, every member of the diplomatic service and every officer had to obtain permission to marry, and the girl of his choice had to have a guaranteed income of 600 *Gulden* a year, known as *Kaution.*
8 With Helen's fortune there was no difficulty about *Kaution.*
9 He died in November, 1914.

10 A flaming brown beauty, she had been Francis Joseph's favourite dancing partner in the days of Archduchess Sophie's *thés dançants*.

11 Aristide Baltazzi's daughter May married on March 9, 1909, Count Ferdinand Wurmbrandt; her daughter Ettie, when Mrs Arpad Plesch, won the English Derby with her horse Psidium in 1961.

12 Lónyay has said that Helen's love affairs with Prince Nicholas Esterházy and Archduke Wilhelm were common knowledge in Vienna—*Crown Prince Rudolf—the Tragedy of Mayerling*, p. 138. Her third lover was Count Vilmos Festetics, who volunteered the statement that intimate relations between Rudolf and Mary began on January 13, 1889. Also on p. 138 Lónyay wrote that it had been established 'beyond doubt that Mary had a love affair with a British officer in Cairo'.

13 E. C. Corti, *Elisabeth, die seltsame Frau*, p. 312.

14 C. Lónyay, op. cit., p. 137.

15 M. Larisch, *My Past*, p. 168; 'Mary was amorous by nature, and the Egyptian episode had transformed her from a girl into a woman, who already knew the meaning of passion.'

16 p. 467; Victor Wolfson, *Mayerling Murder*, p. 75.

17 Ibid., p. 32.

18 A. Monts, Counsellor of the German Embassy at the time, says in his memoirs that Helen Vecsera must have known about Mary's affair with the Crown Prince (p. 106).

19 In the autumn of 1933, a few weeks after my marriage, my mother-in-law took me and my husband to lunch with Mrs Arthur James, a cousin of the Duke of Portland. She suddenly asked me: 'Did you know dear Baroness Vecsera? She visited me with her daughters, Mary and Hanna, in 1888, and she sat in that armchair.' My mother-in-law tactfully answered that this had been 'a little before Judith's time'.

20 Walburge Lady Paget, *Embassies of Other Days*, p. 467.

21 On October 14, at the opening of the *Burgtheater*, the Prince of Wales pointed Mary Vecsera out to Rudolf 'and said how handsome she was. He spoke, I thought disparagingly of her.' The Prince of Wales also said of Mary: 'She seemed a charming young lady and certainly one of the prettiest and most admired in Vienna. I have known her mother as well as her Aunts and Uncles for the last 16 years, when I was in Vienna.' Royal Archives, Windsor, Z 498 49.

Mary Vecsera provides Distraction, pp. 195–204

1 Owned and edited by Paul Dehn, probably financed by Berlin, most of its subscribers were Germans in Germany.

2 F. Stern, *Gold and Iron, Bismarck, Bleichröder*, p. 502: 'The *Kreuzzeitung*, distinguished less for its intellectual tone than for its *clientele*, was the voice of Protestant orthodoxy.'

3 Drumont was also a notorious anti-Semite.

4 Chief of the German General Staff from 1888 to 1891.

5 O. von Mitis, *Das Leben des Kronprizen Rudolf*, pp. 107–10.

6 Extant at the Vienna State Archives.

7 General von Beck-Rzikowsky.

8 Letter to Kálnoky, dated December 20, 1885.

9 Dr Fritz Judtmann, *Mayerling—The Facts Behind The Legend*, p. 48.

10 Eduard Palmer was born in 1838, died in 1914; deputy-director-general of the Alpine-Montan Gesellschaft; then director general of the Osterreichische Landbank.

11 Hirsch in German means stag, and as he built the railway to Turkey, the Turkish stag.

12 One pound in the 1880's was worth £16.50 in 1976.

13 Behind their backs the staff referred to all the princes and princesses by their Christian names.

14 Ibid., pp. 240–41.

15 Elizabeth was in Greek waters to visit Missolonghi, then Corfu, sailing in the worst weather. Marie Festetics recorded in her diary: 'H.M. is very kind, yet she is no longer the same, her father's death has greatly upset her and a shadow has descended on her soul.'

16 Also see Dr Judtmann, op. cit., p. 32; and the Paris newspaper, *L'Éclaire*, of September, 1891.

17 Daughter of Mary's brother Franz, killed in World War I.

18 Hermine was Mary Vecsera's former governness, who at this time lived in London. Mary's letters to her are believed to be in the possession of an American collector.

19 The skull was a present from Dr Emil Zuckerkandl, Bertha Szeps's husband, who had it specially polished for Rudolf. On September 1, 1887, Rudolf wrote to thank him for the beautifully prepared skull. This letter is extant in the Austrian State Archives.

20 Joachim von Küremberg, *Schratt Katalin, a Császárváros, Regénye*, Hungarian edition, p. 139.

Death Planned by his own Hand, pp. 205–210

1 Letter to me dated May 1, 1977.

2 Ibid., p. 129.

3 Ibid. p. 169.

4 There are various types of depression: endogenous, reactive, etc. Even today much more research is needed to cure these various types of depression.

5 V. Bibl, *Kronprinz Rudolf-die Tragödie eines sinkenden Reiches*, p. 154; Johann Orth about Rudolf's suicide plans.

6 Statement of von Fritsche in Lónyay, *Crown Prince Rudolf: the Tragedy of Mayerling*, p. 201.

7 Ibid., p. 134; V. Bibl, op. cit., p. 177, etc.

8 The *Husaren Templ* is a war memorial erected in memory of the Hussars who fell in the Napoleonic wars. See also p. 247.

9 O. von Mitis, *Das Leben des Kronprinzen Rudolf*, p. 226, German edition.

10 Dr Hermann von Widerhofer was Rudolf's personal physician; after his death he became the Emperor's personal physician.

11 Original at Benedictine Monastery of Pannonhalma, Hungary.

12 Princess Stephanie, *I was to be Empress*, p. 256. On February 1, 1889, after the Mayerling tragedy, the German Ambassador reported to Bismarck: 'Internally rent and divided, sceptical and nihilistic in his philosophy of life, and without any religious anchor.' Kaiser William noted on the margin of the despatch: 'Here, in my opinion, lies the crux of the whole drama.' The German Ambassador continued: 'Oversated by the pleasures of life into which he had hurled himself

heedlessly and thereby exhausting himself mentally and physically, he eventually reached for his pistol like a ruined gambler.' Astonishingly, the Ambassador —like Stephanie—had no idea of Rudolf's illness. Psychiatry was not even in its infancy.

13 Ibid., p. 256.
14 Ibid., p. 258.
15 O. von Mitis, op. cit., 1971, German edition, with introduction by Professor Adam Wandruszka, p. 187.

The Last Hours of Rudolf with Mary, pp. 211–223

1 Ibid., p. 259. Stephanie's sister, Louise, in her *My Own Affairs*, however reported: 'In a short conversation Rudolf told me that he would like to free himself from his fatal passion, but could no longer tear himself away from Mary.' (Probably because she was the only woman who at this stage gave him back his virility.)
2 E. C. Corti, *Elisabeth, die seltsame Frau*, p. 311; O. von Mitis, *Das Leben des Kronprinzen Rudolf*, p. 207.
3 Ibid., p. 167. It is an extraordinary fact that not one of the allegedly numerous letters from Rudolf to Mary was found at 11 Salesianergasse. This has led several historians to conclude that Mary Vecsera advertised her love affair with the Crown Prince and that the correspondence was a one-sided one, all on her part. However, as shown on p. 313 below, in the quotation from the book by Count Polzer-Hoditz, the contents of the telegrams exchanged between Mary Vecsera and the Crown Prince are known. According to the *Berliner Börzen Courier* article, Rudolf 'continued with other affairs during the Mary Vecsera period'.
4 General Albert Margutti, *Vom alten Kaiser*, p. 117. The German Ambassador reports to Bismarck, and the British Ambassador to Lord Salisbury, that 'violent and serious altercations' had taken place between the Emperor and the Crown Prince. On April 20, 1889, the Empress Frederick wrote to Queen Victoria that she had heard from Bismarck that a very violent scene between the Austrian Emperor and his son had been the cause of Rudolf's suicide.
5 Ibid., p. 245.
6 O. von Mitis, op. cit., p. 342.
7 Count Alexander Hubner, unpublished *Diaries*.
8 P. 465.
9 *Kaiser Karl, Aus der Geheimmappe seines Kabinettchefs*, p. 343.
10 Ibid., p. 50.
11 Dr Judtmann and several other historians have quoted F. Meissner's report.
12 Ibid., p. 259.
13 Alland is a village near Mayerling.
14 Original at Benedictine Abbey of Pannonhalma, Hungary.
15 It is probably with the Mayerling papers in the Vatican.
16 Ibid., p. 203.
17 For Rudolf's will, see Appendix.
18 From this codicil it is clear that the four letters listed in it were written on January 28 in Vienna and the codicil was added on the 29th in Mayerling. It contains a change in Rudolf's instructions: he no longer wished Stephanie to be present when Szögyény opened his writing desk. The letter to the Empress was obviously written in Mayerling.

19 Original at the Benedictine Abbey of Pannonhalma, Hungary.

20 Also Orsini-Rosenberg statement at the Court of Inquiry, quoted by Lónyay, *Crown Prince Rudolf: the Tragedy of Mayerling* p. 17.

21 E. C. Corti, op. cit., p. 422. 'It is clear that without Mary Vecsera he would not have dared to go into death, but he did not die for her.' According to Lónyay and to the French historian, Maurice Paleologue, the Empress told all this to ex-Empress Eugénie.

22 Archduchess Elizabeth, Crown Prince Rudolf's daughter, to V. Bibl, *Kronprinz Rudolf—die Tragödie eines sinkenden Reiches*, pp. 67 and 69.

23 Wilhelm Polzer; *Crown Prince Rudolf's Tragedy*, p. 231; and G. A. Borghese: *La Tragedia di Mayerling*, p. 273.

24 Baroness Vecsera dismissed both Agnes and her father—who was her gardener—because, had the maid told her the truth, she could have prevented Mary from going to Mayerling. Agnes married a man called Wehling, lived to the age of eighty-one, and never spoke of the tragedy.

25 Dr F. Judtmann, *Mayerling: the Facts Behind the Legend*, p. 152.

26 According to Lónyay, op. cit., p. 172, Braganza had been Mary's lover.

27 Dr F. Judtmann, op. cit., p. 152, and *Figaro* of February 8, 1889, and others.

28 Helen Vecsera's own publication, and others.

'The Truth is Far Worse . . .', pp. 224–237

1 Princess Louis of the Belgians in *My Own Affairs*, p. 114, has written: 'He had sworn to the Emperor to keep silent, as had Rudolf's other friends who had gone to shoot at Mayerling. The secret was well kept. The servants, who might have spoken, have disclosed nothing.'

2 Professor Billroth was sent by the Emperor in a Court carriage to Mayerling on January 31. He had to give his word to Francis Joseph never to speak about what he saw there—not even to members of his family. Billroth kept his word; according to his son, he angrily refused to answer if anyone brought up the subject.

3 At 10.30 a.m. on January 29, 1889, Baron Albert Rothschild rushed into the office of the German Ambassador, Prince Reuss, to tell him that the Baden stationmaster had telegraphed him as the majority shareholder of the railways, the terrible news of Rudolf's death. Reuss told this to his Counsellor, Anton Monts, who reported the episode in his memoirs.

4 I have reconstructed what happened at the Hofburg on the basis of Archduchess Valerie's and Ida Ferenczy's diaries, the Hoyos Memorandum and what E. C. Corti told me in Budapest in 1938, when he was doing his research for the biography of the Empress Elizabeth.

5 Dr Heinrich Slatin was the brother of the famous Major-General Rudolf Slatin, commonly known as Slatin Pasha, the prisoner of the Mahdi. Heinrich was raised to the rank of baron (Freiherr von) in 1906. His Memorandum was published after his death by his grandson, Ing. Dip. Freiherr Heinrich von Slatin, Jr., in the *Neues Wiener Tagblatt* in five instalments, beginning on August 15, 1931. It is interesting that Hoyos was not a member of this Commission, yet he is the one person who could have contributed original information.

6 Dr F. Judtmann, *Mayerling: the Facts Behind the Legend*, pp. 139–40.

7 Slatin Memorandum.

8 The Protocol of Ceremonies was issued by the Department of Ceremonies of

the Lord Chamberlain's Office, which kept a Protocol about all events at Court. The volume for 1889 contains a voluminous appendix about the death of the Crown Prince with important information about the Church funeral.

9 Professor Dr Edwin Stengel, former assistant at Vienna University, dismissed the Austrian verdict 'that the deed was committed in a state of mental derangement'. The so-called proofs 'do not exclude an unsound mind, but they do not prove it'. A. E. J. Hollaender, in *Streiflichter auf die Tronfolgertragödie von Mayerling*, p. 150 in *Festschrift für Heinrich Benedikt*, 1957, says that the doctors had gone to the greatest lengths in their judgment on these pathological points in order to obtain a religious funeral. Professor Gustav Scheuthauer pointed to the gaps in the Protocol and remarked that on the strength of the published dissection report he himself would have certainly concluded that this was a case of murder. F. Judtmann, op, cit., p. 191.

10 Ibid., p. 338.

11 Ibid., p. 338.

12 Ibid., p. 352.

13 In his letter to me of January 11, 1977, Taaffe added: 'One other [person] and the three Counts Taaffe . . .'

14 Dr F. Judtmann, op. cit., pp. 355–56.

15 Now called Nalzovy. The village is called Nalzovy Hory. The castle now houses the Klement Gottwald School for Communist Pioneers.

16 Actually in the basement.

17 Group Captain Taaffe's letter of January 11, 1977, says: 'And one other [person] who conducted the investigation.'

18 In his letter to me of January 11, 1977, Taaffe says: 'Henry may have shown other papers to Skedl in connection with Mayerling, but not the papers handed to the Prime Minister by the Emperor.'

19 Rudolph Taaffe may have proof of this, but in the last eighty-nine years in spite of the most intensive research no firm evidence has been found. In the course of the Soviet advance through Transylvania, Russian soldiers destroyed the furniture of Sáromberke, Samuel Teleki's country house, among it three wooden chests which may have contained vital evidence.

20 A. E. J. Hollaender is of the opinion that the Mayerling papers are not in the Vatican, but in America, possibly in a bank. In his letter of January 11, 1977, Rudolph Taaffe wrote: 'I very much doubt this statement.'

Solution to the Mystery, pp. 238–248

1 Loschek Memorandum.

2 *The Gun Report*, the official publication of the Florida Gun collectors' Association, in its issue of July, 1970, on p. 17 said: 'Crown Princess Stephanie distributed 30,000 *Gulden* and Rudolf's arms among his staff of 67. . . . Vodička received at least one cased revolver. . . . On July 4, 1943, Vodička's widow stated: "My husband received from Crown Princess Stephanie several weapons as mementos to His Imperial Highness. Among them was the case signed R with the crown, which was the mortal weapon of His Imperial Highness." ' But as it was never established which weapon killed either Mary or Rudolf, this is not evidence.

3 Vodička reported all this to the Crown Prince's Private Secretary, Colonel Heinrich von Spindler, who put it in writing. Rudolf's A.D.C., Orsini und

Rosenberg, was a witness to Vodička's statement and commented: 'What motive Bratfisch had to make this statement is unknown to me. . . . The fact remains that Vodička did not proceed as usual to the hunt.' See O. von Mitis, *Das Leben des Kronprinzen Rudolf*, p. 283, and the Hoyos Memorandum.

4 A curious custom of the House of Reuss was that all male members of the family bore the name of Henry (Heinrich), the individual being distinguished by number. *Encyclopaedia Britannica*, Vol. 19, p. 283, 1962 edition.

5 At the end of World War II the secret files of the German Foreign Ministry were brought to London. At the Public Records Office A. E. J. Hollaender read them and used them for an essay. See Prologue, p. 2.

6 Between February 5 and 9 Monsignor Galimberti had made good use of his sources; as a result of what he found out, he completely changed his mind about the Mayerling tragedy. In conversation he hinted that the Vatican may have authorised the church funeral because of knowledge that Rudolf had not committed suicide.

7 Dr. F. Judtmann, *Mayerling: the Facts Behind the Legend*, p. 178.

8 Ibid., p. 179.

9 Hitherto the Austrian authorities have refused to exhume Crown Prince Rudolf so as to ascertain how he was shot.

10 Besides, Loschek saw the Crown Prince, hale and hearty, at 6.15 a.m.

11 When after the death in 1923 of Count Josef Hoyos his memorandum was published, it bore out completely Prince Reuss's information.

12 The Vienna psychiatrists wrote their report after Rudolf's death. Part of it was published in the anonymous article of the *Berliner Börzen Courier* February 24, 1889.

13 Windsor Royal Archives, Z. 498, 52.

14 Rudolf to Anton Monts, *Erinnerungen und Gedanken des Botschafters Anton Graf Monts*, p. 129.

Epilogue, pp. 249–260

1 Marriage: January 23, 1902, divorce June 3, 1924. They had four children: Franz-Josef, b. March 22, 1904; Ernst b. April 21, 1905; Rudolf, b. February 4, 1907; Stephanie, b. July 9, 1909.

2 Archduke Otto.

3 Count Polzer-Hoditz, *Kaiser Karl, Aus der Geheimmappe seines Kabinettchefs*, p. 45.

4 An American duel means two balls put in a box: one black, one white. The seconds agree which one of the two duellists draws first: whoever draws the black ball, must commit suicide.

5 E. C. Corti, *Elisabeth, die seltsame Frau*, p. 412.

6 Windsor Royal Archives, Z 280 53

7 Published after his death in the Sunday supplement of the *Neues Wiener Tagblatt* and in the *Berliner Illustrierte Zeitung*, on April 24, 1932.

8 Heinrich Slatin, in his Memorandum also remarked on Taaffe's strikingly cheerful behaviour after the catastrophe and interpreted it as the Prime Minister's joy to have triumphed over his fallen enemy.

9 Alfred Pick, Viennese local historian.

10 Dr F. Judtmann, *Mayerling: the Facts Behind the Legend*, p. 358.

11 According to Werner Richter, Marie Larisch died in 1940 in an old people's home in Augsburg, *Kronprinz Rudolf von Habsburg*, p. 241.

12 Apart from accounts of this incident by many Viennese, and even members of the Imperial Family, Eugen Ebel has written of it in a biography of the nun with the title: *Das sehr merkwürdige und fromme Leben der Katherine Filljung* (The very remarkable and pious life of Catherine Filljung), published by Verlag Josef Kroll, 1934.

Appendices

1 *The Shackles of Spanish Etiquette*

One of the major influences on Crown Prince Rudolf's life was a survival from the 14th century: the system called Spanish Etiquette. Rudolf and his mother, the Empress Elizabeth, profoundly resented its ceremonial rules and regulations, and its pernicious influences, which prescribed a way of life both of them detested. The personal tragedies of Elizabeth and Rudolf cannot be understood without appreciating the all-pervading influence of Spanish Etiquette and their efforts to escape from its shackles. If only the Empress and the Crown Prince had joined forces in fighting it, they might have achieved something, but unfortunately this they never did.

On the morning after her wedding night, the sixteen-year-old Empress Elizabeth had to attire herself in a formal morning dress and appear at breakfast with the Archduchess Sophie and her suite. The Empress begged her husband to let her have breakfast in her own room, or preferably with him, but under the rules of Spanish Etiquette, which governed the Habsburg Court in the minutest detail, this was impossible. Much though he loved her—and he had written to a friend: '*Ich bin verliebt wie ein Leutnant and glücklich wie ein Prinz*'[1]—he could not grant her this very human wish. The rules of Spanish Etiquette bound everyone, but none so vigorously as the Emperor and his wife.

At breakfast with Archduchess Sophie and the Hofburg entourage, Elizabeth was painfully aware that the whole Court was staring at her. But she had no conception that she and Francis Joseph were, by their presence, re-enacting an ancient tribal custom according to which the great chief and his bride had to show themselves to the tribe after their first mating. It is an open question whether anyone at the Hofburg Court realised the implications of this rigid Spanish Etiquette rule; the study of magic and of primitive religions did not lead to an analysis

[1] 'I am in love like a lieutenant and happy as a prince.'

of such institutions until several decades later, and much still remains to be researched. What Archduchess Sophie did know was that the Spanish Court ceremonial placed the Emperor on an immensely high pedestal, protecting him from his subjects, and giving him absolute powers. She believed implicitly that he could only maintain his position as Emperor if their symbolic ceremonial display was strictly observed.

The roots of Spanish Etiquette, which long pre-dated European Christianity, had been driven underground when the new religion gradually established itself in Europe; but later they re-surfaced in many places—one of them being Burgundy. Cloaked in the trappings of chivalry and the hierarchical ceremonial worked out by Philip the Good (1398–1467), in Spain and in Austria the rules of the system survived right to the end of the 19th century. Philip, after considerable research, had records made of the pagan customs and traditions which had flourished as far back as the 5th century, when the Burgundians first settled between the Oder and the Vistula. He restored some forms of the old Burgundian way of life, re-interpreted according to his own ideas.

Spanish Etiquette is in fact Burgundian Etiquette, whose rites had been developed by Charles the Bold (Philip the Good's son), the greatest master of ceremonies of all times. Eventually they spread to the whole of Western and Central Europe as far as Vienna. Poland, Hungary, Muscovy and the Turkish-dominated Balkans had no use for them. The Turks were Moslems who had rules of their own and of equal antiquity, some of which were counterparts of certain Burgundian rules.

Charles the Bold (1433–1477) had only one child, Mary of Burgundy (1462–1482), who in 1479 married the Emperor Maximilian of Austria (1459–1519). It was she who introduced to the Austrian Court the customs and ceremonial on which she had been brought up. This is how Burgundian Etiquette originally found its way into Austria.

Rules for every move were laid down; for audiences, cercles (when an archduke married, his wife had to hold a cercle), receptions for foreign royalties or for foreign embassies, for gala dinners; for all meals of the All-Highest; for Court Balls and Balls at Court; for receptions and *soirées* at Court; for dinners for the Delegations (when Austrian and Hungarian delegates of the two Houses of Parliament discussed Foreign Affairs, Finance and the Armed Services); for the All-Highest going to church on foot or by carriage; for *Corpus Christi* processions and the Washing of the Feet at Easter;[1] for funeral ceremonies and requiem masses; for presentation of New Year wishes; for marriages and baptismal ceremonies; every conceivable event was provided for. It was even laid down who could speak to the Empress: only 23 men and 229 women could appear at her cercles and speak to her, and 29 persons could visit her in her apartments.[2]

The difference between a Court Ball and a Ball at Court was enormous. To a Court Ball in addition to the high aristocracy a certain number of distinguished persons in responsible positions could be invited, but their wives could only accompany them if they had the right quarterings. To a Ball at Court only persons who had six generations of aristocratic ancestors could go.

At both, apart from chairs for the imperial family on the dais, only a few marble seats were reserved for the princely families; other people were compelled to stand all the evening. A privileged few obtained respite by sitting down for supper, served in separate rooms at small tables, each one presided over by an Archduke. But rigid Spanish Etiquette protocol decreed that both at Court Balls and at Balls at Court, the same people invariably sat next to one another. The soup, which was disgusting, was allegedly cooked according to a three-hundred-year-old recipe.[3]

2 *Crown Prince Rudolf's Will*

Prague, April 15, 1878

'In a few days I shall be starting on a long journey. On account of the pleasure I take in dangerous hunting and difficult enterprises of all kinds, it is quite possible that I may be going into danger and lose my life. For this reason it is incumbent on me to make some arrangement.

'All that I leave in cash is to be used for charitable purposes.

'Bombelles is to give some of the money in equal amounts to each

[1] For this ceremony, which took place on Maundy Thursday, the women had to wear black dresses with six-yard-long trains. Their hair had to be covered with a black veil, falling to the hem of the dress, enveloping the whole figure. In her memoirs, *I Was To Be Empress*, Princess Stephanie described how difficult it was to move, especially to bend down, rise and move on, wrapped in a black veil, dragging a long train (pp. 131–32).

[2] Apart from members of the Imperial Family and other royal relatives and friends.

[3] Lavender Cassels, *Clash of Generations*, p. 3, John Murray.

member of my domestic staff, including those who have served me here in Prague. Whatever remains is for schools. My clothes go to my servants. All my writings, letters and papers which are in my writing desk in Vienna and Prague are to be destroyed by Bombelles. My library is to be divided among all the schools throughout the Monarchy. People who think it worthwhile to possess mementoes of me can have my pictures and other trifles. Anyhow what happens to all these trifles is completely indifferent to me. All my collections are to go in their entirety, as they are, to the University of Vienna, to which institute I owe so much.

'Latour, in memory of me, is to look well after my dog, "Blak", who was my faithful hunting companion; Bombelles is to keep and care for "Kastor" and "Schifferl"; one of them is good and faithful, and the other can smile very wisely.

'My eagle-owls and Schwisshunds, as well as the Dachshunds, are to go to poor huntsmen.

'My island, Lacroma, I lay at my father's feet. May he graciously accept it, grant it his protection and allow it to fall in no other hands. It is a remembrance of poor Uncle Max and a really Southern Slav territory which one should not despise nowadays.

'I recommend my staff to the gracious protection of His Majesty. They are good people who have always served me faithfully. Likewise I beg you from the bottom of my heart graciously to consider Major Spindler and his family. Ever since I was in my third year he has been with me and he has always carried out his duties conscientiously.

'I enclose a letter for Wilczek and he is also to be given Florins 20,000 of my money in cash.

'I forgive my enemies, all those who, particularly in recent times, have angered me. I have trodden a different path from that of most of my relatives but I always had the purest motives. Our age calls for new viewpoints. Everywhere, particularly in Austria, there is reaction, the first step towards downfall. Those who preach reaction are the most dangerous enemies. I have always pursued them. I warn you against them.

'God save Austria and her great Empire! God save the Austrian Army! Victory to its banners! Greetings to the 36th Regiment, my real home.

'A last farewell kiss in spirit to all the beautiful women in Vienna whom I have so dearly loved!

'In complete devotion I kiss my parents' hands. I beg them to forgive any trouble I have caused them.

'I embrace my family.

'I thank you for your love.

'My last greetings to all my friends, to my whole dear Austria.

Rudolf'

3 *Crown Prince Rudolf's second Will*

Vienna, March 2nd, 1887

'The following testament was written by me in my own hand, with a completely lucid, conscious mind, and I most humbly request His Imperial and Royal Apostolic Majesty to be good enough graciously to take upon Himself the burden of being executor of this testament and also to assume the guardianship of my daughter Elisabeth.

'I appoint my daughter Elisabeth to be heiress-general of all my movable and immovable estate; to my wife Stephanie I assign life-long enjoyment of my entire estate. In the event of her re-marriage the usufruct shall cease totally and pass to my daughter. In the event of my daughter's marriage the usufruct shall be divided between the two.

'I further dispose as follows:

'1. I leave 50,000 florins to Colonel von Spindler, the head of my Secretariat; in the event of his death, to his son or, if he is no longer alive, his daughter.

'2. I leave 20,000 florins to Count Carl Bombelles, my Lord Chamberlain; if he is no longer alive the sum shall revert to the heiress-general.

'3 The sum of 30,000 florins is to be distributed, upon directions and judgment of my wife, to my valets, gun attendants, stabling staff, and all those persons of the hunt staff in the Vienna Woods, at Görgény, at Laxenburg, and in the Danube reserve, whom she knows to have served me particularly well.

'4. The large cupboard with the water colours (wedding presents from the Viennese industrialists) I leave to the Court Collection.

'5. My swords in use and modern hunting guns, as well as all my hunting trophies and mementoes, are to be distributed to friends and relations, according to my wife's directions; anything that is left I leave to my valets and personal attendants.

'6. All my hunting and pet dogs I leave to my huntsman and gun attendants, as well as the staff in the Vienna Woods and Danube reserves.
'7. All my clothes, linen, and footwear I leave to my valets.
'8. My natural history collections I leave to Viennese educational institutions, according to my wife's judgment. I further command that the existing hunting leases at Görgény Szt. Imre, Sipton, and in the Vienna Woods are to be relinquished immediately upon my death, likewise—after liquidation of my possessions—the lease of the lodge of Görgény Szt. Imre.

'My writing desks in Vienna and Laxenburg are to be opened, in my wife's presence, by Herr Ladislaus von Szögyény Marich, departmental head in the Ministry of Foreign Affairs, and my papers partly destroyed and partly kept according to his judgment.

'I confirm with my signature and my seal that these dispositions written down in my own hand represent my free will.

Crown Prince Archd. Rudolph
Lt.-Gen.'

4 *Excerpt from Crown Prince Rudolf's Report of a conversation with Prince Bismarck on February 28, 1883*

Berlin, March 1, 1883

'On the afternoon of February 28 I called on the Chancellor and found him greatly altered. He is looking ill, wears a beard, and, having violent pains in his legs, can only walk slowly with the aid of a stick. He received me in the most cordial manner, and after a few ordinary remarks concerning his health, current festivals, etc., he went on to talk of politics. Above all the Prince stressed his pleasure in the ever-stronger development of the Austro-German alliance, and the fact that it responds to the convictions and desires not only of the two Emperors and their statesmen, but also those of the peoples of the two countries. He was of opinion that peace and the future of the two countries was ensured by this alliance, which alone gives a guarantee of effective resistance against external enemies, and against the republican tendencies which were surging so strongly in every country.

'Emphasising his words rather sharply, he incidentally made the following observations: "I am glad that we have prolonged the alliance again. I am old and like to see this work secured beyond all doubts and disputes; in this alliance lies the future of Europe; it must for all times be insured against any possible misconception and every untoward accident. And even though our relations are satisfactory for the moment, the future, as I foresee it, will call for yet closer union." Then followed a long explanation of the alliance as established by law, which could only be dissolved by the common consent of both monarchs and both parliaments—he mentioned our delegations. He used practically the identical words I had already heard on the same subject at two other interviews, and which I have already twice reported to Vienna.

'In the same way he went on to speak of the closer commercial alliance, and accentuated the fact that it is just as necessary, though he realised that it cannot be effected quickly, and he concluded with the words, "It is a favourite idea of mine in this respect also to link up the two great Central European Powers."

'This subject drew Prince Bismarck on to speak of the domestic politics of Austria-Hungary, and from his remarks I gathered that Hungary was the stumbling-block to the closer union of the two Empires. Yet he added, "It is just the Magyars who ought to be the most faithful supporters of this alliance." He was, accordingly, often irritated by the tactlessness of German professors and journalists who lament so exaggeratedly the oppression of the Saxons in Siebenbürgen and the Germans in Hungary stirring up ill-feeling; for, whenever possible, his compatriots ought to be glad to strengthen the Magyar stock and the Hungarian State, who might be regarded as faithful allies.

'In connection with our Slavs, Bismarck said he was convinced that in the furtherance of their own interests the cultured and far-seeing section of them must support the Austro-German alliance.

'The political attitude of the Germans in Austria does not seem to please the Chancellor. He laid stress on the fact that Austria can only exist by the help of German influence, education, culture and language. Therefore it is the mission of Germany to support the State ideal, to prove herself indispensable, a useful help to the Emperor, but not "to play about with constitutional sophistry, with lamentations and opposition to the Emperor". These are his own words, of which I made particular note.'

5 *Noble Window Smashers*

[This article appeared anonymously on March 18, 1883, in the *Neues Wiener Tagblatt*]

'The following is reported to us from Prague: The sound of the crash of breaking window glass must be specially pleasant, because a few days ago certain young gentlemen decided at an elegant private gathering where they were assembled to give themselves this entertainment. They did so in a most exclusive manner, as they belong to the most exclusive society, not to the dirty and uncouth lower orders. On the evening in question a small select company of these young men took themselves to the Josefstadt, to the old Jewish ghetto that is, and picked on the windows of one of the houses there as the target of their well-aimed stone-throwing. Unfortunately the police soon interfered with this otherwise harmless form of amusement. With the exception of one of their number, a young Count Sylva Taruce, who succeeded in escaping, the other members of the stone-throwing gang—with young Count Clam Martini at their head—were arrested and brought to police headquarters. There they had to spend the night in the cells. Next morning, after a well-deserved reprimand, the young gentlemen were released to their respective palaces. Broken window-glass, as can be seen, also sometimes has a disagreeable sound, even when broken by noble stones.'

6 *Crown Prince Rudolf's Royal Petition to his Father, The Emperor, for permission to write a history of the Monarchy in words and pictures Vienna, March, 1884*

'Your Majesty,

'In spite of much excellent preparation, the Austro-Hungarian Monarchy still lacks a great ethnographical work, which, founded on the most advanced scientific research of the present day, and embellished by the highly perfected artistic means of reproduction shall, while stimulating and instructing, present a comprehensive picture of our Fatherland and its race of people.

'The study of these peoples living within the boundaries of this Empire does not only present a highly important sphere of activity for scholars, but is also of practical use in the development of united patriotism.

'By the growing recognition of the qualities and characteristics of the single ethnographical groups, and of their mutual and material dependence that feeling of solidarity, which is to unite all the peoples of our Fatherland, must be strengthened.

'Those groups of races which through language, custom and through partly dissimilar historical development, feel themselves separated from the other sections of the population, will be beneficially affected by the fact that in the scientific literature of the kingdom their individuality finds due recognition, and to a certain degree respect; they will be encouraged to seek their intellectual centre of gravity in Austria. It would therefore be of the highest importance to cultivate in our Fatherland ethnology and its kindred sciences, as the latter, removed from all immature theories, from all-party feeling, represents material from which alone an objective comparison and estimation of the different peoples can be formed.

'Up to now this has not been the case. We should not conceal from ourselves the fact that in Austria ethnology has been far less cultivated than in England, France or particularly in Russia, although we perhaps possess to a greater degree than any other country those specialists who are excellently qualified for it.

'Nevertheless, invaluable studies on individual races do appear; but these are generally included in technical libraries or lie fallow in almost unknown local papers, or—all too often, alas—are published abroad.

'Therefore my mind is filled with the idea of collecting this rich material still available in Austria, and thereby facilitating the production of a work which, flattering the scientific and artistic sensibilities of individual nations within the boundaries of this Empire, will do honour to the Monarchy as a whole and to all its parts. And where is there another State so rich in variety, which manifests within its boundaries such glorious multiformity in natural history, scenery and climate, or can provide, by the ethnological combination of different groups of peoples, more interesting pictures for a great work?

'*Austro-Hungary in Picture and Story* can, in scientific and artistic respects, and also as a real national book, have great partriotic significance.

'The literary and artistic circles among all the peoples of this Empire would be united in a common undertaking; well-known names would shed lustre on the work, and opportunity would be provided for the younger, aspiring intellects to make themselves known and use their gifts; many of them might be helped over the difficult beginnings and protracted struggles which they would otherwise have to face, to rise above circumstances and take their place in the ranks of the known and esteemed scholars and artists.

'This work shall show at home and abroad what a rich treasury of intellectual power this Monarchy possesses in the peoples of all her countries, and how these co-operate in a splendid achievement, which is bound to serve to develop the consciousness and power of the common Fatherland.

'If the sanction of the All Highest and Imperial patronage is accorded to our long-cherished hopes, then the work shall see the light under the most favourable auspices and accompanied by our most enthusiastic patriotic sentiments.

'Rudolph'

7 *The article Crown Prince Rudolf sent to Maurice Szeps in August 1885 before the meeting at Kremzier of Emperor Francis Joseph, Czar Alexander III and Prince Bismarck, representing the aged Emperor William I. Szeps refused to print it.*

'With traditional splendour and pomp, the Austrian Court is preparing to receive the Emperor from the North, and on August 25 the quaint little town of Kremzier and the normally peaceful palace of the aged Prince of the Church (the Bishop of Olmütz) will witness magnificent Court ceremonies and the dignified and imposing comings and goings of dignitaries and great diplomats.

'Here and there amid all the noisy and dazzling play-acting grins the disturbing countenance of naked reality, and we Austrians, mindful of our position, ask ourselves a very real question: "What value and what success will result to our country from these days at Kremzier? And was this meeting, this ostentatious conclusion of an alliance with Russia, really necessary?"

'Today we must answer—yes. Kremzier is the result of Skiernevice, and an inevitable result tending to our advantage. Yet our Emperor's visit to Skiernevice was not a gesture prompted by Austrian policy and care for the future. The episode at Skiernevice has been of no use to us, for with Russia no honourable friendship is possible, so long as we cherish aspirations in parts of the Balkan Peninsula, occupy provinces of it, and dream of future domination in the East. Our interests are conflicting. The days of Reichstadt, when the division of the Balkan countries was still within the bounds of possibility, are long past. The Russo-Turkish War, St. Stefano, and then the Treaty of Berlin, have changed everything fundamentally, and, as matters now stand, the choice lies between a complete renunciation of all aspirations of power in the East, or a decision by force of arms. How little can be arranged under such circumstances, and at interviews of this kind, and how absolutely worthless to us is all that was decided, and served up, ought to be clear to anybody who is in a position to study Eastern politics.

'Damage, real damage, was done us at Skiernevice, and particularly on account of the fact that the visit was paid to the young Czar by a very much older Emperor of Austria; this will be represented by the Russians to the Balkan Slaves as "Canossa", or at least as an obligatory attendance by weak Austria on powerful Russia. Formalities of this kind make a deep impression on uncivilised peoples, and one can be perfectly certain that the Russian emissaries have made full use of this episode. This circumstance has not failed to impress even our more cultured Slavs in Austria-Hungary.

'For this reason Kremzier has importance . . . but alas, too late. In order to diminish the unfavourable impression of the Skiernevice incident, the return visit of the Russian Emperor should have taken place soon after it.

'Skiernevice was the greatest mistake made by our present Minister of Foreign Affairs, who is so partial to the Russians. The sin was financial as well as political, for the interview at Kremzier, result of Skiernevice, is costing a fabulous sum, which might be very much better invested in the Balkan Peninsula, in those countries where Ministers, officers and politicians of all kinds can be won over for small amounts. Whilst the Emperors are swearing friendship and warmly embracing each other, the Russians are exploiting the credulity and shortsightedness of our diplomats to undermine the position of the pro-Austrian King Milan (of Serbia) to subsidise richly the agitators in Bulgaria and Montenegro, to send out agents and to establish arms depots on the Serbian and Bosnian frontiers, in order to prepare for the rising which they have planned in our occupied territories and in Serbia.

'In Kremzier splendid festivals are being held, joyous holiday attire is flaunted, the statesmen are going to negotiate—about what, they do not know themselves, and amid all this hollow magnificence the fact remains: we Austrians must either renounce all influence, all sphere of dominion in the East, or prepare for a desperate but inevitable struggle.'

8 *Rudolf's illegitimate Son in America*

When Rudolf was twenty, he met two charming Russian girls, the illegitimate daughters of Czar Alexander II. The younger one, known to her friends as K., was enchanting: pretty, vivacious, full of mischief. He fell in love with her and she with him. It was a gay flirtation, but when a year later the Emperor wanted Rudolf to marry and settle down he begged his father to allow him to marry Princess K. The Emperor was appalled at the very thought—an illegitimate princess to become Empress? 'Rudolf must be mad!' Less understandably the Czar was equally opposed to the match, probably because he too subscribed to the principle that the illegitimate daughter of a monarch—even his own—was not fit to become Empress.

Rudolf was not too upset by all this, for soon he set out to look over three suitable Catholic princesses—and lost his heart to the Belgian Stephanie.

Over the years it became crystal clear that they had nothing in common, and Rudolf was miserably unhappy with her. Divorce was impossible in the House of Habsburg; he had failed in his political and military ambitions, and his health was undermined. His threat to shoot first Stephanie and then himself, shows what a state his nerves had reached.

In this condition his mind began to wander back to the past, and the picture of the charming Princess K. as she had been at fifteen, emerged more and more vividly. She had not married. Suddenly Rudolf felt that he had to see her again. Perhaps she would cheer him and give him new vitality. He got in touch with her, and they arranged to meet in Switzerland in strict incognito.

There must have been correspondence between Rudolf and Princess

K, though there is no sign of it in the Vienna archives. Therefore either Szögyényi destroyed these letters,[1] or Rudolf left them with his cousin Johann Salvator, who burnt them before leaving Austria for good.

There can be no doubt that Rudolf went to Switzerland on September 16, 1888, for two reasons. Ten years later, the day before her death,[2] the Empress Elizabeth went from Geneva to Prégny, to lunch with Baroness Julie de Rothschild.[3] She was accompanied only by her lady-in-waiting, Countess Irma Sztáray.

After signing the visitor's book, Elizabeth handed the pen to Countess Sztáray, who looked back over several pages to see what distinguished people had been to Prégny. Suddenly, in the middle of an otherwise blank page, she saw a familiar signature: Rudolf. In September 1888 he had lunched at Prégny. Baroness Julie noticed Countess Sztáray's start—and quickly spirited the visitors' book away so as not to upset the Empress.

The second reason why there can be no doubt about the brief encounter is that Princess K. became pregnant as a result of it. She did not inform Rudolf of her plight, although at that time, and in her position, it was a plight indeed. The account about Rudolf's illegitimate son comes from Marie Larisch, a suspect source, but there is so much corroborating evidence that it cannot be ignored.

Hans Wilczek who, although much older than Rudolf, had been a close friend of his, a few years after Mayerling told Marie Larisch that 'a lost putative Habsburg offspring existed somewhere in America'. Hearsay had it that Francis Joseph had told someone that 'that young woman' (as he had once referred to Princess K. in Marie Larisch's presence) had born Rudolf's son, and that after his mother's death the boy was being raised in an American orphanage. Wilczek went on to say that in order to trace the child the Emperor had solicited the assistance of General James Longstreet. This famous Confederate

[1] This is unlikely as Mr de Szögyény-Marich told the German Ambassador on April 8, 1889, that he had finished sorting Rudolf's papers and had destroyed nothing, as Rudolf had done this himself.

[2] See Countess Irma Sztáray's *Erzsébet Királyné Kiséretében* (In the suite of Queen Elizabeth), p. 153. Next day, when walking from her hotel in Geneva to the steamer, the anarchist Luigi Lucchini stabbed the Empress in the heart and she died a few hours later.

[3] She was the wife of Baron Adolf de Rothschild, in charge of the Neapolitan affairs of his House. He helped Queen Marie of Naples, the Empress Elizabeth's sister, to escape from Naples.

soldier had represented the United States at Rudolf's and Stephanie's wedding, and later remained on friendly terms with Crown Prince Rudolf. General Longstreet instituted a search, which lasted for more than a decade. It was on the point of yielding results when he died in 1904.

Marie Larisch's story is that Princess K. confided in her elder sister who, aware of her mother's extremely strict Victorian attitude, consulted General Cassius Marcellus Clay. President Abraham Lincoln had appointed him as his representative to the Russian Court in 1861; Clay served in this position for eight years. He became a close friend of the Czar and his family, and retained friendly connections with them even after his departure from St Petersburg. Clay's advice was that Princess K. should go to America and have her baby there; if it was a boy, he believed that Crown Prince Rudolf would recognise him as his morganatic child and at all events would provide for the baby and its mother, with whom—in Clay's opinion—Rudolf may still have been in love.

Then K.'s sister had to face the terrifying task of informing her mother of what had happened. Her father, Czar Alexander II, had been murdered in 1881. The reaction of the mother was worse than expected. She and her relatives were shocked, unsympathetic and instead of helping the wretched K., disowned her and refused to let her have one penny. The elder sister sent her as much as she could, and K. sailed with her nurse for America, where she heard of Rudolf's death. The baby was born in the Middle West; presumably the nurse looked after him while there was any money at all; then she left for Europe in the hope of bringing help to her beloved young mistress. This simple peasant woman believed that if she described the pitiful conditions under which Princess K. lived, the family would relent and at least send her some money. In this she was proved wrong; what happened to her is another mystery. Marie Larisch heard from Wilczek that K. managed to convey to her elder sister that her baby had been born, that it was a boy, and that they were desperately poor. Then the nurse disappeared; in Marie Larisch's words, 'It is not unlikely that she disappeared in order to save her own and the Austrian Court from embarrassment.[1]

The baby was born on June 21, 1889,[2] at Hot Springs, Arkansas.

[1] *My Royal Relatives; Secrets of a Royal House.*

[2] From the obituary notice of James Cleveland in the *Columbia Missourian* of July 2, 1938.

As to why Princess K. trekked to the Middle West, with the intention of reaching California, there is no explanation. Possibly Generals Clay and Longstreet had made arrangements for her to stay with someone there. But it is odd, to say the least, that they did not enquire into K.'s finances (perhaps because of the immense wealth of her family in Russia it did not occur to them that she might be destitute) and did not realise that she would have difficulties in getting there.

Here there is a gap in the story. Where did Princess K. and her baby stay for the next ten months? It is documented that in 1890 she entered the charity ward of St Louis Hospital in St Louis, Missouri, where she died a few weeks later. In November, 1890, her son was placed in the Roman Catholic orphanage of St Ann's; because he had a rosary wound round his right arm, the nuns took it that he was a Roman Catholic. They gave him the name of James, and because a label they found in his clothes, added Cleveland as his surname.

The facts about James Longstreet Cleveland's life between 1889 and 1926 have been pieced together with the help of the *State Historical Society of Missouri*, whose Director, Mr Richard Brownlee, has provided further photo-copies of documents relating to Rudolf's illegitimate son.

9 *Graphological Analysis of Crown Prince Rudolf's Handwriting by Klára Ács*

Crown Prince Rudolf inherited many qualities from his mother: her vitality, her passionate disposition and to a certain degree her tainted heredity. Rudolf was wonderfully gifted, and not the offspring that might have been expected of the frigid, obtusely single-minded Francis Joseph and Elizabeth, who was ineffective with her children.

According to his handwriting, Rudolf was a very precocious child. At the age of five he manifested the qualities of a child of ten. As a small boy he was happy; he loved sports and was tough, yet he tired easily. His eyes were weak, he should have worn glasses as soon as he started school work. Later his eyes were affected by an illness and were constantly inflamed.

Between the ages of thirteen and sixteen his handwriting showed great impatience. At thirteen Rudolf was already willful and in a state of constant tension; his conscious personality was beginning to emerge; stubbornness was an important element.

At seventeen his intelligence, his willpower, his manifold interests emerged; his internal tensions were also growing; he began to realise that his future responsibilities would be quite different from what he had imagined. About this time he became infected with gonorrhoea, which he had to conceal even from General Latour, his devoted tutor, who taught him to face up to his own shortcomings.

Rudolf adored his mother in spite of seeing very little of her. Mother and son loved each other very much, yet they could never completely relax in each other's company; indeed they remained almost strangers to each other.

In his entourage, Rudolf would not allow anyone to contradict him; he was very sensitive, easily hurt; injustice made him positively ill.

At the age of eighteen, Rudolf's actions were already incompatible with the Court's point of view; he had a strong social sense and wanted to fight for his ideals. Everything that life had to offer interested Rudolf. Besides politics, he was attracted by various branches of art, primarily literature, his great ambition was to become a writer.

According to his handwriting, at the age of twenty-seven his blood was not in order; because of his gonorrhoea he had a painful inflammation of the loins, his feet also hurt. Later he also got syphilis; this can only be deduced because in the 1880's this illness could only be diagnosed in its later stages.

At the end of 1886 his handwriting betrayed frustrations as well as passionate emotions. At the beginning of 1887 his physical condition was very poor, but his temperamental ability to rise to an occasion partly overcame this. Outside circumstances also kept him very tense. In the spring of 1887 his handwriting showed that his willpower had almost doubled; he was determined to realise his political conceptions at any price.

From his signature of January 9, 1888, it is clear that Rudolf sensed grave danger. In spite of this, his talents were evident in all directions. Traces of syphilis were apparent in his eyes and in his handwriting; his sight had become so poor that it approached blindness.

On November 7, his handwriting showed him to be lethargic; on November 17 that he lived a double life. At this time he was less depressed; he had once more confidence in himself. Then on a letter written in December he again forgot to put a date. He had a premonition that something horrible was going to happen. He was convinced that his life was running down.

Judging by Rudolf's handwriting, at Mayerling it was Mary Vecsera who insisted that they should put an end to their lives. She probably staged a hysterical scene and demanded that Rudolf should shoot her. Rudolf's shot killed Vecsera. After it Rudolf was demented—his mental condition was appalling. He wanted desperately to escape from the world, but had no strength to do anything.

Bibliography

Acsay, Ferenc: *Rónay János Jácint Élete*, Györ, 1906

Anonymous: *The Martyrdom of an Empress*, Harper, New York, 1902

Bagger, Eugen: *Francis Joseph, Emperor of Austria—King of Hungary*, G. P. Putnams Sons, 1927

— *Licht über Mayerling*, Graz, 1954

Barkeley, Richard: *The Road to Mayerling: Life and Death of Crown Prince Rudolf of Austria*, Macmillan, London, 1958

Benedikt, Professor Dr Heinrich: *Die Monarchie der Gegensätze*, Ullstein Verlag, Wien, 1947

Bibl, Victor: *Kronprinz Rudolf—die Tragödie eines sinkenden Reiches*, Gladius Verlag, Leipzig, 1938

Bismarck, Otto von: *Reflections and Reminiscences*, Harper, New York, 1899

Borgese, G. A.: *La Tragedia di Mayerling—Storia di Rudolfo d'Austria e di Mary Vetsera*, published by Milano, Milan, 1925

Cassel, Lavender: *Clash of Generations*, John Murray, London, 1973

Chapman-Huston, Desmond: *Bavarian Fantasy*, John Murray, London, 1955

Christophe, Paul: 'Gift für den Kronprinzen. Ein Rezeptbuch der k. und k. Hofapotheke und seine Geheimnisse', in *Neue Illustrierte Wochenschau*, September 18, 1955

Corti, Egon Caesar Conte: *Elisabeth die seltsame Frau*, Styria Verlag, Wien, 1934

— *Die Rothschilds*, Styria Verlag, Wien, 1949

Corti, Egon Caesar Conte, and Sokol, Hans: vol. 3 of the *Franz Joseph Trilogie: Der alte Kaiser—Vom Berliner Kongress bis zu seinem Tode*; chapter 6: 'Death of the Crown Prince in 1889', Graz, 1955

Cunliffe Owen, M.: *Keystone of Empire*, Harper, New York, 1903

Dombrowski, Raoul Ritter von (anonymously): *Rudolf, Kronprinz von Österreich-Ungarn als Forscher und Weidmann*, Gedankenblätter, Wien, 1899

Doutrepont, Georges: *La litérature à la Court des Ducs de Bourgogne*, Bibiliotheque du XVo[e] Siècle, tom. 8, Paris, 1906

Ebel, Eugene: *Notes biographiques sur la Mystique Lorraine, Catherine Filljung, Religieuse Dominicaine, Fondatrice de l'Orphelinat de Biding*, Paris, 1929

Ebenthal, Hildegarde: *The Tragedy of a Throne*, Funk & Wagnall, New York, 1917

Engel-Jánosi, Friedrich: *Österreich und der Vatikan, 1864–1918*, Verlag Styria, Graz, 1958

— *Die politische Korrespondenz der Päpste mit dem Österreichischen Kaisern, 1804–1918*, Harold Verlag, Wien–Munchen, 1964

— *Einige Dokumente zum Tode des Kronprinzen Rudolf*, in Mitteilungen des Österreichischen Haus, Hof und Staatsarchives, two volumes, published in 1966

Fésüs, Dr György: *Kortársaink, Életrajzi Vázlatok*, biography of J. J. Rónay, published by Károly Stampel, Pozsony–Budapest, 1887
Franzel, Emil: *Kronprinzen Mythos und Mayerling-Legenden*, Herold Verlag, Wien–Munchen, 1963
Frischauer, Berthold, 'Kronprinzenlegenden—aus meinen Erinnerungen, an den verstorbenen Kronprinzen Rudolf', in *Neue Freie Presse*, August 21, 1921
Fuhst, Herbert: *Mary Vetsera im Lichte ihrer Abstammung und Verwandschaft—eine familiengeschitchtliche Untersuchung*, privately published, Wien–Berlin, 1930
Glaise-Horstenau, Edmund von: *Franz Josefs Weggefährte*, Wien, 1930
Gorup, Ferdinand Freiherr von: 'Der Tod des Kronprinzen Rudolf. Die Wahrheit erzählt vom Polizeipräsidenten A. D. Ferdinand Gorup', *Wiener Morgenpost*, September 26 to November 7, 1927
Grant, Hamil: *The Last Days of Archduke Rudolf*, Grant Richards, London, 1917
Grünwald, Kurt: *Türkenhirsch*, Israel Programme for scientific translations, 1966
Habsburg, Archduke Albrecht of: *Letter about Rudolf*, 1882, Vienna State Archives
Habsburg, Crown Prince Rudolf of: *Random Thoughts*, Vienna State Archives, 1873
— *Letter to King Ludwig of Bavaria*, Vienna State Archives, 1878
— *Fifteen Days on the Danube*, 1879
— *Eine Orientreise*, 1881
— *Die Österreich-Ungarische Monarchie in Wort und Bild*, 1892. All writings of the Imperial Family were published by the State Publishing House.
Harding, Bertita: *The Golden Fleece*, Bobs Merrill Co., Indianopolis–New York, 1937
Haslip, Joan: *The Lonely Empress*, Weidenfeld and Nicolson, London, 1965
Herbert, Vivian: *Francis Joseph and his Court*, Lane, New York, 1917
Höhnel, Ludwig Ritter von: *Zum Rudolf-See und Stephanie-See*, Verlag Hölder, Wien, 1892
Hollaender, Albert E. J.: *Streiflichter auf die Kronprinzentragödie von Mayerling, in Festschrift für Heinrich Benedikt*, o.ö. Professor für neuere Geschichte an der Universität in Wien, Wien, 1957
Hóman, Bálint, and Szekfü, Gyula: *Magyar Történet*, Királyi Magyar Egyetemi Nyomda, Budapest, 1935
Hudal, Bishop Alois: *Die Österreichische Vatikan Botschaft, 1806–1918*, pp. xiii, 326, Munchen–Inssbruck, printed in 1952
Hummelberger, Walter: *Maria Caspar und Josef Bratfisch: Biografische Notizen*, Annals of the City of Vienna Historical Society, vols. 19–20, 1963–64
Judtmann, Dr Fritz: *Mayerling: The Facts behind the Legend*, Harrap, London, 1971
Kohn, Hans: *The Habsburg Empire, 1804–1918*, Anvil Books No. 52, Van Norstrand, Princeton, 1961
Krist, Josef: *Kronprinz Rudolf und seine Lehre*, Neue Freie Presse, February 11, 1952
Küremberg, Joachim von: *Schratt Katalin, a Császárváros Regénye*, Béta Irodalmi R. T. kiadása, Athenaeum, Budapest, 1941
Lamsdorff, Graf: *Tagebuch des Grafen Lamsdorff*, State Publishing House, Moscow, 1926
Larisch-Moennich, Countess Marie: *My Past*, Eveleigh Nash, London, 1913
— *Secrets of A Royal House*, John Long, London, 1935
— *My Royal Relatives*, John Long, London, 1936

Lernet-Holenia, Alexander: *Mayerling*, Paul Zsolnay Verlag, Wien, 1960

Lónyay, Karl Count: *Rudolf, the Tragedy of Mayerling*, Scribner, New York, 1949

Louise, Prinzessin von Coburg: *Throne die ich stürzen sah*, Amalthea Verlag, Zurich, 1926

— *My Own Affairs*, Cassell, London, 1921

Macartney, C. A.: *The Habsburg Empire*, Weidenfeld and Nicolson, 1968

Magnus, Sir Philip: *Edward VII*, John Murray, 1964

Malortie, Carl Ernst von: *Handbuch zur Einrichtung und Führung eines Hofhaltes*, Hahn, Hanover, 1866–67

Marek, George R.: *The Eagles Die*, Hart-Davis MacGibbon, London, 1975

Margutti, General Albert Baron von, *Vom alten Kaiser*, Leonhardt Verlag, Leipzig–Wien, 1921

Márki, Dr Sándor: *Erzsébet, Magyarország Királynéja*, Franklin Társulat, Budapest, 1899

May, Arthur: *The Habsburg Monarchy*, Harvard Press, New York, 1951

Mayer-Gross, W.: *Clinical Psychiatry*, Cassell & Co. Ltd, London, 1960

Mayerling Original: Offizieller Akt des K. K. Polizei Präsidiums Facsimile der Dokumente des Authentischen Bericht, Nr. I. 1889. (Nach sorgfaltiger Auswahl der Dokumente durch Beamte des Österreichischen Staatsarchives.) Frick Verlag, Wien, 1955

Menger, Carl, and Crown Prince Rudolf: *The Austrian Nobility and its Constitutional Profession. A Warning To Aristocratic Youth by an Austrian*, published anonymously in Munich in 1878

Mitis, Oskar, Dr Freiherr von: *Das Leben des Kronprinzen Rudolf*, Insel Verlag, Leipzig, 1928

Monts, Anton Graf: *Erinnerungen und Gedanken des Botschafters Anton Graf Monts*, Berlin, 1932

Motley, John Lothrop: *Correspondence*, Harper, New York, 1899

Neck, Rudolf: *Über die Abschiedsbriefe des Kronprinzen Rudolf*, Bulletin of the Austrian State Archives, vol. 2. Wien, 1958

Paget, Walburga Lady: *Scenes and Memories*, Smith Elder, London, 1912

— *Embassies of Other Days*, Hutchinson, London, 1923

— *In My Tower*, Hutchinson, London, 1924

— *The Linings of Life*, Hurst & Blackett, London, 1928

Planitz, Ernst Edler von der: *Die volle Wahrheit über den Tod des Kronprinzen Rudolf von Österreich*, B. Pichler, Berlin; 1st edition 1889, 46th edition 1900

Plener, Ernst von: *Erinnerungen*, 3 vols. Wien, 1921

Polzer, Wilhelm: *Die Tragödie des Kronprinzen Rudolf*, Verlag Oskar Karinger, Graz, 1954

Polzer-Hoditz, Arthur Graf von: *Kaiser Karl, aus der Geheimmappe seines Kabinettchefs*, Amalthea Verlag, Zurich–Leipzig–Wien, 1929

Pór, Antal: *Rónay Jácint életrajza, Rónay Jácint szabadkömüves*, Budapest, 1890

Prescott, Hilda F. M.: *The Unhurrying Chase*, Eyre and Spottiswoode, London, 1954

Redlich, Josef: *Emperor Francis Josef of Austria*, Macmillan, New York, 1929

Richter, Werner: *Kronprinz von Österreich*, Eugen Retsch Verlag, Zurich, 1941

Romer, Flóris Ferenc: *Rónay Jácint Élete*, Magyar Tudományos Akadémia, Budapest, 1897

Rónay, Father J. J.: *Napló Töredékek*, privately printed in Pozsony, 8 volumes, 1887
Rumbold, Sir Horace: *Final Recollections of a Diplomatist*, Edward Arnold, London, 1902
Skedl, Dr Arthur: *Der Politische Nachlass des Grafen Eduard Taaffe*, Rikola Verlag, Prague, 1922
Sosnosky, Theodor von: *Franz Ferdinand, der Erzherzog Tronfolger*, Deutscher Verlagsanstalt, Stuttgart–Berlin, 1929
Stephanie, Princess of Belgium: *I Was To Be Empress*, Nicolson & Watson, London, 1937
Stern, Fritz: *Gold and Iron, Bismarck, Bleichröder*, Allen & Unwin, London, 1977
Stockhausen, Julia von: *Im Schatten der Hofburg, Gestalten, Puppen und Gespenster*, Donau Verlag, Wien, 1952
Szeps, Julius: *Politische Briefe an einen Freund 1882–1889*, published by author in Wien, 1922
Szittya, Emil: *Selbstmörder*, published in Leipzig, 1925
Sztáray, Countess Irma: *Erzsébet Királyné Kiséretében*, privately printed in Budapest, 1910
Taylor, A. J. P.: *The Habsburg Monarchy*, Macmillan, London, 1946
Urbas, Emanuel: *Kronprinz Rudolf in Preussischen Jahrbüchern*, Band 219, 1929, pp. 1–28
Vajay, Szabolcs von: *Der Eintritt des ungarischen Stammesbundes in die Europäische Geschichte, 862–923*, von Kase und Kohler Verlag, Mainz, 1970
Van Deventer, H. R.: *He did not die at Mayerling*, Lippincott, Philadelphia, 1937
Wandruszka, A.: *The House of Habsburg*, Sidgwick & Jackson, London, 1964
Welcome, John: *The Sporting Empress*, Michael Joseph, London, 1975
William II of Hohenzollern: *My Early Life*, Methuen & Co., London, 1926
Wolfson, Victor: *The Mayerling Murder*, Prentice-Hall, New Jersey, USA, 1969
Wölfling, Leopold (former Archduke Leopold Ferdinand): *My Life Story—from Archduke to Grocer*, Hutchinson, London, 1930
— *Habsburger Unter Sich*, Verlag O. Goldschmidt-Gabrielli, Berlin–Wilmersdorf, 1921
Zanardi-Landi, Countess Caroline F. M.: *The Secret of an Empress*, Cassell & Co. Ltd, London, 1914
Zuckerkandl-Szeps, Bertha: *My Life and History*, Cassell, London, 1938
The Austrian and the Hungarian Press from January 30 to February 14, 1889

Index